HITLER'S TRAITORS

HITLER'S TRAITORS

DISSENT, ESPIONAGE AND THE HUNT FOR RESISTERS

EDWARD HARRISON

Pen & Sword
MILITARY

AN IMPRINT OF PEN & SWORD BOOKS LTD.
YORKSHIRE - PHILADELPHIA

First published in Great Britain in 2022 by
PEN AND SWORD MILITARY
An imprint of
Pen & Sword Books Limited
Yorkshire – Philadelphia

ISBN 978 1 39900 732 0

A CIP catalogue record for this book is available from the British Library.

Typeset in Times New Roman 11.5/14 by SJmagic DESIGN SERVICES, India.
Printed and bound in the UK by CPI Group (UK) Ltd.

Pen & Sword Books Limited incorporates the imprints of Atlas, Archaeology,
Aviation, Discovery, Family History, Fiction, History, Maritime, Military, Military
Classics, Politics, Select, Transport, True Crime, Air World, Frontline Publishing,
Leo Cooper, Remember When, Seaforth Publishing, The Praetorian Press,
Wharncliffe Local History, Wharncliffe Transport, Wharncliffe True Crime and
White Owl.

For a complete list of Pen & Sword titles please contact
PEN & SWORD BOOKS LIMITED
47 Church Street, Barnsley, South Yorkshire S70 2AS, United Kingdom
E-mail: enquiries@pen-and-sword.co.uk
Website: www.pen-and-sword.co.uk

Or
PEN AND SWORD BOOKS
1950 Lawrence Rd, Havertown, PA 19083, USA
E-mail: Uspen-and-sword@casematepublishers.com
Website: www.penandswordbooks.com

In memory of the Reverend John Morris Harrison, present at the liberation of Bergen-Belsen.

Contents

Acknowledgements

I would like to thank those who edited the original versions of the articles, namely Renate Bihl, Betsy Breuer, R.J.W. Evans, Hermann Graml, Mirella Kraska, Thomas Schlemmer and Manfred Weissbecker.

I should also mention those who provided decisive help in other respects. My siblings John and Patricia, both accomplished Germanists, have been an unfailing source of encouragement. The late Bill Calder gave strong support at an early stage. Through clouds of pipe smoke the late Dr Erich Langstadt of the Brotherton Library introduced me to primary sources about the Catholic Church in Nazi Germany. My first meeting as a graduate student was in Munich, where I spent an unforgettable afternoon with the late Martin Broszat and Elke Froehlich. With exemplary generosity, Jonathan Duering OSB made available to me the private records which he was using for his own doctoral thesis. The late Sir Alistair Horne of St Antony's College Oxford provided the opportunity to complete my essay on Helldorf. Blair Worden gave invaluable guidance as Literary Executor to Lord Dacre of Glanton [Hugh Trevor-Roper]. The presence of two essays on Trevor-Roper is also very much due to exceptional help from Judith Curthoys, the Christ Church archivist. At Pen and Sword Charles Hewitt expertly redesigned the project as two volumes – the first on *Secret Service* has already appeared. Lester Crook was a most thoughtful and enthusiastic editor. On the production side Harriet Fielding went beyond the call of duty in solving my IT issues, and provided unfailing guidance. Paul Middleton was a meticulous copy-editor and Richard Munro skilfully compiled the index. Invaluable help with image permissions was provided by Dr. Hannah Hien, Enrico Litschko, Julia Martin, Abbot Michael Reepen OSB and Ursula Schedl.

The six essays included in this volume were originally published as follows:

ACKNOWLEDGEMENTS

'May 1941: Rudolf Hess, the Uninvited Guest' in Kurt Paetzold and Manfred Weissbecker, *Rudolf Hess. Der Mann an Hitlers Seite* (Militzke Verlag, Leipzig 1999), pp. 368–92.

'Count Helldorf, the Nazi Movement and the Opposition to Hitler' *Vierteljahrshefte fuer Zeitgeschichte* vol. 45/3 (July 1997), pp. 385–423.

'The Red Flag and the Cross' *European History Quarterly* vol. 22/1 (Jan. 1992), pp. 104–119.

'The Nazi Dissolution of the Monasteries: a Bavarian Case-Study' *English Historical Review* vol. CIX /431 (April 1994), pp. 323–55.

'Hugh Trevor-Roper and *The Last Days of Hitler*', *Vierteljahrshefte fuer Zeitgeschichte* vol. 57/1 (Jan. 2009), pp. 33–60.

'Funeral in Berlin: Hugh Trevor-Roper's Special Missions in 1945–46 and his Evidence for *The Last Days of Hitler*', *Vierteljahrshefte fuer Zeitgeschichte* vol. 65/4 (Oct. 2017), pp. 507–44.

I would like to thank *The English Historical Review*, *The European History Quarterly*, Militzke Verlag and the *Vierteljahrshefte fuer Zeitgeschichte* for kind permission to republish articles which first appeared in their pages.

Edward D.R. Harrison

Abbreviations and Glossary

AaM	Abteiarchiv [Abbey Archive] Muensterschwarzach
Abwehr	German Secret Service, namely the intelligence, counter-intelligence and sabotage service of the High Command of the Wehrmacht
AdIfZ	Archiv des Instituts fuer Zeitgeschichte [Institute for Contemporary History (Munich)]
Axis	Association of Germany and Italy
BAK	Bundesarchiv Koblenz
BAP	Bundesarchiv Potsdam
BBC	British Broadcasting Corporation
BDC	Berlin Document Centre
BHSA	Bayerisches Hauptsstaatsarchiv [Bavarian Main State Archive]
BL	British Library
'Black'	Opprobrious term for German Catholics
Bundesarchiv	German Federal Archive
C	Letter denoting either the Chief of the Secret Intelligence Service or the Service itself
CCG (BE)	Control Commission for Germany (British Element)
CE	Counter-Espionage
CIA	Central Intelligence Agency [USA]

ABBREVIATIONS AND GLOSSARY

CIC	Counter Intelligence Corps [USA]
C in C	Commander in Chief
COS	Chiefs of Staff
Cossac	Chief of Staff to the Supreme Allied Commander
CSDIC	Combined Services Detailed Interrogation Centre
CSU	Christliche Soziale Union [Bavarian]
DBFPFS	Documents on British Foreign Policy first series
Deutsche Arbeitsfront [DAF]	German Labour Front
Enigma	German coding machine
Fifth Columnists	Hidden subversive elements controlled by Fascists
FO	Foreign Office
Frontbann	Ernst Roehm's organisation for military training of radical right
Gauleiter	Regional leader of the Nazi Party
GC & CS	Government Code and Cypher School with responsibility for devising British codes and breaking foreign ones
GHQ	General Headquarters
Gruppenfuehrer	Nazi paramilitary rank equivalent to lieutenant general [UK army]
GSO	General Staff Officer
Hauptsturmfuehrer	Nazi paramilitary rank equivalent to captain [UK army]
HMG	His Majesty's Government
Humint	Intelligence from human sources
Intendantur Ley	Agency of Robert Ley, head of organisation of the Nazi Party
IWM	Imperial War Museum
JIC	Joint Intelligence Sub-Committee

KGB	Soviet security and intelligence agency
Kreisleiter	District leader [of Nazi Party]: the lowest rung of its salaried officials
Kulturkampf	Bismarck's attempt to restrict the Catholic Church in Germany
LAB	Landesarchiv Berlin
MI5	British Security Service: agency responsible for preventing espionage, sabotage and subversion on UK territory
MI6	Popular name for Secret Intelligence Service
MO	Medical Officer
Napola	Nationalpolitische Erziehungsanstalt: National Political Educational Institute: an 'elite' Nazi secondary school
NSDAP	Nationalsozialistische Deutsche Arbeiter Partei: National Socialist German Workers' Party
New Beginning	Movement of revolutionary socialist cadres within Third Reich
Obergruppenfuehrer	Nazi paramilitary rank equivalent to general [UK army]
Obersturmbannfuehrer	Nazi paramilitary rank equivalent to lieutenant colonel [UK army]
OSB	Order of Saint Benedict
OSS	American Office of Strategic Services, precursor of CIA
PID	Political Intelligence Division [of the British Foreign Office]
POW	Prisoner of war
PS	Private Secretary
PWE	Political Warfare Executive
Reichsgau	One of eleven regions established after Germany's annexations
RSHA	Reichssicherheitshauptamt: Reich Security Head Office, with authority over the Gestapo, Criminal Police and SD

ABBREVIATIONS AND GLOSSARY

RSS	Radio Security Service: British organisation for intercepting the wireless messages of foreign spies during the Second World War
SA	Sturmabteilung: Storm Troops of the Nazi Party
SAW	Staatsarchiv Wuerzburg
SD	Sicherheitsdienst: Nazi Party security service within the SS
SHAEF	Supreme Headquarters Allied Expeditionary Force
Sigint	Intelligence from the interception and decryption of signals
SIS	British Secret Intelligence Service, also known as MI6: responsible for gathering intelligence and counter-intelligence outside UK territory
SOE	British Special Operations Executive: responsible for sabotage, subversion and fomenting resistance overseas
SO1	SOE department for secretly spreading misinformation
SO2	SOE department for stimulating resistance and organising sabotage
Sopade	Social Democratic Party of Germany [in exile]
SS	Schutzstaffel: protection squad of the Nazi Party
Stahlhelm	Steel Helmet: right-wing paramilitary organisation of German veterans
Standartenfuehrer	Nazi paramilitary rank equivalent to colonel [UK army]
Sturmbannfuehrer	Nazi paramilitary rank equivalent to major [UK army]
TNA	The National Archives [UK]

UK	United Kingdom
Ultra	Security classification for intelligence derived from decoding German wireless messages enciphered by the Enigma machine
VOMI	*Volksdeutsche Mittelstelle*: Liaison Office for Ethnic Germans [with responsibility for their resettlement]
USSR	Union of Soviet Socialist Republics
Wehrmacht	German Armed Forces
WLL	Wiener Library London [now Wiener Holocaust Library]
WO	War Office

Introduction

At the end of his life Adolf Hitler suffered from the delusion that the Third Reich had lost the war not because the Allies were more powerful but because he was betrayed by army generals. Nor was such treachery confined to soldiers. Hitler felt overwhelmed by it. First his armaments minister Albert Speer tried to persuade him that the war was lost, then his nominated successor Hermann Goering tried to supplant him by demanding the total leadership of the Reich, and finally he discovered that SS leader Heinrich Himmler was attempting to negotiate surrender. This was the worst treachery of all. In *The Last Days of Hitler* Hugh Trevor-Roper identified Himmler's defection as the catalyst that prompted Hitler to take his own life.

Rudolf Hess, the Fuehrer's Deputy for Party Affairs, had been the first leading Nazi to try and make peace. Without informing Hitler of his plans, Hess landed in Britain by parachute on 10 May 1941. His mission was an attempt to work towards the Fuehrer by achieving Hitler's early ambition of Anglo–German understanding. The bizarre quest of the Fuehrer's Deputy is the first topic in this collection of six essays examining the Nazi regime and German resistance.

Hess promised a generous peace, but insisted that Churchill had to be sacked. His proposals were of no interest to the British Government. Disappointed by the failure of his mission, Hess fell mentally ill. He provided little useful intelligence, and in particular nothing of value about German intentions towards Russia. Britain could have derived much propaganda value from Hess, for example by claiming he had revealed Hitler intended to attack America or even Italy and Japan. Instead the Foreign Office opted for a policy of mysterious silence, which delighted the Nazi Propaganda Minister Joseph Goebbels because Britain had missed opportunities to cause mischief. Goebbels attributed Hess's erratic behaviour to his being a health freak and guzzling grass.

While Hess was a true believer in Hitler, the subject of the second essay is a more ambiguous figure. Count Wolf-Heinrich von Helldorf was the only person who played a significant role in both the Nazi seizure of power and the July Plot against Hitler. A decorated veteran of the Great War, afterwards Helldorf found it difficult to adjust to civilian life and gravitated to right-wing extremism. By 1931 he was leading the Berlin Storm Troopers and mounted a violent anti-Semitic pogrom on a principal shopping street of the capital. This pogrom was instigated by Joseph Goebbels, who was also the Nazi Gauleiter of Berlin. Helldorf's violence won Goebbels' patronage. Hitler's propaganda expert advanced Helldorf's career and reported on his aristocratic friend in voluminous diaries.

After Hitler became Reich Chancellor, Helldorf was made Police President first of Potsdam and later of Berlin. But his career in the Third Reich never matched his influence during the seizure of power. Helldorf was lazy and ideologically lacklustre. He saw the persecution of the Jews as an opportunity to fill his own pockets by extorting enormous bribes in return for passports. Helldorf did not impress Himmler, the Chief of German Police, who blocked his further promotion. This humiliation was one of the reasons Helldorf turned to resistance. He was also a natural conspirator, and never developed an unconditional faith in Hitler. He drew his own conclusions from Germany's military disasters of the later war years. After the abortive military revolt in Berlin on 20 July 1944, Hitler ordered that Helldorf was to be executed last in his batch of plotters. Then he could watch the others die in protracted agony, dangling on piano wire from meat hooks, before his own turn came.

Helldorf seemed to Goebbels the worst traitor of all because he had taken everything he could get from the regime before trying to stab Hitler in the back once Germany's fortunes turned.

Helldorf and the military resistance threatened a revolution from above. But Hitler also feared a revolution from below. Indeed, the political parties representing industrial workers and Roman Catholics had long seemed subversive to powerful elements in the German state and society. For their part Hitler and the Nazis wrongly believed that Germany had not lost the Great War on the battlefield but on the home front, where treacherous left-wing politicians had stabbed the army in the back. After the Nazi seizure of power in 1933 the Social Democrat and Communist parties had to be obliterated to ensure German unity in a future conflict.

INTRODUCTION

Despite the efforts of the Gestapo and the burgeoning concentration camps, there was extensive resistance from Communists and Social Democrats. Chapter 3 includes an extensive review on New Beginning, a movement that developed from Social Democracy. The adherents of New Beginning believed that the overthrow of Nazism would be achieved within Germany by secret cells avoiding direct action in order to prepare for the day of revolution. Waldemar von Knoeringen was the mentor for New Beginning in southern Bavaria, but despite his energy and dedication the movement's strategy proved a fallacy, as the revolutionary cells were never strong enough to mount a serious threat to Hitler's regime.

After 1933 the Catholic Church in Germany was in a much stronger position than the forces of the Left. The Church retained its essential structure and support from the laity. The difficult questions were exactly how much support it could expect and whether it should try to mobilise that support. When the Nazi regime interfered with the Church's influence, should the Bishops make formal protests in writing or appeal directly to the laity and ask Catholics to defy the regime? The possibilities and boundaries of dissent are illustrated vividly by the crucifix struggles that flared up at different times in the Catholic regions of Germany. Chapter 3 includes discussion of the Oldenburg crucifix struggle, during which the Church succeeded in mobilising the laity to force the regime to put back into classrooms crosses that it had unilaterally removed. Although this success was repeated later in Bavaria, elsewhere in Germany it was sometimes a different story, with the Nazis removing crosses with impunity.

While Hitler himself wished to avoid trouble with the Church until the war was over, his secretary, Martin Bormann, was a militant atheist only too eager to seize any chance to undermine Catholicism. Chapter 4 examines the Nazi dissolution of the monasteries, which Bormann instigated. In January 1941 he urged the Nazi Gauleiters or regional leaders to make the most of opportunities to transform monasteries into hospitals or Nazi schools. During the first half of 1941 many monasteries were dissolved throughout Germany and Austria. The closure of Muensterschwarzach Abbey in Bavaria on 9 May was remarkable because the dissolution provoked large demonstrations of local people on three successive days. But Catholic outrage over the closure was limited to the local region, and the dissolution was not reversed.

During the second week of July 1941 the Gestapo began closing religious houses throughout the Muenster diocese of Bishop Galen. Galen denounced the closures in extremely frank and eloquent sermons, the last of which culminated in his denunciation of the Nazi mass murder of the mentally ill. Galen was a prominent figure with a powerful diocese behind him. Whereas the Nazis had ignored written complaints from Bishops about the closure of monasteries, Galen's public denunciation could not be ignored. It was expedient to give way. Hitler called a halt to both the dissolution of the monasteries and large-scale Nazi 'euthanasia'. Galen's successful appeal to public opinion showed that for some issues mass publicity and not secrecy was the way to stop the Nazis.

Although the RAF dropped Galen's sermons on Germany, for the most part German resistance achieved little credibility in London. Hugh Trevor-Roper of MI6 suggested that all the July Plot had achieved was to blow up Hitler's trousers.

During the war Trevor-Roper earned a reputation as the leading expert on the German Secret Service in British Intelligence. In particular, he made a very positive impression on Dick White of MI5. After White was appointed head of Counter-Intelligence in the British occupation zone of Germany, he chose Trevor-Roper to investigate Hitler's death, as Stalin's calculating silence on the matter was encouraging stories that Hitler had survived.

Trevor-Roper's research into Hitler's end is discussed in Chapters 5 and 6. His enquiry was exemplary in its shrewd sifting of evidence, its tempo and tenacity: it was a model intelligence operation. Trevor-Roper assembled overwhelming proof that Hitler was dead. In this way he provided the logical conclusion to the wartime successes of British Counter-Intelligence. He capped this triumph with a winter descent on Germany at Christmas 1945 to locate copies of Hitler's will. His success in doing so was his best achievement as an intelligence officer.

Once again, Dick White helped Trevor-Roper by suggesting that he write up his research on Hitler as a book. He did so with impressive speed and style. *The Last Days of Hitler* has stood the test of time remarkably well. Although Trevor-Roper was taken in by Albert Speer, his understanding of Nazism and its leaders was usually penetrating, and his account of Hitler's death largely accurate. It is a macabre story, beautifully told. As the book was designed to prevent the creation of a Hitler myth, the British Joint Intelligence Committee thought the Foreign

Office should disseminate a German translation. But the Foreign Office missed its opportunity to request the translation rights.

Trevor-Roper's investigation in autumn 1945 and his subsequent book have been reappraised by Professor Geoffrey Parker and Sarah Douglas in *The Journal of Military History*. Parker questions whether a single person could have interrogated numerous witnesses single-handed and sifted their evidence in less than six weeks. Instead he suggests that Trevor-Roper spent most of his time in Germany reading the transcripts of interrogations carried out by others. Douglas writes that a collective effort of countless interrogators from all over Europe became *The Last Days of Hitler*. The final essay in the present collection refutes these assertions. It uses primary sources to show that during his autumn enquiry Trevor-Roper personally questioned many witnesses, indeed he was an exceptionally effective interrogator who elicited detail and meaning that had previously been missed. His eagerness to question witnesses himself was not least due to recurrent problems with interrogations carried out by others. Indeed, the majority of evidence in his book did not come from interrogations, but from a great range of other sources.

Although Trevor-Roper carried out a superb investigation into Hitler's death, he underestimated the difficulties presented to the Nazi regime by the Christian churches. After all, Bishop Galen did halt a phase of Nazi euthanasia. The essays in this collection illustrate the possibilities of dissent and resistance inside a tyranny that, for all its propaganda bluster, was always fearful of the enemy within.

Chapter 1

Rudolf Hess: The Uninvited Guest

The image of Britain amongst the Nazi leadership owed more to fantasy than knowledge. British policy was supposedly controlled by great lords who could change its direction whenever they wished. Britain's influence in world affairs was due not only to the invincible battleships of the Royal Navy, but also to the hidden power of the mysterious and omnipotent British Secret Service. The legendary ruthlessness of this vast organization maintained Britain's huge empire. Operating through the Boy Scouts movement, the Secret Service supposedly toppled dynasties and assassinated the enemies of Britain everywhere. It was the most powerful intelligence service in the world, with countless agents in every corner of the globe. In its glittering headquarters security was so tight that no one dared even to open a drawer. Little was known about the shadowy figures who ran this mighty organization. One Nazi writer suggested their names would scarcely be included in *Who's Who*. As to funds, the Secret Service was believed to have enormous means at its disposal, perhaps 138 million pounds a year.[1]

The realities of the British Secret Intelligence Service [SIS] on the eve of the Second World War were sadly different to Nazi legend. Its activities mostly focused on Europe, and Germany's expansion from 1938 to 1941 meant the loss of many SIS stations. In its headquarters, sets of drawers that refused to shut were marked: 'this cupboard is to be considered secure'. The three most senior SIS personnel were all included in the 1941 edition of *Who's Who*. The SIS budget in 1939 was probably much less that 1 per cent of the sum specified by the Nazi writer. Far from being overwhelmed by a sense of mysterious power, some new recruits to SIS felt there had been a mistake and the organization they had joined was only a cover. Somewhere else there must be a real Secret Service that lived up to its awesome reputation. Another reaction to the working environment of SIS was that if this was our intelligence system,

England was doomed to defeat. Nor were the problems of British Intelligence in the early years of the Second World War confined to SIS. The official history suggests that well into 1940 MI5 also suffered from disorganisation and poor morale.[2]

Nevertheless, the myth of British Intelligence persists in Germany, where it has been claimed that an exchange of letters between the British Secret Service and Rudolf Hess, the Fuehrer's Deputy for Party Affairs, provoked the latter's flight to Britain in May 1941. This theory is based on an anonymous and unconfirmed report and post-war speculation by Karl Haushofer, the father of Hess' personal adviser Albrecht Haushofer. Furthermore, it has been claimed that Ernest Bevin, the British Minister of Labour, received a coded message from Germany that Hess was on his way, so the British knew the exact date he would arrive. Based on a single newspaper article by an old friend of Bevin's seeking to make himself important, this theory also fails to convince.[3] By contrast, much solid evidence undermines the notion that Hess was expected.

MI5 documents suggest there was no exchange of letters between British Intelligence and Hess prior to his flight. According to an MI5 report, on 2 November 1940 British censors intercepted a letter dated 23 September addressed to the Duke of Hamilton, House of Lords. This letter came from Albrecht Haushofer. It referred to an earlier letter written in July 1939 and suggested that if possible Hamilton should meet the writer 'somewhere on the outskirts of Europe, perhaps in Portugal. I could reach Lisbon any time (and without any kind of difficulties) within a few days after receiving news from you.' On 6 November the Censorship Department sent the original of the letter to MI5 and a copy to the Foreign Office. MI5 discussed the matter with SIS and it was decided to run the case as a potential double-cross operation, namely a channel under British control for providing the Germans with misleading information. The Duke of Hamilton was an officer serving in the Royal Air Force. If he was willing to take part in the operation, he would pose as a German agent while actually working for Britain. MI5 arranged with Air Commodore Boyle, Director of Intelligence in the Air Ministry, for the Duke to be sent to Lisbon, even though as MI5 later admitted 'at that time the Duke of Hamilton had not himself been consulted or even told about the letter'.

At this point it was realized the original letter had been lost. MI5 noted that 'what happened to the letter is not quite clear, but it is certain that it never reached the Duke of Hamilton and must be assumed to have been lost in the [MI5] Registry'. Although copies had been made, MI5 felt the loss of the original 'presented certain difficulties as it was felt to be a little awkward to ask the Duke of Hamilton to do something for us on the basis of a letter the original of which could not be produced. However, it was decided that this could not be helped.' On 20 January 1941 MI5 discussed the matter with Air Commodore Boyle, who then brought in Group Captain F.G. Stammers of RAF Intelligence. Stammers was instructed to send for the Duke of Hamilton and obtain a statement from him about his connection with Albrecht Haushofer. Stammers saw Hamilton in early March and showed him a copy of the September 1940 letter from Albrecht Haushofer. Stammers explained that as Haushofer had close links with the German Foreign Office, British Intelligence thought that it might be of considerable value to make contact with him. At this stage MI5 was clearly unaware of the link with Hess. It was hoping to use Haushofer to get material from the German Foreign Office. Following this meeting with Duke of Hamilton, Stammers reported back to MI5 on 11 March 1941 that Hamilton had known Albrecht Haushofer since 1936 when he met him in Berlin. Through Haushofer the Duke had been introduced to Goering and several other important men.[4]

As Hamilton's previous contacts with Haushofer seemed promising, on 25 April 1941 the Duke was interviewed at the Air Ministry by Group Captain D.L. Blackford and T.A. 'Tar' Robertson of MI5. They pressed Hamilton to volunteer to go to Portugal so he could pump Albrecht Haushofer for intelligence. Hamilton unenthusiastically replied he would go if he was ordered to, whereupon he was told it was a job for a volunteer. Hamilton's caution was reasonable as he was a pilot serving full-time in the RAF not a part-time secret agent. All the same, it was perhaps not quite the reaction his interviewers had expected from a dashing young officer, though MI5 did not lose hope. They later reported that 'Hamilton did not seem to be altogether averse to this plan but was given some time to think it over.'

Three days later Hamilton wrote to the Air Ministry that he was willing to go on two conditions '1) that H.M. Ambassador in Lisbon should be notified of his mission and Hamilton should explain the position to Sir Alexander Cadogan [permanent under-secretary] at the Foreign office before leaving and 2) he must be given a reasonable cover for not having answered Haushofer's letter of seven months before.' The first of these conditions was problematic because if Hamilton was in touch with the Ambassador and something went wrong it would compromise this important official. So the Air Ministry told MI5 'action on the lines suggested at the present moment might be misunderstood'. While the matter was still unresolved Hess dropped from the skies and on 11 May MI5 'decided it was better not to press the matter and that the approach should be dropped'.

This evidence suggests MI5 had not sent Haushofer any letter under Hamilton's name. Only after Hess arrived did British Intelligence realize that Haushofer had written his letter of September 1940 at the behest of the Fuehrer's Deputy. The abortive MI5 negotiation with Hamilton, initiated in agreement with SIS, has clear implications. If British Intelligence were really trying to lure Hess from Germany, would they have taken so little interest in the matter as to lose Haushofer's letter? Indeed, the dilatory and unsatisfactory way MI5 went about this business suggests that at this early stage in the war British Intelligence was not really up to luring Hess to his ruin.[5]

MI5 was subordinate to the Earl of Swinton in his capacity as Head of the Home Defence (Security) Executive. When Swinton read MI5's account of this sloppy business he was enraged. On 20 May he wrote a stinging rebuke to Sir David Petrie, the newly appointed Director-General of MI5: 'I have read the minute sent by Abbot [of MI5] on the Haushofer letter, and I must take strong exception to the way in which this matter was handled. It is intolerable that a matter of this importance should not have been brought to my notice ... I cannot understand how officers dealing with this can have failed to appreciate the importance of the material in their possession ... It is perhaps idle to enquire now how the letter came to be lost ... a classic example of how not to do it.'[6]

Much the same can be said of the way Hess was treated during the hours immediately after his arrival. Hess descended by parachute shortly after 11 pm on the night of 10 May 1941, and announced to a Scottish ploughman that he had come to see the Duke of Hamilton. The first British officer to reach the scene was Lieutenant Clarke of the Third Battalion, Renfrewshire Home Guard. Clarke arrested Hess, who was taken to Battalion Headquarters at Giffnock. The Home Guard Commander told the nearest regular troops, the 14th Argyll and Sutherland Highlanders, that his prisoner was an officer of some importance and should be taken in charge by a regular unit. The 14th Argyll and Sutherland arranged for an escort, which was some time in coming. The delay was unfortunate, as a circus developed with Hess forming the centre of attention as an exotic and unidentified exhibit with open access for all those present. Roman Battaglia, a Polish interpreter summoned to the scene, later commented that he had formed an extremely unfavourable impression of the way this initial interview was conducted.

Battaglia's account was summarized in a report of 30 May forwarded to Brigadier Stewart Menzies, the Chief of SIS. Battaglia said that 'no attempt was made, as far as he knew, to check up on his own identity or integrity; that of the fifteen or twenty persons present there seemed to be no official interrogator, and that he was asked to put questions from all corners of the room, some of which he considered offensive and which he refused to ask. No accurate report, as far as Battaglia knew, was made of the interrogation, and people wandered around the room inspecting the prisoner and his belongings at their leisure.' Meanwhile, one of the officers present asked the prisoner if he was Rudolf Hess as he was 'the split image of him'. The prisoner denied he was Hess, but the Battalion Commander, as he put it in his report, 'recognised that the prisoner was not an ordinary Pilot'. So when the escort finally arrived he detailed a senior officer, Major Barrie, to accompany the party to Maryhill Barracks in Glasgow. When he learned in due course of Hess' interrogation by the Home Guard, Menzies wrote to H.A. d'A. Hopkinson of the Foreign Office that, 'It seems incredible that this should have been permitted,' and Hopkinson agreed that 'the matter seems to have been badly handled'.[7]

Captain Anthony White, the night Duty Officer at Glasgow Area Command, had telephoned Maryhill Barracks in Glasgow at about quarter to one. After a few minutes he roused the night Duty Officer in the barracks, Second Lieutenant Fulton. As White later reported, 'I asked him his name and informed him that I had considerable trouble in getting a reply from him.' Fulton seemed 'rather sleepy' so White told him, 'Pull yourself together. Are you awake now?' Fulton replied that he was awake and was told to expect a German prisoner within an hour. He was to make all necessary arrangements for the safe custody of the prisoner in accordance with his rank. Instead Fulton went back to bed. When Barrie and his party arrived at 2.30 am there was no sentry and Barrie had to blow his car horn until someone came out. No preparation had been made to receive an officer prisoner and Hess was taken to an ordinary cell in the guardroom. While the Corporal of the Guard was half-dressed, Fulton was still sound asleep in his pyjamas. He had made no provision for suitable quarters, an officer guard or medical attention. But at least he now sat up in bed and rang around making arrangements. At a quarter to three he telephoned Captain White, who told him to get the prisoner 'out of the guardroom, get a bedroom for him and a bed. Give him any food that he may require and see that his [slight] injury is attended to by the M.O. and above all that an adequate guard is provided.' Only now was Hess dealt with in the proper fashion. In view of the chaos following the arrival of the Fuehrer's Deputy in Scotland, the notion that he was expected defies belief.[8]

The Duke of Hamilton had been told in the early hours of 11 May that the German pilot was asking for him. At 10 am Hamilton duly visited the prisoner. Although Hamilton did not recognize him, the German claimed that he had seen him at the 1936 Olympics and, revealing his true identity for the first time, announced: 'I am Rudolf Hess.' Hess mentioned that his friend Albrecht Haushofer had told him that the Duke was an Englishman who would understand Hess' point of view. So he had tried to arrange a meeting with the Duke in Lisbon. It now became clear to the Duke that the letter of September 1940 from Haushofer had been written in collusion with Hess. Hess went on to give the Duke an account of the purpose of his mission, and asked for 'parole' from the King, that is, the right to leave the country, as he had come unarmed and of his own free will. But this was not a matter for the King to decide.[9]

Convinced the prisoner was indeed Hess, Hamilton flew south to report to the Prime Minister, whom he saw late in the evening of 11 May. Churchill's reaction was, 'Hess or no Hess I am going to see the Marx Brothers.' When the film showing was over Churchill went into the matter carefully and the following morning, 12 May, passed on Hamilton to the Foreign Secretary, Anthony Eden. Having summoned his senior official, Sir Alexander Cadogan, Eden talked things over with Hamilton. Eden also proposed involving Ivone Kirkpatrick, who had served at the Berlin Embassy. After consulting Menzies, Cadogan asked Kirkpatrick to go to Scotland immediately to determine whether the visitor was Hess. If Hess' identity was confirmed, the matter would gain great political significance. Rudolf Hess was one of Hitler's most fanatical adherents. In 1924 he had written down the first volume of *Mein Kampf* from

Hitler's dictation. It was Hess who introduced Hitler when the Fuehrer spoke at the annual Nuremburg Party Rally. Long and devoted service by Hess had culminated in the influential post of Fuehrer's Deputy for Party Affairs, which gave him the authority to comment on a wide range of government business and appointments. Although in recent years Hess had lost some of his former closeness to Hitler, this diminished standing was not known to the outside world.

Kirkpatrick travelled to Scotland with Hamilton and the two of them saw Hess shortly after midnight on 12 May. As if holding forth at a Party Rally, the Fuehrer's Deputy gave a long and well-rehearsed discourse on Germany's grievances against England, claiming that his country's legitimate aspirations had always been thwarted by the treacherous brutality of British policy. Although Hess was still in full flow, by 3 am Kirkpatrick wanted to go to bed and rudely interrupted to demand the purpose of his visit. Hess replied that he wanted to convince the British Government Germany was bound to win the war and so bring about a negotiated peace. If Britain did not choose peace, Hitler would be very angry and the consequences for the British would be appalling. Germany would build so many bombers and submarines that those British who did not die from bombs would perish through starvation, as there would be a total blockade. After such further defiance if Britain did surrender there was no guarantee food would be provided. Hess was making a characteristically Nazi offer: peace or extermination.[10]

Hess urged Kirkpatrick to avoid national suicide. Instead there could be a generous peace under which Germany would guarantee the British Empire. The German Army and the Royal Navy would rule the world together. However, Hitler would not negotiate these indulgent terms with Churchill, who would have to go. Hess stressed that although he could speak with complete authority as someone in the Fuehrer's closest confidence, the sudden mission was his idea alone. Kirkpatrick's report on his interview with Hess was only shown to Eden, Deputy Prime Minister Attlee and Max Beaverbrook, the Minister of War Production. It was not seen at this stage by the Minister of Information, Alfred Duff Cooper. When Kirkpatrick telephoned the Foreign Office on 13 May he was told that the Government was embarrassed by the whole affair and did not know exactly how to handle it. So if Kirkpatrick spoke to the press he was just to give trivial details of Hess' appearance, diet etc. This decision was to have unfortunate consequences.[11]

The first Nazi communiqué following Hess' flight said he was mentally disturbed. In contrast, the Political Intelligence Department of the British Foreign Office commented in a secret report that neither Hess' demeanour immediately after landing nor his successful piloting of a fast aircraft for several hundred miles supported the German position that he was deranged. Although the British psychiatrists who examined him during 1941 differed in their views of Hess' sanity, it seems he was not suffering from active mental illness when he arrived in Britain. On 13 May 1941 Colonel Gibson Graham of the Royal Army Medical Corps examined Hess and concluded: 'The patient does not look ill; while guarded in his conversation he did not strike me as being mentally of unsound mind. Such information as he gave with regard to his health was given in a rational and coherent manner.' But once Hess had registered that his mission was not bringing the anticipated triumph of Anglo–German peace he went into a rapid psychological decline. On 14 May he told Kirkpatrick that the sentries were deliberately stamping outside his room just to annoy him. Kirkpatrick began to wonder about Hess' sanity and questioned the doctors who had seen him. They assured Kirkpatrick that although Hess was distinctly odd, he was certainly neither insane nor certifiable. But the Fuehrer's Deputy continued to deteriorate and by the following day was convinced there was a plot to poison him.[12]

The mystified reaction of the British Government to Hess's appearance demonstrates clearly that he was not expected. All the same, the sudden arrival of the Fuehrer's Deputy provided opportunities that had to be exploited carefully. First, Hess could be pumped for intelligence. Second and more importantly, his flight to Britain had vast potential for domestic and overseas propaganda. It could be given a slant that would boost domestic morale and give further stimulus to anti-Nazi feelings abroad. Finally, and most important of all, Hess' arrival was an event of primary diplomatic importance, which would set Britain's allies, her enemies, and the neutral states buzzing. There was a unique opportunity to drive a wedge between Germany and her allies by imputing treacherous motives to Hess' mission. Yet the level of attention Hess generated was a double-edged sword, as there was a danger foreign states might jump to the conclusion that Britain really was trying to make peace with Hitler.

The task of extracting intelligence from Hess was allocated to the Secret Intelligence Service [SIS], although for the most part SIS operated on foreign territory, whereas MI5 had responsibility for secret service in Britain. Cadogan noted in his diary for 13 May that MI5 were trying to butt in on Hess. But the same day Churchill ruled that General A. Hunter, Director of Prisoners of War under the War Office, was to be responsible for guarding Hess and the Foreign Office was to be responsible for all contact between Hess and the outside world. As the Foreign Office supervised SIS, it naturally gave the job of quizzing Hess to the intelligence organization under its own control.

Mytchett House, which became known as 'Camp Z', was chosen for Hess' prison. Bugging devices were installed by post office engineers for taping Hess' conversations before he was transferred there on 20 May. But who was to engage Hess in chat and discover his secret thoughts? SIS chose Frank Foley, its former Head of Station in Berlin, Thomas Kendrick, who had occupied the same post in Vienna, and an unidentified officer known as 'Captain Barnes'. General Hunter introduced Hess to his new friends when he arrived at 'Camp Z', but the relationships failed to blossom, as Hess became convinced that he was surrounded by secret agents, as indeed he was. The morning after his arrival Hess was seen by Colonel Graham, who noted that the prisoner 'evidently regarded with great distrust the three officers immediately concerned with him'. 'Captain Barnes' aroused Hess' suspicions because his uniform fitted so badly and it was very obvious the badges had been removed.

Hess became convinced that these gaolers intended his death, either by poison or driving him to suicide. Was surrounding Hess with intelligence officers the best way of getting material from him? Perhaps something a little more subtle could have been attempted. On 22 May General Hunter reported to Cadogan that, 'When I saw Rudolf Hess installed in Camp Z ... I wondered if the three "companions" were such as would have much success in getting information out of him.' Eden queried on Hunter's letter that, 'We do not seem to have handled this very happily?'[13]

Surrounded by spies, Hess' paranoia unsurprisingly became much worse. On landing in Britain, he had been appraised as odd but sane. But his mental health deteriorated in tandem with his vanishing hopes of success. By 29 May 1941 Colonel Graham was reporting that 'this man shows definite abnormal traits which have become suddenly acute ... the problem is one for a skilled psychiatrist'. Hess had diminishing potential as an intelligence source, but was becoming increasingly likely to kill himself. Overall, it seems the SIS operation against Hess produced little. In particular, Hess revealed nothing of value about German intentions towards Russia.[14]

Even before the SIS failure to get much out of Hess, Churchill had agreed to a Foreign Office suggestion that Viscount Simon, the Lord Chancellor and head of the national legal system, should interview Hess and deploy his skill as a lawyer to draw him out. Simon had met Hess in March 1935 when he visited Berlin as Foreign Secretary. Perhaps Simon's eminence would flatter the Fuehrer's Deputy into making the confidences he had denied less distinguished figures. On 27 May Simon wrote to Eden confirming that, 'If the P.M. and you think that I would be the suitable choice for this piece of "intelligence" work, I am entirely ready ... could I have any information useful as background on supposed German strengths and on *lacunae* [gaps] in our present information?' The Armed Forces provided Simon with notes indicating points on which he could try to get information from Hess. For his part Cadogan hoped for clarification on whether or not Hitler had actually sent Hess, even though Desmond Morton, who advised Churchill on intelligence matters, was already convinced that Hess had come without Hitler's prior knowledge. Kirkpatrick was to accompany Simon during his visit to Hess. As it was considered essential that no one should know that a Government Minister had seen Hess, Simon and Kirkpatrick were to assume the names of Dr Guthrie and Dr Mackenzie and pose as psychiatrists.[15]

Kirkpatrick described the discussion that ensued between Simon and Hess on 9 June 1941 as a 'Mad-Hatter's tea-party'. Although Hess vaunted himself as a peace-maker, his diatribe on this occasion had a distinctly reproachful, indeed aggressive, tone as he criticised British policy at length. Simon sat through three hours of this one-sided and provocative ramble so he could discover Hess' actual proposals. But there was no new substance in what Hess had to say to Simon, who left little the wiser. After reading the typescript pages of the Hess–Simon interview, Churchill wrote that 'they are like a conversation with a mentally defective child who has been guilty of murder or arson'. From his involvement in the Hess case Simon reached two conclusions, namely that Hess was in no way authorized to come and that the 'plan' of the Fuehrer's Deputy was 'his genuine effort to reproduce Hitler's own mind, as expressed to him in many conversations. He would never dream of making proposals of his own.' But Simon could have reached these conclusions without spending an afternoon with Hess.[16]

Following the new disappointment of the unsatisfactory interview with Simon, which even Hess could scarcely regard as a success, his mental condition continued to get worse. On 16 June Hess tried to commit suicide by throwing himself from a landing and broke a leg. Colonel J.R. Rees, Consultant in Psychological Medicine to the Army, having examined Hess on both 16 and 18 June, decided that 'there is no doubt ... that Hess' mental condition, which was somewhat masked before, has now declared itself as a true psychosis (insanity). There is no form of treatment which holds out a good prospect of recovery from this type of disorder.'[17]

Hess had proved a disappointment from the intelligence perspective. Nor was his exploitation for propaganda any more successful. At first sight his arrival was a godsend to the Ministry of Information. More than any other news story of the war, it seemed a unique opportunity to boost popular morale and score a propaganda triumph over the Nazis. If the Ministry of Information could get control of the story, it might work with the British media to turn this gift from the heavens to considerable national advantage.[18]

Unfortunately at the time of Hess' arrival British propaganda was in a state of chaos, with overlapping jurisdictions and uncertainty over who was responsible for what. In theory the Ministry of Information was in charge of 'white propaganda', namely the official spreading of material that was believed to be true in order to damage the enemy. In contrast, Department SO1 of the Special Operations Executive was responsible for 'black propaganda', which sought to undermine the Nazis by spreading lies in secret. Unfortunately much information was grey rather than black or white. In other words, it was uncertain whether the material was true or false. Furthermore, both the Ministry of Information and SO1 aspired to control all British propaganda. The Foreign Office also took an interest, as did Members of Parliament [MPs]. These competing influences produced incoherence and a lack of direction. One civil servant commented in August 1941 that the energy of the whole propaganda effort for the previous year had largely been dissipated in inter-departmental intrigues and strife. British propaganda could scarcely have been worse situated to exploit the Hess story.[19]

Late on 12 May the Government had issued a short statement admitting that Hess was in Britain, but when pressed in the House

Commons the following day Churchill refused to add to this. One MP asked that the Minister of Information should handle the news with skill and imagination, but unfortunately this was precisely what did not happen. In response to pressure from the British Broadcasting Corporation [BBC] and SO1, the same day Churchill approved as a temporary measure 'Preliminary Propaganda about Hess for immediate use on all British and Foreign [radio] broadcasts'. This merely stated that '(a) Hess is in good health and bears all signs of being in his right mind. (b) He has come entirely on his own and brings no communication from the German Government. (c) It is already clear that Hess' flight from Germany is a sign of the stress and strain caused by preoccupation as to the course of the war which are prevalent in high German circles and also of tension in the relations between high personages in Germany.' These modest propaganda guidelines nevertheless indicated the British Government would countenance some creativity with the details of the Hess case. There was no evidence in British hands that his flight was due to tension within the Nazi leadership. But how much further was the British Government willing to go?[20]

The question of whether to issue a detailed statement was discussed at 6 pm on 14 May by Churchill, Eden, Menzies, Cooper and Cadogan at 10 Downing Street. Churchill and Duff Cooper pressed for an immediate statement whereas Cadogan argued for silence. Hitler had claimed that Hess was a misguided idealist searching for peace. Cadogan wanted to avoid anything that would confirm this claim. Instead he wanted the Germans to fear Hess was a traitor. Although Churchill and Duff Cooper brushed Cadogan aside, the Prime Minister then had dinner with Lord Beaverbrook, the Minister of Supply, who also argued against a statement. Eden too wanted silence, telling Churchill on the telephone that the Germans must be kept in the dark as to what Hess had said. Beaverbrook and Eden had more influence with Churchill than Duff Cooper, and eventually Churchill agreed not to make a statement for the time being. The problem was that once a policy of silence had been adopted, it was the route of least resistance to continue with it.[21]

Indeed, the failure to define a clear propaganda line later compounded the missed initial opportunity. The root of the problem was, as Duff Cooper remarked, 'the P.M. is not really interested in propaganda'.[22] The Government's handling of the Hess affair produced a crisis in the Ministry of Information. On 21 May the Ministry's senior officials,

Walter Monckton who was Director-General and Cyril Radcliffe, the Controller of News and Censorship, sent their Minister, Duff Cooper, a memorandum on the problems facing their department. Their main theme was that, 'The Ministry of Information is so constituted by the Government that it has no control over information. It can decide neither what to make public nor when to make something public nor what line or shape to give to such information as is made public ... each department deals independently with its own news, and there is no central or co-ordinated direction of any kind. In such circumstances it is idle to speak of the British Government as having a policy with regard to news ... we are generally a few days behind the Germans ...We are pitted against Goebbels and we are asked to give away weight to him ... From time to time there has been widespread dissatisfaction with the way in which our propaganda weapons have been wielded. There is great dissatisfaction at the moment.'[23]

Monckton continued to fume and six days later he wrote to Duff Cooper complaining how 'we never even saw in the Department the reports about Hess [by Hamilton and Kirkpatrick] after his arrival in this country, though it ought to have been our task to handle the publicity side'. Monckton also resented criticism the Ministry had attracted for leaking the news that Hess had indirectly tried to contact the Duke of Hamilton. All this was the final straw for Monckton, who asked to be relieved of his post. The Government's handling of Hess had completed the demoralisation of its official propagandists.[24]

Meanwhile, in Washington a pro-British Presidential Assistant, James Rowe Jr. had quickly realized how the Hess case could be used to boost Britain's cause in America. Rowe prompted President Roosevelt to send Churchill a message on 14 May 1941 requesting any information revealed by Hess that would help convince Americans that Germany was a real threat to the United States. Roosevelt stressed that it would be very valuable for shaping American opinion to discover from Hess any Nazi plans for the military domination or encirclement of the United States. Three days later Churchill replied there had been nothing much from Hess about America except some disparaging remarks that he did not even spell out. Roosevelt had pressed Churchill for propaganda material to help the British cause but to no effect. Yet American opinion was of vital importance to the British war effort. Hess' derogatory comments on the United States should have been used for a systematic attempt by British propaganda to portray Hess as anti-American. Instead, US opinion was left largely to its own devices, and rumours circulated that British silence about Hess meant peace talks were taking place through him. Although Eden commented that even Britain's best friends showed a lack of understanding, precious little attempt was made to explain things to them.[25]

So what other propaganda lines should have been attempted? There was no lack of interesting suggestions. During the war Dr Kurt Hahn, a Jewish–German refugee from the Nazis and famous educator, was working as a translator for the Foreign Office. On 20 May 1941 Hahn submitted a report to his employer arguing that 'there was a great longing for peace in Germany of which Hess had become the unconscious and silent Ambassador. Now was the moment to encourage the German Resistance and to make it clear to the German people that the British would never make peace with Hitler, but that a cleansed and liberated Germany had nothing to fear from Britain.' Along similar lines the ex-Nazi Hermann Rauschning suggested to Lord David Davies, a former Liberal MP, that now was the time for Churchill to broadcast to the German people. Davies remarked in a paper that was seen by Churchill that, 'It is a unique opportunity, when large numbers of Germans must be bewildered and dazed, to make it perfectly clear that we are fighting to destroy Nazi-ism and not the German people … it is essential that we should try to drive a wedge between Hitler and the millions of Germans who at the bottom of their hearts really loathe the Nazi regime, which they stupidly and foolishly imposed upon themselves without realizing where it was going to lead them.' But this perceptive insight was ignored.[26]

From the time Hess arrived the British department responsible for disguised propaganda, SO1, had taken a keen interest in the Fuehrer's Deputy. SO1 was looking for material for its subversive radio broadcasts and its printed and spoken propaganda. On 13 May SO1 tried to send Sefton Delmer, who knew Hess personally, 'to undertake a preliminary examination of the prisoner in order to establish lines for the exploitation of the incident in propaganda to Germany'. But neither Delmer nor his colleague Valentine Williams was allowed to see Hess. SO1 pointed out that, 'Hess must be fully aware of the bitter internecine conflicts between the Nazi Party leaders. The German is full of malice and, duly encouraged, Hess might easily be induced to defame for our purposes one or other of his personal enemies among the Party bosses … the essential point about the Hess case is that we, and not the Germans, are or will be in possession of the facts. The whole of Germany is agog to know the truth, and it must take what we care to tell it. The interest value of the Hess incident is prodigious and its skilful exploitation in our broadcasts should add immeasurably to our listening audience in Germany.'[27]

Cadogan saw things differently. As he commented on 14 May 1941, he felt the writer was jumping to conclusions about Hess' willingness to tell on the Party and Eden agreed. Two days later Cadogan noted that, 'I have often been told, during the last 8 years, that we must "keep Germany guessing". All the guessing was being done by us, as I frequently pointed out. Now at last Germany is guessing, and we must be very careful not to give her any reassurance. Silence about Hess may be very dull, but for a while it may be the more effective [policy].' Once again Eden agreed, though on 20 May Cadogan relented to the extent of letting SO1 put questions to Hess via Menzies, as 'For Intelligence purposes he is under 'C' [Menzies]'. On 23 May, nearly a fortnight after Hess' arrival, the Foreign Office approved the exploitation of the incident through 'whispers' passed via underground channels abroad. But shouting was needed not whispers, and the Foreign Office still preferred silence. William Strang, its assistant under-secretary for Europe, noted on 29 May that, 'I have always doubted whether there is much to be gained by active exploitation of the Hess affair. The fact is in itself sensational enough, and disturbing enough to the German public. If we are silent about it, we can't go wrong, and may create uneasiness in the minds of the directors of German policy. If we try to exploit it, we are pretty certain to open a flank, since we are not really very good at that sort of thing.'[28]

The British media resented the condescending official silence over Hess. On 21 June the *Daily Mail* commented that 'common sense ... seems to have been lamentably lacking in the whole official conduct of this affair ... we cannot congratulate the government on the way they have handled this matter either in regard to the information conveyed to our own people or to the use made of the event in foreign propaganda ... particularly propaganda in enemy countries'. The same sense of a missed opportunity was always felt by Sefton Delmer, a former newspaper correspondent in Berlin, who was responsible for 'black' radio propaganda to Germany. Many years later Delmer commented that he still found it hard to understand Churchill's orders to play down Hess's flight to Britain.[29]

Far from creating uneasiness amongst the directors of German policy, as Strang supposed, the British silence delighted them. From the moment that Goebbels learned of Hess' flight the Nazi propaganda minister was alarmed that British propaganda might exploit the incident to damage morale within Germany and undermine the country's international standing. On 14 May Goebbels noted in his diary that Hess had shown 'a crazy lack of discipline. This all comes from being a health freak and guzzling grass.' But Goebbels sensed Britain was botching the propaganda opportunity: 'once again Duff Cooper is confirming he is a real amateur'. On 15 May Goebbels observed that there was still no strong theme in the British propaganda: 'The danger is that invented atrocity stories could be attributed to him. But that has not yet happened.' And on the following day he recorded: 'London has not seen the obvious trick of simply by-passing Hess and issuing statements in his name. That would be the only danger for us, but a terrible one.' But by the time he made his diary entry on 17 May, Goebbels was beginning to gloat: 'The Hess affair is losing steam … Increasing perplexity in London over the matter. Duff Cooper deserves a reward from us. He really is remarkably stupid. What I could have done with this story!'[30] Indeed one of the few sentiments shared by Goebbels and Cadogan was their opinion that Duff Cooper was an idiot. Yet this was not wholly fair, as his freedom of action was so limited.

The Nazis remained baffled that Britain had exploited Hess so feebly. In September 1943 Goebbels was still discussing the Hess disaster with Hitler, who speculated on the possible damage if Britain had seized the initiative and used his Deputy to sow distrust amongst Germany's allies, perhaps with catastrophic results if the Italians had deserted and the Japanese stayed out of the war. Hitler concluded that England had fumbled its best political opportunity of the war. Of course Nazi criticism of British propaganda has to be treated with caution. Nevertheless, it seems British propaganda about Hess was stifled to no obvious gain by the Foreign Office. In the absence of fresh material, by mid-July the story had lost its value for propaganda to Germany, where all watched with hope or fear the invasion of the Soviet Union launched on 22 June.[31]

The opportunities for British domestic propaganda were also missed. This was all the more disappointing, as hardly any incident throughout the war grasped the attention of the British public so completely. According to the Ministry of Information, people felt 'amazement at what was regarded as the most astonishing event of the war ... Strangers spoke to one another with animation in trains and buses on the way to work.' The immediate popular reaction was that Hess was the "answer to a propagandist's prayer", but within a few days people felt that the news might have been handled with greater effect.'[32]

Some citizens felt so strongly about the Hess affair that they wrote directly to influential figures, including the Home Secretary Herbert Morrison. Taken together, letters sent directly to Morrison and censored letters about Hess give an excellent insight into British popular reactions to Hitler's Deputy. Between 13 and 27 May about 450 letters were censored that referred to Hess. Most writers greeted his arrival as 'the greatest moral victory for us and moral defeat for Germany ... he could have gone anywhere to escape, but he chose the freedom of England and democracy', as a writer in Cowes expressed it. A correspondent in Doncaster thought that, 'I bet old Hitler is having a fit for if he [Hess] talks we'll know all the inside plans. Everybody is talking about it and what a good thing it is for us.' A writer in St Anne's on the Sea thought it was 'a welcome gleam of hope in a dark time. Also it offers good propaganda – so good even our puerile Ministry of Information can make something of it.' Many letter writers took hope that it was the beginning of the end: 'I think the Germans have started to rot,' as one correspondent in Leeds put it, or in the words of a Glasgow writer, 'The worms must be turning in Germany as Hess had to make his escape to the land of freedom.' Some thought that Hess must have fallen out with Hitler and fled in fear of his life. There was speculation over 'who would rat next' and generally Hess was regarded as the harbinger of better times ahead.[33]

There was some popular concern that Hess had been able to penetrate Britain's air defences so easily. As a writer from Argyllshire complained, 'I think it's terrible. It just shows how well Scotland is guarded when he landed so easily. It will just show the Germans how easy it would be to land an army here.' Other writers felt that Hess had only come to prepare the way for an army of invasion. A Halifax writer noted: 'Isn't there an old story about the WOODEN HORSE OF TROY??? I'd suspect any enemy landing in this country of being a modern counterpart of that animal.' Another writer noticed by the censors thought Hess might be 'a super spy in England to prepare for parachute troops landing during the night'. A Mr Hiley of Halifax wrote to the Home Secretary Herbert Morrison to ask whether 'Hess has come here for a prearranged purpose of directing operations during any intended invasion? Or to be the signal for a set of pre-arranged Fifth Column moves here?' Quite a few people believed that Hess had come to assassinate Churchill. One anonymous correspondent asked the Home Secretary, 'Who can tell, except his own scientists, what subtle poisons are now being used by Hitler? Beware of Hess. Guard our Prime Minister.' Miss Leigh Pemberton of Wrinsted Kennels warned the Home Secretary that 'we are very nervous about the safety of Mr. Churchill. We feel convinced that the German man has come over for some foul purpose. Please don't let them meet ... Nothing is beyond the cunning and wickedness of these Germans.' British civilians felt the Germans were capable of any deception. As Mr Winsbury of London told the Home Secretary, 'Please don't be duped by anything the Germans do as their cunning is far ahead of ours and we have already been duped too many times.'[34]

Left to their own devices with little information from on high, people worried that the cunning Germans were being helped by aristocratic British traitors. It was felt that the silence over Hess was due to his friends in high places. The Ministry of Information reported that, 'The Hess affair has revived the idea of an active Fifth Column in this country, composed of people in "high society" and even among those in important political positions. Some suspicion is now expressed of the Duke of Hamilton being a Fifth Columnist.' Some censored letters also showed social resentment and suspicion that Hess was colluding with the upper classes. A writer in Essex commented that, 'I suppose he has plenty of friends in this country and he is over to have a parley with them, but the working class will have to pay for his expenses. I suppose he will be among the many European wasters we have to keep free in Hampton Court.' A writer from Carnarvonshire wondered 'if there is any truth in the tale that this wretched man was intimate with the Duke of Hamilton. There seem to be far too many of our nobility mixed up with the Nazis.' Along similar lines, a Mr Harbord of Somerset wrote to the Home Secretary suggesting that Hess' real object in coming to Britain was lust for Unity Mitford, an aristocratic enthusiast of Hitler's who had tried to kill herself on the outbreak of war. Hess was a 'woman's man' and 'with such characters "cherchez la femme" may be a sufficient explanation'. A writer from Caithness felt as early as 14 May that, 'It is quite time already that the Government give a public statement as to why the man is here. The British public will demand to know the reason, but what can one do with such mugs as A. Eden and Duffer Cooper about – they are hopeless and should be sent to the dogs' home.'[35]

A recurring popular reaction was that Hess was being treated too well. As one regional officer of the Ministry of Information noted, 'Press reports of Hess enjoying a light diet of fish, chicken and eggs have caused widespread disgust and indignation, especially in view of the kind of difficulty experienced by housewives in obtaining these kinds of food.' A writer in Ayrshire commented on Hess' 'damn cheek coming over here after murdering all the poor Polish people for he is one of the worst … and just think of him getting chicken to eat'. Ordinary people wanted Hess to get a taste of his own medicine, as a correspondent in Bicester put it: 'It makes me want to vomit the way the BBC say he is quite "comfortable", "resting nicely" etc. etc.. Give the bastard a seat in the middle of Plymouth one night of Blitz. Pfui!'[36]

As Churchill realized popular feeling about Hess' treatment, he took a harder line. On 13 May Churchill had told the Foreign Secretary that, 'His health and comfort should be ensured; food, books, writing materials and recreation being provided for him … He should be treated with dignity as if he were an important General who had fallen into our hands.' However, three days later Churchill told Cadogan that, 'His treatment will become less indulgent as time goes on … The public will not stand for any pampering except for intelligence purposes with this notorious war-criminal.'[37]

Not only did the British Government's handling of the Hess affair puzzle and disappoint the British public, it also baffled and worried the Soviet Union. After the defeat of France in June 1940 the Soviet leadership had noticed with concern the retention in the British Cabinet of appeasers such as Lord Simon. In July 1940 the Soviet Ambassador in London, Ivan Maisky, confided in English friends of his fear that Britain might be stabbed in the back by its ruling class in the way France had been betrayed by Pétain and his allies. In spring 1941 Soviet concern at the prospect of Anglo–German rapprochement was boosted by the clumsiness of the British Ambassador in Moscow, Sir Stafford Cripps. The Ambassador impulsively warned Molotov, the Soviet Foreign Minister, that a protracted war might tempt Britain to reach some arrangement to finish it. The Soviet Government then told Maisky to keep a vigilant eye for any Anglo–German peace feelers.[38]

With particularly unfortunate timing, at this point Hess arrived in Scotland. Maisky promptly called on R.A. 'Rab' Butler, the Under-Secretary for Foreign Affairs. As Butler reported to Eden, 'The Soviet Ambassador took the view that Hess was a great exponent of "Mein Kampf". He said earnestly that Hess was the most anti-Russian of the Nazi leaders, and … that Hess believed in alliance with this country [Britain] rather than Russia.' But Butler did nothing to reassure Maisky. He stuck to the policy of silence and did not volunteer any information, winning Eden's approval. The Foreign Secretary considered that Butler had spoken very well, as he commented the next day. In fact, he had added to the blunders of the silence policy. In reality Britain was resolute against Hitler and Hess' self-imposed mission to arrange peace was an absurdity. It is difficult to see the benefit of allowing mystery to develop in the Soviet perception of such fundamental issues.[39]

The Soviet Union was eager for all the material it could get on Hess, and its top agent, Kim Philby of British Intelligence, was eager to oblige. On 14 May news from Philby arrived in Moscow. He claimed Hess had brought peace proposals, and much the same was reported by Soviet agents in the United States, Germany and Japan. On 18 May more material from Philby arrived, according to which Hess wanted a compromise peace but was still loyal to Hitler. Philby also claimed Hess had been visited by Eden, though such a visit never took place. Soviet Intelligence reported from London that although Philby thought the time was not yet ripe for peace negotiations, Hess might later become the focal point for negotiations towards a compromise peace. Philby's malign speculation can only have harmed Britain in Soviet eyes.[40]

The superficial and misleading intelligence from Philby reinforced the impressions collected by Maisky. When Hitler invaded Russia on 22 June 1941, it seemed in Moscow as if Hess had been sent to arrange peace with Britain before this new attack took place. According to the former Soviet Foreign Minister Maxim Litvinov, on the morning of 22 June everyone in the Kremlin was expecting the Royal Navy to join up with the Nazis for an attack on Leningrad. When it became clear Britain was not taking part in *Barbarossa*, at least for the time being, an

Anglo–Soviet Agreement was concluded on 13 July that provided for mutual assistance and committed both parties not to make a separate peace.

Yet Anglo–Soviet relations continued to be blighted by the Hess factor. The negative effects of the foolish policy of silence over Hess were made even worse by the choice of Simon to visit Hitler's Deputy. To the Soviet Union, Simon typified the kind of British leader who might come to terms with Hitler, and inevitably Simon's visit eventually became known. Soviet fears of a unilateral Anglo–German peace agreement persisted. British officials understandably regarded Moscow's fretting as highly ironical in view of the Soviet Union's own shifty record of making sudden deals with the Nazis. Hess became an open wound in Anglo–Soviet relations. Whenever these deteriorated, the Russians resurrected their concern over Hess.[41]

Official silence over Hess not only annoyed foreign allies, it also led to misunderstandings within the British war effort. Secret departments in Whitehall were unaware of Hess' deterioration. This led the British Special Operations Executive [SOE] to consider the use of Hess as an assassin in Nazi Germany. SOE had been set up in 1940 to foment resistance in Nazi-occupied Europe. As mentioned above, its Department SO1 had been concerned with subversive propaganda. But it also had a Department SO2 responsible for stimulating resistance and sabotage. In September 1941 responsibility for subversive warfare was transferred to a new body, the Political Warfare Executive, but SOE retained control of sabotage. As the end of the war approached, this function was gradually eroding, and some SOE staff began to consider how their organization could survive into the post-war world.

Some unique triumph was called for. In 1942 SOE had sponsored the successful assassination of Reinhard Heydrich, head of the Gestapo and regarded by some as Hitler's logical heir. In June 1944 SOE revived plans to assassinate Hitler himself. The project was approved by Churchill, Eden and the British Chiefs of Staff, but although a wealth of intelligence was assembled about Hitler's lifestyle at Berchtesgaden, no operation actually took place, not least due to the difficulty of finding a suitable assassin. SOE also worked on similar projects to assassinate other Nazi leaders such as Himmler and Goebbels. In December 1944 SOE's planning staff raised the proposal of using Hess to assassinate one of his former colleagues: 'Hess might either be bluffed into doing it [as a way of opening peace negotiations] ... or, alternatively, be hypnotised into doing it. Hess is known to be an extremely nervous individual and should be very susceptible to hypnotic treatment ... Can Hess be psychologically induced, by producing the necessary 'evidence', into believing that Himmler, or any other Nazi leader, is the only person who prevents the possibility of re-approachment between Germany and Great Britain?' This absurd proposal was never implemented. If Hess had been set free to roam around Germany with a rifle, the indignation of Britain's allies can easily be imagined.[42]

The unexpected arrival of Rudolf Hess was an event of great potential for Britain. The Italian Foreign Minister Count Galeazzo Ciano noted in his diary that it was 'the first real victory for the English'. Hess was a straw in the wind, an early and spectacular signal that Hitler's plans were going astray. Unfortunately the British Government failed to exploit the opportunities presented by Hess' escapade. This fumbling owed much to other urgent claims on the War Cabinet's time and energy, as the war continued unabated even though Hitler's Deputy had dropped in to visit. Yet Churchill was badly advised by the Foreign Office, where gentlemanly reticence prevailed. The key figures in shaping British policy on Hess were Eden and Cadogan. In their social remoteness they developed an ill-judged policy of silence that not only displayed contempt for the British public but also botched the opportunities for propaganda overseas. The Hess affair turned into an international relations disaster. Not least, Anglo–Soviet misunderstandings over Hess proved a catalyst in the onset of the Cold War.[43]

Chapter 2

Nazi Against Hitler:
Count Wolf-Heinrich von Helldorf

In 1931 Count Wolf-Heinrich von Helldorf was brought before a court in Berlin for inciting Nazi Storm Troopers to acts of violence against Jews. Thirteen years later Hitler gave special instructions that Helldorf was to be executed last in his group of 20 July conspirators so that the Party veteran could watch the slow agonizing strangulation of the others before his own turn came. As both a Nazi activist in the early 1930s and later a member of the July Plot to overthrow Hitler's regime, Helldorf is one of the most contradictory figures of the Third Reich. Amongst contemporaries he had a bad reputation. In 1944 Konrad Heiden described Helldorf as 'an adventurer and military profiteer of the worst sort'. The French Ambassador to Germany, André François-Poncet, saw Helldorf as an *'aventurier sinister'*. Immediately after news of the July plot broke, Helldorf's participation gave rise to considerable suspicion in Britain about the conspirators' motives, as he was a prominent Nazi. Only Helldorf's former subordinate, Hans-Bernd Gisevius, regarded him indulgently. But Gisevius went to the other extreme and provided a whitewash.[1]

While many contemporaries despised Helldorf, historians have ignored him instead. His face does not fit easily into the portrait galleries of resistance heroes. None of the volumes providing biographical chapters of participants in the July Plot includes a study of Helldorf. Indeed there is a tendency to obliterate Helldorf from the events of 20 July completely. One German dictionary of the resistance more than four hundred pages in length did not even include Helldorf in the index.[2] Despite this neglect, Helldorf remains a significant figure. His transformation from SA hooligan to participant in the July Plot was extraordinary, and as the only figure who played a significant role both in

23

the Nazi seizure of power and in the elite resistance, his career deserves closer examination than it has previously received. In particular, why did Helldorf rise to prominence in the Nazi Movement? Why did he later become disillusioned with Nazism and what did he contribute to the attempts to remove Hitler? The historian Klemens von Klemperer, who described Helldorf as 'a drunken vainglorious lout', admitted that 'the former Nazis in the resistance present a special case and a puzzle in many respects. I have no answer to the question of why Count Helldorf went down this path.' This chapter sets out to provide an answer to this problem.[3]

Helldorf was born on 14 October 1896 in the Saxon town of Merseburg, 20 miles west of Leipzig. His family were landed nobility of obscure beginnings. In the early fifteenth century the name was used by robber barons whose castle was destroyed by angry neighbours. The link between Helldorf and the robber barons is uncertain, but he resembled them more than his immediate ancestors. These led conventional lives as state officials and landowners, forming marriage ties with other aristocratic families such as the Buelows and Schulenburgs.[4]

Helldorf was born with a silver spoon in his mouth. Initially he was educated by private tutors and then at local grammar schools and a private monastery school at Rossleben. This traditional humanist education made the most of his natural intelligence. In August 1914 Helldorf joined the 12th (Torgau) Regiment of Hussars. He arrived at the front line on his eighteenth birthday. Joachim von Ribbentrop, the future Nazi Foreign Minister, served in the same regiment. In March 1915 Helldorf was promoted lieutenant. After taking part in the first Battle of Ypres, he served on the eastern front before returning to France in August 1918. Helldorf mostly commanded machine gun units, and was decorated with the Iron Cross First and Second Class. He was ill several times during the war and missed three months' service at the end of 1915 due to venereal disease. Later in the war Helldorf qualified as an army interpreter. Participation in warfare from the age of eighteen unsettled Helldorf and made it difficult for him, like many other veterans, to find his way back into civilian life.[5]

The German Army was one of the few institutions for which Helldorf felt lasting commitment and under pre-war circumstances he might well have followed a military career. After his demobilization Helldorf served in various *Freikorps*, which suppressed Communist insurrections. As a leader of the *Freikorps* Rossbach, Helldorf took part in the Kapp Putsch of 1920. After the Putsch failed Helldorf took refuge in Italy for several months. In October 1920 he married Ingeborg von Wedel, with whom he was to have five children. It was an appropriate match, as the Wedels were a distinguished Prussian family with large estates in Pomerania. After his marriage Helldorf was presented with a golden opportunity to adopt a traditional way of life. The Helldorfs owned the large estate of Wohlmirstedt in the Unstrut valley near Naumburg an der Saale. The property comprised a country house built in 1836 and extensive lands. In 1921 Helldorf's father, whose marriage was in difficulties, renounced the Wohlmirstedt property in favour of his son. It was an unselfish but rash decision.[6]

Despite his valuable inheritance, Helldorf could not content himself with farming and family life. He became interested in the *Stahlhelm* [Steel Helmet], the paramilitary organization of German veterans, and worked as adjutant for the Halle *Stahlhelm* leader Theodor Duesterberg. At the end of October 1923 Helldorf visited Munich with Duesterberg, who was seeking to persuade General Karl von Lossow to march on Berlin and establish a right-wing government. Lossow was Commander of the Bavarian section of the *Reichswehr*, the post-war German Army. Helldorf visited Munich again on 8 November 1923. He saw both Lossow and the State Commissioner for Bavaria, Gustav von Kahr, and probably pressed for action by Bavaria against the Reich Government. Later the same day Helldorf held discussions with two politicians close to Hitler, General Erich von Ludendorf and Max-Erwin von Scheubner-Richter. As Quarter-Master General of the Imperial Army, Ludendorf had been one of the leading figures in Germany's war effort. Scheubner-Richter was one of Hitler's more able associates. In the evening Helldorf travelled back north and Scheubner-Richter accompanied Hitler to the Buergerbraeukeller, where the Nazi leader sought to exploit the presence of Kahr and Lossow to launch a Putsch. During the defeat of the Putsch the following day Scheubner-Richter was killed. Helldorf's association with the Nazi Movement dated back to the crucial period of the November Putsch.[7]

Helldorf was undoubtedly impressed by the fact that, unlike Duesterberg and the *Stahlhelm*, Hitler and the Nazis had risked a coup to back up their denunciations of the Weimar Republic. Following the trial in spring 1924 of the leaders of the Munich Putsch, Hitler was sent to prison but Ernst Roehm, though convicted of treason, was discharged a free man. Helldorf met Roehm for the first time at the May 1924 German Rally in Halle. Roehm told Helldorf and a group of others about his plans to establish a new organization that would unite in one association all the young men from the racialist paramilitary groups who were capable of bearing arms but had not yet received military training. Roehm made such an impression on Helldorf that immediately after the German Rally he left the *Stahlhelm*. As he told a judge investigating Roehm and his Munich associates in November 1924, 'I myself am a National Socialist, whereas the leadership of the *Stahlhelm* is not National Socialist. Although my attitude is one of extreme Nationalism and extreme social consciousness, that does not mean that I approve all the points of the National Socialist programme concerning economic matters.' As the Nazi programme called for the expropriation of land without compensation, this was a prudent reservation for a large landowner to make.[8]

Some time after the Rally in Halle, Roehm wrote to Helldorf asking him if he would like to head the Centre Region of his new organization. At the German Rally in Weimar in mid-August 1924 Helldorf spoke at a closed evening session about the new association, which was to be called the *Frontbann*. Helldorf later told the Munich judge that 'the *Frontbann* is to make the German people once again capable of bearing arms so that it can wage a war of liberation abroad. There was no talk of war against the enemy at home ... We never thought in terms of a repetition of 9 November 1923.' Helldorf probably took much the same line at the Weimar meeting, which was attended by about fifty nationalist paramilitary leaders, including Roehm and Ludendorf. Those present included Karl Friedrich Freiherr von Eberstein, whom Helldorf had appointed as his private secretary a few days previously. According to Eberstein's account of the Weimar meeting, Roehm explained to those present that the paramilitary associations were now to be dissolved and subordinated to the military leadership of the *Frontbann*. Not surprisingly, the stronger paramilitary associations had little enthusiasm for such a move. The Nazi Party's paramilitary organization was called the S[turm] A[bteilung] or Storm Troops. Hitler did not want the swallowing up of SA members in the *Frontbann* in case this endangered his early release from prison. After the Weimar Rally Helldorf and Eberstein tried to persuade the *Stahlhelm* in their region to enter the *Frontbann*, but without success. This doomed the Centre Region of the new organization to failure.[9]

Despite Helldorf's slender achievements for the *Frontbann*, Roehm paid him a glowing tribute in his memoirs: 'the personal sacrifices which Count Helldorf in particular made not just for the paramilitary association but for the whole National Socialist Movement will always be a proud record for him'. Helldorf's sacrifices were in the first place financial. The Centre Region of the *Frontbann* had no funds. According to Eberstein, 'there was no money at all. Count Helldorf financed the whole show in Merseburg from his own resources.' Furthermore, in late 1924, when Roehm was wanted by the judicial authorities in Munich, Helldorf hid him in a hunting lodge on the Wohlmirstedt estate. Later Eberstein recalled fondly how in the evenings Roehm came up to the big house and played arias from *Siegfried* and *Die Meistersinger* on the splendid grand piano in the concert room.[10]

From 28 February to 2 March 1935 Helldorf and his wife acted as hosts at their mansion to a conference of *Frontbann* leaders. In his memoirs Roehm wrote that Helldorf and his wife had done everything to get the preparations for the conference right. Not only did they entertain forty-two *Frontbann* leaders, they also provided food and accommodation for 250 of their followers. Hitler was now out of prison and a car was sent to Bayreuth to fetch him to the conference but he could not be found. In this way he registered disapproval of the proceedings. After the Wohlmirstedt conference Roehm and Hitler were unable to agree on the future role of the *Frontbann* and so at the end of April 1925 Roehm stepped down as its leader and transferred command to Helldorf. It was not much of an inheritance. Roehm had not only alienated Hitler but Ludendorf as well. For all his wealth, Helldorf lacked the industry to bring the organization to life. According to Eberstein, the *Frontbann* 'went to sleep', and on 22 September 1925 Helldorf resigned as national leader.[11]

Helldorf had been elected to the Prussian state assembly in December 1924 and held the seat until March 1928. Otherwise, with the collapse of the *Frontbann* he turned away from politics. In 1927 he became President of the Saxony Chamber of Agriculture. The evidence on Helldorf's farming and property dealings is very fragmentary, but it seems the problems caused many estates by low prices were compounded in his case by extravagance. Helldorf spent at a pace that even his substantial purse could not match. For example, the party to celebrate a son's baptism cost 5,000 RM. Eventually he lost the Wohlmirstedt estate, to judge from a flurry of legal documents probably in 1928, when he became part-owner of a racing stud in Harzburg. Helldorf owned at least one very lucrative horse, *Narcissus*, which won nearly 44,000 RM in 1929 and over 40,000 RM in 1930. But these winnings were eaten up by heavy costs and debts. Helldorf also lost money from betting on horses. In 1931 *Narcissus* brought in nothing at all. Bankrupt and with no conventional way of retrieving his fortunes, Helldorf committed himself once again to racialist politics.[12]

The catalyst was Roehm's arrival back from self-imposed exile in Bolivia. Roehm became SA Chief of Staff on 5 January 1931 and within months Helldorf had joined the SA. He had already joined the Nazi Party itself on 1 August 1930 with the membership number of 325,408. In May 1931 Helldorf became Leader of the Second Regiment of the Berlin Sub-Division of the SA. On 21 July he reported to Joseph Goebbels, Gauleiter [Nazi Party Regional Leader] of Berlin, who noted in his diary that Helldorf wore perfume and was very presentable. The Gauleiter wondered whether he was homosexual like Roehm. He later discovered Helldorf's addiction to young women matched his own. Goebbels eventually concluded in his enlightened way that, 'Helldorf is a reprobate. But isn't every real man like that?' Later Goebbels had to console the weeping actress Else Elster when she told him she was expecting Helldorf's child.[13]

By July 1931 it was clear that the head of the Berlin SA, Petersdorf, was not up to the job. In early August Roehm appointed Helldorf acting head of the whole Berlin SA in Petersdorf's place. Roehm made this appointment permanent on 15 September 1931, three days after Helldorf's notorious anti-Semitic demonstration mentioned above. This had proved his suitability for high office in the SA. Helldorf's attack on the Jews took place along the Kurfuerstendamm [Kudamm], a showcase shopping street in central Berlin, and so became known as the 'Kudamm Pogrom'. As it provided the basis for Helldorf's career in the Nazi Movement, the Kudamm Pogrom deserves close attention.[14]

The idea for the pogrom came from Goebbels, who during a meeting of the Berlin Nazi leaders proposed a demonstration by unemployed supporters on the evening of the Jewish New Year Holiday. The SA leaders objected to restricting the demonstration to the unemployed, so it was decided to involve all their members. Helldorf gave the necessary orders by word of mouth. On the evening of 12 September 1931 about 1,000 Storm Troopers took part in the demonstration, which took on the character of a violent pogrom in which several dozen or more Jews were viciously assaulted down a great stretch of the Kudamm. Most of the SA men involved were under thirty, younger than Helldorf. His part was to incite them to acts of racialist violence. Groups of about fifty men marched down the Kudamm on either side of the road. The early groups shouted in chorus slogans like 'We are hungry … We want work'. The later groups turned to menacing chants such as 'perish Judah' and 'strike the Jews dead'. They also attacked passers-by. Many Jews including elderly people were beaten up.

When the violence was already well under way, Helldorf showed up in the back of a chauffeur-driven car wearing a distinctive naval cap with gold braid. Accompanied by his chief of staff, Karl Ernst, Helldorf drove up and down the Kudamm at walking pace encouraging his young followers, giving them instructions and prolonging the tumult. In particular Helldorf told the SA to attack the Café Reimann on the Kudamm. This was smashed up and its patrons assaulted. Eventually Helldorf's car was deliberately driven in such a way that it hemmed in another vehicle, one of whose passengers was called a 'Bank Jew' by Helldorf. After the driver complained to the police, the latter asked Helldorf for identification and he was taken to the Bahnhof Zoo police station so his identity could be established.[15]

The large number charged for taking part in the pogrom came before the courts at a series of trials. On 23 September 1931 twenty-seven participants were sentenced by the Charlottenburg Summary Court to short prison terms for breaches of the peace and related offences. The Summary Court acknowledged that the accused were mostly youths without previous convictions who had been incited and led astray by Helldorf and Ernst. Helldorf was not prosecuted at this first trial. Deferring to his social status, the police omitted to hold him when he was identified at the station and he then successfully hid for a week before finally surrendering himself to give evidence in defence of his followers. After he had done this, Helldorf was held in Moabit Gaol awaiting his own trial. As the Summary Court had already sentenced his chauffeur to eighteen months in prison, his prospects were bleak.

But a rescuer was to hand. The Kudamm Pogrom had cemented Helldorf's relationship with Goebbels, the real instigator of the atrocity. The Gauleiter was determined to help such a useful and congenial ally. On 25 September Goebbels visited the Reich Chancellor, Otto Bruening, and told him that his friend Helldorf was in great danger as he was due to come before the same judges who had sentenced his chauffeur. Bruening informed Goebbels that he 'could not interfere in a procedure which was under way, particularly as I could not be sure whether the Nazis and the SA of Count Helldorf might not then disturb the visit of the French Ministers'. [Two days later a team of French government ministers was due to arrive in Berlin]. Goebbels understood immediately and assured the Reich Chancellor he could prevent any such disruption. The bargain was struck: Helldorf would appear before different judges and the Nazis would behave themselves during the French visit. Helldorf's trial had been set for 29 September. But the Public Prosecutor was briefed verbally and on 28 September he cancelled Helldorf's trial date, as he reported to the Prussian Minister of Justice on 6 October.[16]

Due to Chancellor Bruening's manipulation of the legal system, Helldorf evaded summary justice and came up before a regular court. On 7 November Charlottenburg Regular Lay Court gave Helldorf and Ernst sentences of six months. Helldorf was immediately released from custody due to ill-health. Furthermore, he and his followers in the Kudamm disturbance appealed against their sentences. The appeal proceedings began in January 1932. Goebbels gave evidence at this hearing and turned it into a circus. He had to deal with the accusation made by a police spy that Goebbels and Helldorf had worked out together the plans for violence on the Kudamm. Goebbels noted in his diary that, 'I immediately make very sharp attacks on the Police Presidium and until the police spy is named refuse to make any statement on grounds of propriety ... I tussle with the Public Prosecutor and finally shout at him so much that he completely disintegrates ... The SA men on trial shake with laughter.' At the summing up Helldorf spoke on behalf of the accused, claiming that, 'The events on the Kurfuerstendamm sprang from idealism and passionate love of the Fatherland.' He himself was present 'because as SA Leader he had to go to every place where his people were in danger'. The appeal court quashed Helldorf's prison sentence due to lack of evidence and he was fined only 100 RM for insulting the Jewish car passenger. Thanks to Goebbels and to his lawyers, who included the Nazi advocate Roland Freisler, the Berlin SA Leader emerged from the Kudamm trials largely unscathed. Helldorf had spent six weeks in custody awaiting trial and was later so proud of this sacrifice that he increased it to two months in his *Who's Who* entry.[17]

It seems Helldorf's anti-Semitism was opportunistic rather than ideological. Soon after his trial he was chatting easily with the Jewish novelist Vicky Baum at a party given by Sefton Delmer, the Berlin Correspondent of the *Daily Express*. Delmer summed up Helldorf as 'a reckless soldier playboy, laughing and boasting', a concise and telling description of the Count at this point in his life.[18] Whether he was serving an ideology or himself, Helldorf's willingness to orchestrate anti-Semitic violence impressed the Nazi elite, to whom he was also useful as a political go-between. Despite his ruffianly behaviour, his aristocratic title helped win access to the conservatives who dominated the final years of the Weimar Republic. Helldorf was ideal as a non-binding channel of communication. On 19 April 1932 he was involved in negotiations with Alfred Hugenberg, the leader of the German Nationalists. On 26 April he visited General Kurt von Schleicher, the political voice of the Reichswehr, to pave the way for negotiations between Schleicher and Hitler.[19]

From the perspective of the Nazi leadership, Helldorf stepped briefly out of line following the Nazi success in the Reichstag elections of July 1932. This triumph went to his head, and Helldorf allowed himself to become the vehicle for the revolutionary ardour of the rank-and-file SA. On 9 August 1932 Goebbels was with Hitler on the Obersalzberg when the Nazi propagandist Karl Hanke telephoned from Berlin that the SA was making a fool of itself. Hanke came to Berchtesgaden the next day and reported that Helldorf had developed 'big plans'. Helldorf, always ready for a Putsch, was contemplating a violent coup d'état with his Berlin SA. Goebbels noted in his diary that 'this must be stopped. We report to Hitler ... Roehm will get his instructions tomorrow.' The SA was to bluff a coup d'état under the control of the Party leadership, not attempt a real coup of its own. Helldorf was put in his place. On 10 August Helldorf warned the Berlin SA against illegal measures in a proclamation and demanded that 'now above all' the SA had to prove that it was 'under strict discipline in the hands of the Fuehrer'.[20]

Within days of his 'big plans' collapsing, Helldorf resumed his role as a political go-between, taking part in the negotiations to secure Nazi participation in the Reich Cabinet. The Chancellor at the time, Franz von Papen, recalled in his memoirs how 'on the morning of August 12 [1932] I was visited by Roehm ... and Count Helldorf ... Roehm ... looked remarkably like a bulldog and provided a considerable contrast to Helldorf, a man of the most aristocratic appearance. Helldorf I had known for many years, and between us we monopolized the conversation.' Papen's comments are redolent of the snobbery that seldom failed Helldorf in his political climb. Helldorf's appearance was also an asset in the Nazi Movement. His hawk-like mien conformed to a Nazi stereotype, and so he cut an appropriate figure on public occasions. Helldorf could also rant well enough at political meetings to warrant sharing a platform with Goebbels, as Sefton Delmer witnessed on one occasion.[21]

With Roehm's support, Helldorf continued to make a rapid career in the SA. By December 1931 he had risen to the command of the Brandenburg Group of the SA in addition to its Berlin Sub-Group. In September 1932 five Senior Groups to cover the whole of Germany were created in the SA hierarchy. Helldorf was one of the five men appointed as a Senior Group Leader, with responsibility for Germany east of the Elbe excluding the Free State of Saxony. This was the highest post he achieved in the Nazi Movement, though he was unable to make it a serious power base. During 1932 Helldorf also facilitated Ribbentrop's entry into the NSDAP. Afterwards Ribbentrop systematically tried to attract Hitler's attention by standing outside the lift of Berlin's Hotel Kaiserhof. 'What's the name of the man who's always standing there?' Hitler asked Helldorf. 'He's someone with a great deal of money and very good foreign contacts, perhaps we can make use of him later,' came the reply. Helldorf arranged a meeting between Hitler and Ribbentrop, which took place on 13 August 1932 in Berchtesgaden.[22]

Helldorf's brisk career in the SA was only possible because Roehm did not emphasize traditional standards of behaviour. In the aftermath of the Kudamm affray the Berlin police investigated Helldorf's private life. They discovered that he had separated from his wife. On searching his flat they found letters that suggested he was on bad terms with his mother and siblings. They also found a number of unpaid bills.[23] In June 1932 one of Helldorf's angry creditors wrote to Gregor Strasser, Leader of the Nazi Party Organization. In December 1932 another disgruntled creditor complained to Wilhelm Frick, the later Reich Minister of the Interior. While some Nazis thought Helldorf was poor because of the sacrifices he had made for their cause, others thought it was a shortage of money that had brought him back into politics. His rapid career in the SA was resented by some of his Berlin subordinates. On 1 November 1932 an anonymous member of the Berlin-Brandenburg SA Group wrote to Hitler criticizing Helldorf: 'Apparently people in Munich [Party Headquarters] think that none of the old Party leaders in Berlin is capable of filling such a post. Of course it has to be a Count. We up here have had enough of his sort, who have done nothing for the Movement but immediately get the rich pickings. Now Mr Hitler what has this Mr Helldorf achieved up to now? When he was stinking rich none of us knew him. Once he had squandered everything he remembered there was an NSDAP ... and thanks to Mr Roehm he was able to bring it off.' In February 1933 another disgruntled Nazi veteran wrote to Hitler complaining it was hard to imagine anyone more depraved than Count Helldorf, who had ruined himself through womanizing and gambling away hundreds of thousands of marks. This veteran reproached Hitler with greeting Helldorf in public as if he were 'one of the chief matadors of our great movement'.[24]

This was the crux of the matter. Despite the griping from below, Helldorf retained the confidence of the bosses. During the Nazi seizure of power he was one of the figures Hitler turned to in a crisis. On 29 January 1933, the eve of his appointment as Reich Chancellor, Hitler heard rumours that Schleicher was planning a coup d'état to prevent the formation of a Hitler cabinet. Thereupon Hitler ordered Helldorf to place the whole Berlin SA on alert. But no coup materialized. Schleicher decided resistance was impossible as it would contravene the authority of the venerated Reich President, Paul von Hindenburg, and might lead to civil war. At the beginning of the Nazi regime Helldorf enjoyed high standing with Hitler.[25]

Hermann Goering was appointed Minister of the Interior for the state of Prussia in the coalition government Hitler formed with the German Nationalists on 30 January 1933. During February Goering removed the Chiefs of Police in fourteen of Prussia's cities. For the most part their successors were non-Nazi conservatives. The British Ambassador to Berlin, Sir Horace Rumbold, reported to London on 22 February that 'the Nationalists appear to exercise some control of the new appointments, and the more scandalous nominations seem to have been vetoed by them. Thus, the appointment to the presidency of the Berlin police of young Count Helldorf ... was frustrated.' However, Goering did install Helldorf as the new Police President of Potsdam.[26] As he was lazy, dishonest and dissolute, Helldorf was not perhaps the obvious choice to lead a police force. Indeed, his indolence and apathy meant that despite this early preferment, Helldorf's career in the Third Reich would never quite match his influence during the seizure of power.

After becoming Police President of Potsdam, Helldorf celebrated with a spending spree. He ordered a Mercedes he forgot to pay for, and in June 1933 spent 400 RM at 'Wendt's Exclusive Tailoring' in Berlin-Schoeneberg, although his official income that month was only 756 RM. During his time in Potsdam Helldorf had constant money troubles, even though in December 1933 he was elected to the Reichstag, whose members drew generous expenses. His conduct of police business showed his inexperience. When the Potsdam butchers were accused of charging excessive prices, Helldorf took them all into protective custody, so that for a day it was impossible to buy meat in the city. In the evening Helldorf apologized to the butchers and released them.[27]

For years the right-wing conservatives in the German nobility had looked down on Helldorf and those like him for losing class through their association with a mass movement like the NSDAP. So Helldorf was irritated by the ease with which new aristocratic converts to Nazism found a place in the Third Reich. In particular, he was annoyed by the success of the right-wing Association of German Nobles in currying favour with Hitler. In February 1933 Prince Adolf zu Bentheim-Tecklenburg-Rheda became Chairman of the Nobles' Association. Prince Bentheim was not a man of progressive views. The previous year he had told the annual Conference of Nobles that 'nobles do not belong in the ranks of whingeing pacifists, but where the blood is flowing'. In June 1933 Bentheim met Hitler and promised him the Association's unconditional obedience. In reply Hitler assured Prince Bentheim that many nobles had been excellent fighters for his Movement. Hitler was willing to forgive and forget because support from the nobility helped him to achieve respectability in the eyes of President Hindenburg and the army.

Helldorf was stung to protest. On 16 December 1933 he wrote to Hitler asking him not to encourage the endeavours of the Association of German Nobles, as this mainly comprised the non-Nazi section of the German nobility. Hitler rebuffed Helldorf's request.[28] Helldorf's fears that Johnnies-come-lately in the nobility would achieve preferment at the expense of veterans like himself were exaggerated. The vagueness of Nazi ideology left a vacuum in which long service and loyalty conferred particular status in the Third Reich. Helldorf could always count on this until his final betrayal offended against the very mechanism that had made him.

Following his appointment as Potsdam Chief of Police, Helldorf had been relieved of his duties as an SA Senior Group Leader on 20 February 1933. Yet for the time being he remained head of the Berlin-Brandenburg SA and in this capacity he played a significant role in the Nazi reaction to the Reichstag Fire. Our knowledge of this role comes from Helldorf's testimony at the Reichstag Fire trial on 20 September 1933. Helldorf was called as a witness by the prosecution to give him an opportunity to clear his reputation, as he had been labelled an arsonist by the Communist-sponsored *Brown Book* published in Paris by Willi Muenzenberg during summer 1933. The *Brown Book* alleged that Helldorf had been one of a group of Nazi plotters who had set the Reichstag on fire using a Dutch Communist Marinus van der Lubbe as a fall guy. Muenzenberg himself conceded privately that he had included much fantasy and invention in the *Brown Book*. With his reputation for violence and corruption, Helldorf was gift-wrapped for Communist propaganda.[29]

Helldorf told the court that on the night of 27 February 1933 he had worked in his office until about 7 pm and then joined Professor Sixt von Arnim, his chief of staff at the time, for dinner at Klinger's in the Rankestrasse. While they were dining, news came that there was a fire at the Reichstag. Other Nazi leaders hurried to the Reichstag when they learned of the fire. With characteristic indolence – *pas trop de zèle* could have been Helldorf's motto – he did not bother to go to the Reichstag himself. Instead he sent along Arnim to find out what was going on. Later that night Helldorf ordered his SA Group to arrest Communist and Social Democrat leaders. Helldorf told the court that he gave the orders completely on his own responsibility, for as head of the Berlin SA he felt thoroughly entitled to arrest enemies of the state. Helldorf's testimony reminded the Nazi elite of his role in the destruction of the Left following the Reichstag Fire.[30]

Helldorf's good standing with Hitler and Goering was reinforced by skilfully distancing himself from his old patron Ernst Roehm. When the Reichstag Fire Trial took place, Helldorf had already been replaced by Roehm as head of the Berlin Brandenburg SA. At the time of the Roehm Putsch in June 1934, when Hitler slaughtered much of the SA Leadership, Helldorf did not have specific SA regional responsibilities. He had deftly abandoned the sinking ship and found the new political line.

According to Erich von Manstein, at the time Chief of Staff of the Army District for Berlin, Helldorf had recognized the dangers of Roehm's plan to replace the army with the SA and indeed warned the army that the SA Leadership was planning a coup d'état. During the Putsch, General von Schleicher and his wife were murdered within Helldorf's jurisdiction as Police President of Potsdam. The local police informed the Public Prosecutor, who asked Helldorf for homicide detectives from the criminal police. After the detectives had begun taking depositions at Schleicher's house, Helldorf appeared and told them not to record witness statements but just to write a report on the crime scene. Soon afterwards a team of Gestapo and SS arrived and replaced the criminal police in the enquiry. Helldorf's role had been to minimize the investigation of the Schleicher murders. Helldorf never seems to have commented on the slaughter of his old friend Roehm.[31]

Because of his long association with Roehm it was rumoured that Helldorf was among the slain. On 24 July 1934 the Helldorfs were amongst the guests at a dinner party Ribbentrop gave at his home in Dahlem. Believing him to be dead, the other guests were amazed to be introduced to Count Helldorf, the Potsdam Chief of Police. The American Ambassador, William E. Dodd, was among those present. While Helldorf was a taciturn figure in Nazi uniform, his Countess lectured the Ambassador on the need to sterilize all American 'negroes' and declared that the Jews never worked, a complaint in which her husband joined.[32]

As Ambassador Dodd had discovered, the reports of Helldorf's death were much exaggerated. Yet in the aftermath of the Putsch, Helldorf presented an inviting target for those entrusted with cleaning up the SA. These included Police General Kurt Daluege and SA *Standartenfuehrer* Gottlieb Roesner, both of whom were old enemies of Helldorf's. Daluege had been one of the *Frontbann* leaders in 1925, when the organization was planning to seize the formerly German port of Memel, which had been occupied by Lithuania after the First World War. Four ships were waiting with munitions in Stettin when they were seized suddenly by the Prussian Government. Daluege suspected that Helldorf had tipped off the authorities. Gottlieb Roesner had founded the first local branch of the Berlin SA at Spandau in 1925. Roesner referred to the Stettin affair when he met Helldorf in 1930, and claimed that Helldorf never forgave him for this and blocked his promotion. In the aftermath of the Roehm Putsch Daluege became Acting Leader of the SA Groups in north-east

Germany, including Helldorf's old Berlin-Brandenburg Group. Daluege entrusted the cleansing of this particular group to Roesner. The *Standartenfuehrer* carried out a search in the flat of *SA-Gruppenfuehrer* Ernst, who had been among the victims of the Putsch. There he found receipts signed by Helldorf for sums of money received from the Jewish spiritualist Erik Jan Hanussen.[33]

Helldorf became the target of an official SA enquiry that rumbled on for nearly a year. The SA Court assembled a protracted list of complaints against him ranging from drunkenness to corruption. It was charged that in 1932 he had often visited the Monocle Bar in Berlin's Kurfuerstenstrasse wearing SA uniform and in the company of other SA leaders. Under the influence of drink, Helldorf's party would request the band to play the Horst Wessel Song, the SA anthem that celebrated a Berlin pimp and illustrious martyr in the fight against Bolshevism. The SA Court also collected a great deal of evidence on Helldorf's debts. He owed 10,000 RM to a horse trainer in Hoppegarten, whom Roesner telephoned for the details, and nearly 500 RM to his landlady there. He had also given his word of honour to pay his mother's rent but had not done so. He also owed money to a bookkeeper. Helldorf had used his title to gain a great deal of credit, which he had little prospect of repaying. However, the most serious charge against Helldorf was that he had taken money for the SA from a Jew, Hanussen, and then embezzled it.[34]

Helldorf's former SA adjutant, Sixt von Arnim, stoutly defended his old chief in a letter of 25 January 1935 on his impressive new stationery as Vice-Chancellor of Berlin Technological University. Arnim wrote that Helldorf did not know that Hanussen was Jewish. Arnim conceded that he might well have passed on a cash donation from Hanussen to Helldorf, but this did not mean that Helldorf had spent the money on himself. Arnim not only defended Helldorf's financial probity, he also defended the Count's lifestyle: 'In view of all that I know from living with Count Helldorf, the stories about his extravagant way of life are completely baseless. Count Helldorf lived relatively simply. I never once saw him drunk.'[35]

The enquiry against Helldorf stalled due to lack of evidence. It was hard to prove embezzlement. The key figure Hanussen had been murdered in mysterious circumstances so could not give evidence. Although Helldorf was suspected of involvement in the murder, there was no proof of this. Furthermore, Helldorf's patrons Goering and Goebbels were consolidating their position in the Nazi regime and were determined that Helldorf should rise too. The new SA Chief of Staff, Viktor Lutze, gradually realized there was no dividend in hunting someone with such powerful friends. In May 1935 he transferred the proceedings to the Party Court, which dropped them in August. Roesner was expelled from the SA on the grounds that his actions against Helldorf were prompted by a desire for revenge. A nobody like Roesner stood little chance in a feud with someone who not only had friends in Hitler's circle but also occasional access to the Fuehrer himself.[36]

Helldorf's most active patron was Reich Minister of Propaganda Joseph Goebbels. As Gauleiter of Berlin, Goebbels was determined that his friend Helldorf should be Chief of Police in his city in place of Rear Admiral Magnus von Levetzow, who had only joined the Nazi Party on 1 August 1932, the day after his election as one of its Reichstag deputies. Von Levetzow had been appointed Police President of Berlin in early 1933 after Helldorf's candidacy had been vetoed by the German Nationalists. In June 1935 von Levetzow intervened to stop violence by Nazi mobs against cafes in Jewish ownership. As long as von Levetzow was Police President, anti-Semites could not do what they liked on the streets of Berlin. Goebbels repeatedly urged on Hitler that von Levetzow should be replaced by Helldorf. In the middle of July 1935 Hitler took a short holiday with Goebbels on the Baltic Coast – Helldorf was amongst the others present – and once again the Propaganda Minister returned to the charge. A telegram arrived from Berlin reporting a Jewish demonstration against an anti-Semitic film. A group of Jews had taken advantage of the cinema's darkness to make a brave protest. Goebbels skilfully deployed this as the final straw. As he noted in his diary on 15 July, 'The Fuehrer has now had enough. He wants to remove Levetzow at once.' Von Levetzow was pushed out and on 18 July Helldorf was appointed Acting Police President. On 19 July Goebbels recorded jubilantly: 'Levetzow removed, Helldorf appointed. Bravo!'[37]

Von Levetzow was dismissed because he tried to police Berlin in accordance with the law. Helldorf replaced him on the strength of the credentials he had gained from the Kudamm affray in 1931. This pogrom had been the catalyst for Helldorf's meteoric rise in the SA. Now once again it was the making of him, as Hitler and Goebbels wanted the racial policing of the Reich capital in the hands of a proven anti-Semite. Helldorf appeared to be the man to clear Berlin's streets of Jews, just as he had tried to clear the Kudamm in 1931. At a press conference Helldorf announced that fighting the Jews in Berlin would be one of his major tasks and, bowing to Goebbels, he declared that 'he could only work in the Reich capital in very close co-operation with the relevant Party authorities, in particular the Gauleitung of Berlin'.[38]

As the new Police President of Berlin, Helldorf deferred not only to Goebbels but also to Reinhard Heydrich, head of the Gestapo. One of Helldorf's most important new tasks was to plan the involvement of the Berlin police in the arrangements for the 1936 Olympics. Police preparations were co-ordinated by a 'Police Command Staff', which included a Gestapo officer. Helldorf appointed as his representative Hans-Bernd Gisevius, a right-wing lawyer in the Prussian Civil Service. Gisevius had wanted to become head of the Gestapo and was bitterly resentful of Himmler and Heydrich, who had frustrated his ambition. In February 1936 Heydrich wrote to Helldorf that if Gisevius were to take part in the Olympic preparations it would impair co-operation with the Gestapo. Helldorf sacrificed his representative without a murmur. He replaced Gisevius with another deputy and told Heydrich in an attempt to make light of the matter that he hoped 'by this means the stone of offence will be removed'.[39]

One reason for Helldorf's diffidence was that he had not been able to enrich himself in Potsdam, and his finances were still in disarray. Others suffered more from this than did Helldorf himself. At the end of July 1935 his father wrote to a Jewish friend that 'it is not easy for me as someone who was once very prosperous and a landowner still to have to earn my bread at the age of sixty-seven ... My son is really overloaded with special tasks in his new office so that for the time being he is still unable to do anything for me.' Helldorf's debts put a question mark over his new appointment. In August State Secretary Grauert of the Ministry of the Interior informed him that his appointment could be confirmed only after they had discussed his debts. Helldorf claimed that Himmler had helped him to settle the first half of his debts and had promised in the event of Helldorf's confirmation to see to the regulation of the second half of his debts as well. Indeed, through Himmler's good offices in March 1935, Goering, in his capacity as Prussian Prime Minister, had made Helldorf a loan of 10,000 RM. It was made clear that he was not expected to repay it. Helldorf's appointment as Police President of Berlin must have been confirmed in August, as more of his debts were then sorted out. On 20 August Helldorf drafted a document estimating his debts at 20–25,000 RM. Himmler apparently took this document to Hitler, who signed it to approve payment.[40]

The assistance Helldorf received during 1935 from Himmler, Goering and Hitler himself suggest his political standing was high and much was expected of him. But despite their help, Helldorf's money problems continued and undermined his efforts to defend his jurisdiction as Police President of Berlin. One dangerous rival was his long-standing adversary, General of Police Kurt Daluege, the national Chief of Constabulary. Daluege had become one of Himmler's instruments for the centralization and reorganization of the German police. Helldorf's Police Presidium was a potential obstacle to these processes. On 15 March 1937 Daluege wrote to Helldorf complaining that his officials had difficulty in getting information from departments in the Berlin Police Presidium. Daluege pointed out that Helldorf was his subordinate, and should have mentioned that his salary was mortgaged due to long-standing debts. Daluege further complained that Helldorf's officers never referred to their boss as the Police Chief but always as 'the Count': 'the Count has ordered', 'the Count has commanded' etc. Daluege reminded Helldorf that Himmler had forbidden such forms of address. The pettiness of this particular complaint suggested considerable bad blood between Daluege and Helldorf.[41]

In his reply Helldorf wrote that he had forbidden the officers of the Police Presidium to have any direct contact with superior agencies except in matters of secondary importance. As to his debts, Helldorf claimed that he had chosen to discuss these with Himmler rather than Daluege because the latter was very abrupt and wounding when he raised personal matters. Helldorf continued: 'I am aware that because I am called Count Helldorf I have a black mark against me ... I place damned little value on this title of Count and would gladly renounce it.'[42]

Following his brush with Daluege, Helldorf worried he might lose his job. On 20 May 1937 Goebbels noted in his diary: 'Helldorf is afraid that Himmler wants to topple him. I am able to reassure him. Himmler is too ambitious.' Two days later Goebbels noted that perhaps Helldorf was only seeing 'white mice'. But Himmler was anything but a white mouse. He had tried to aid Helldorf with his debts, perhaps in an initial belief that Helldorf was an energetic and radical Nazi who could be used in the building of the SS state. Daluege seems to have convinced Himmler that Helldorf was not only obstructive but that his sloth, womanizing and financial carelessness outweighed his credentials as a Party veteran. Even Goebbels was critical of Helldorf's apathy and reluctance to stick up for himself. But Goebbels would not let his old friend lose the Police Presidency, commenting that 'Himmler must not take everything from him.' Helldorf may have benefited from Hitler's extreme reluctance to dismiss long-standing Nazis even if they were lazy and corrupt. On 15 December Goebbels discussed the question of the Berlin Police Presidium with Himmler, who in making senior police appointments sought to achieve co-operation with the Gauleiter rather than to ride roughshod over them. Himmler was by now reconciled to Helldorf staying on and made this clear.[43]

After retaining his post as Police President despite pressure from Himmler, during late January 1938 Helldorf was involved in the most dangerous crisis the Nazi regime had faced since June 1934. On 12 January 1938 the Minister of War and Commander in Chief of the Armed Forces, Field Marshal Werner von Blomberg, was married in a small private ceremony at which Hitler and Goering were the witnesses. Some days after the wedding the Berlin Gestapo heard that the city's prostitutes were delighted that one of them had done so well as to become 'Frau Feldmarschall'. The Gestapo discovered that there was indeed a file and index cards on the new Frau Blomberg in the Police Presidium. Frau Blomberg's residence card combined the address of the Field Marshal with details of her vice conviction.[44]

Within the Gestapo, discussion of the case reached as high as the chief, Reinhard Heydrich. Heydrich came from the same part of Germany as Helldorf and the two had served in the same Freikorps. Not only was it natural for Heydrich to involve Helldorf, Frau Blomberg's conviction was for modelling pornographic photographs and so technically it was a matter for the Police President rather than the Gestapo. Certainly there was little between Heydrich and Helldorf in terms of their suitability for dealing with a matter of honour. Indeed, the Blomberg affair gave a wide range of scoundrels an unaccustomed sense of moral superiority. Even Goebbels believed that at last he had found someone whose behaviour was worse than his own.[45]

After their initial enquiries the Gestapo passed the matter on to Helldorf and gave him an opportunity to assert the authority of his office. Helldorf's priority was to check that the photograph in his records really was of Frau Blomberg. He remembered having seen a newspaper announcement to the effect that the son of General Wilhelm Keitel was to marry Blomberg's daughter. Keitel was Blomberg's right-hand man in the Ministry of War. He had both a professional and a private interest in avoiding a scandal. Helldorf went to see him on 21 January 1938. But Keitel could not make an identification one way or the other. Helldorf then tried to see Blomberg himself, but the Field Marshal was absent. Keitel offered to show Blomberg the photograph the following day, but Helldorf refused to hand over the evidence. He wanted immediate clarity to spare both army and regime a scandal. Then Keitel suggested Helldorf should go to Goering, who had seen the young woman when acting as a witness at the wedding. Helldorf immediately agreed to this idea. Goering was someone Helldorf wished to cultivate. Furthermore, Goering's political seniority was such that once he knew about the matter Helldorf would lose any responsibility for it. It suited Helldorf to invite a much larger vulture to inspect the carcass. On seeing the photograph Goering confirmed that the nude woman was indeed Frau Blomberg: 'It is a catastrophe!'

Now the criminal past of his wife was established, Blomberg was finished whatever he did. Even if he divorced his new wife he could not survive the ridicule and by involving Hitler as a witness he had made the Fuehrer look ridiculous as well. This was borne out by the reaction of Reich Criminal Police Director Arthur Nebe, who gazed at the image of Frau Blomberg clad only in a string of pearls and exclaimed: 'to think the Fuehrer kissed this very woman's hand!' Despite his annoyance over being made a fool, at first Hitler unrealistically tried to retain the congenial Blomberg but abandoned the attempt when the Field Marshal refused to give up his new wife. But even if Hitler had persuaded Blomberg to divorce, the army would no longer have accepted him as Commander in Chief of the Armed Forces.[46] Helldorf's role in the crisis had been restrained and effective. He had passed the matter quickly upwards with the minimum of fuss. Helldorf could feel that he had handled a difficult problem carefully. Now there could be no further talk of removing him as Police President.

Goebbels had wanted Helldorf to become Police President of Berlin primarily because his friend had previously been a useful instrument in Goebbels' radical anti-Semitic measures. By June 1938 Goebbels saw Helldorf and the police as the means through which he could drive the

Jews out of Berlin. On 4 June 1938 Goebbels noted in his diary that he 'discussed Berlin's Jewish Question with Helldorf. He still sees a great number of difficulties. But we will master them. (Our) goal is to drive the Jews out of Berlin. And indeed without sentimentality … (Helldorf) is resolved upon it.' On 11 June Goebbels addressed three hundred officers of the Berlin police: 'I really whip them up. Against any sentimentality. The slogan is not legality but brutality. The Jews must get out of Berlin. The police must help me in this.' On 19 June Goebbels noted that 'Helldorf is now taking radical action in the Jewish question. The Party is helping him. Many arrests … The police have understood my instructions.' Yet three days later it became apparent that Helldorf at least had not understood Goebbels' instructions. Goebbels complained in his diary: 'The Jewish question in Berlin has now become very complicated. The Party has daubed (the windows of) Jewish shops, probably at Helldorf's instigation. Thereupon Funk (the Reich Minister of Economics) intervened. He wants everything to be done legally. But that takes such a long time … Helldorf has turned my orders into the direct opposite; I had said that the police were to take action legally [he had not: see above] while the Party looked on. Now the reverse is happening. I summon all Party authorities and issue new orders. No illegal measures are to take place. The Jews are to make their shops clean again themselves.'

Goebbels had wanted the police to break the law and do his dirty work rather than his own Berlin Nazi Party, but Helldorf was wary of criticism and had incited the Party instead. To restore his credibility with Goebbels, later in June Helldorf did take some action to meet the Gauleiter's wish for the police to help tighten the screw on Berlin's Jews. On 29 June Helldorf informed the Berlin police of his fear that in removing the Nazi slogans from their shop windows Jewish businesses were trying to obscure their names. Helldorf requested the police 'to control particularly severely the placing of names on Jewish businesses, and in all cases where the names cannot be read clearly from the outside to demand that they be placed in accordance with the regulations as soon as possible'. Helldorf was now taking an interest in legal measures against the Jews of Berlin. In early July he sought to please Goebbels by proposing the establishment of a ghetto in Berlin to be paid for by the rich members of the Jewish Community. Later in the month Helldorf provided Goebbels with a list of anti-Semitic measures. Goebbels noted with satisfaction that these were 'truly rigorous and comprehensive. This way we will drive the Jews out of Berlin in the foreseeable future.' On the limited archival evidence of documents on which Helldorf's name appears rather than merely the designation 'Police President', it seems that in his official capacity Helldorf was an eager advocate of sharper 'legal' actions against Berlin's Jews, although he had now abandoned hooligan anti-Semitism. In this way, the following year on 12 October 1939 Helldorf sent a report on economic developments to the Governor of Brandenburg. He wrote that 'in order to prevent the provisioning of the Jewish population with foodstuffs before the Aryan population, which unfortunately takes place, it is suggested that all Jews ... should include the names which are supposed to show Jewish origin [Israel and Sara] on their ration cards'.[47]

If it suited him, Helldorf would have contact with Jewish Germans in a private capacity. In July 1938 the Reichsfuehrer SS and Chief of the German Police, Heinrich Himmler, wrote to Helldorf suggesting that he change his dentist. An SA man had reported that Helldorf and his brother-in-law Count Wedel visited a Jewish dentist. This was during the very period in which Helldorf was pressing forward anti-Semitic measures. Himmler had arranged for the report to be investigated and discovered that the dentist in question was indeed Jewish. Himmler told Helldorf that, 'I assume ... that in future you will no longer visit him.' Helldorf's file includes a cheque for 160 RM made out in favour of the dentist, who was fortunate indeed to get payment from this particular patient.[48] Many of the documents in Helldorf's SA file dating from between 1931 and 1937 concern his indebtedness. There are no such documents for the period after 1938. Helldorf had now found a lucrative new source of revenue.

With the increasing tempo of anti-Semitic measures, many Jews became increasingly desperate to leave Germany. Department Two of the Berlin Police Presidium supervised passport and emigration documents for the largest and richest Jewish community in Germany. Two accounts survive in the Wiener Library of the way Helldorf treated desperate Jews trying to escape from Berlin. In March 1938 a non-Jewish actress went to see him after the Gestapo had confiscated the passport of a Jewish playwright. It seems likely the actress already knew Helldorf. Although at first he was astonished by her intervention, Helldorf promised to arrange for a passport, which he did. Later in the year a civil servant in the Reich

Chancellery promised to help a rich Jew overcome the obstacles to his emigration. On the morning of 10 November 1938 the Jew in question, 'trembling and white as death', called on a friend to say goodbye: 'that morning he had received his emigration permit from Count Helldorf personally in return for a payment of several hundred thousand marks'. Although it is difficult to generalize from only two cases, both suggest that for a Jewish German to have a non-Jewish advocate swayed Helldorf. Furthermore, the second-hand evidence that he exploited a rich Jew's terror to extract a bribe tallies both with Helldorf's long-standing willingness to exploit anti-Semitism for his own benefit and with his lack of any scruple in financial matters. Hans-Otto Meissner claimed that 'Helldorf protected many Jews in a remarkable way and enabled a number to emigrate.' This is too indulgent. For Helldorf, anti-Semitism was always a matter of calculation as well as ideology. He was unscrupulous in exploiting anti-Semitism for his political advancement or, it seems, to line his pockets.[49]

Goebbels had initially been disappointed by the legalism of Helldorf's public anti-Semitism in 1938. Even though Helldorf had tried to appease Goebbels by pushing ahead with legal measures, his political meddling and lack of a work ethic had further annoyed the Gauleiter. On 10 July Goebbels noted in his diary that, 'Himmler complains to me about Helldorf ... He doesn't work hard, instead he always just meddles in high politics.' On 12 July Goebbels returned to the same theme: 'He is too slack and passive. I parade all his faults before him. It makes him very dejected. But he can't escape from his skin.'[50]

Although Helldorf was proving a disappointment to his patron, he did offer Goebbels effective support during his lengthy and dangerous liaison with the Czech actress Lida Baarova. In 1938 the long-suffering Magda Goebbels finally took revenge by having an affair with Goebbels' deputy Karl Hanke, the State Secretary in the Propaganda Ministry. In October 1938 Helldorf told Goebbels about this relationship and was his closest ally during the ensuing rumpus. Hitler was determined that Goebbels and his wife should be reconciled, and on 24 October he summoned the Propaganda Minister to Berchtesgaden for this purpose. Goebbels noted in his diary that, 'Helldorf is called for and has to confirm explicitly some of the statements made by me. He does so with considerable and impressive firmness.' Hitler ordered Goebbels and his wife to attempt a reconciliation. On the way back to Berlin, Goebbels had a long talk with

Helldorf, 'who showed the deepest human sympathy for my position'.[51] But although Helldorf had proved a friend in need for Goebbels, the Count's disregard for the Gauleiter's wishes concerning anti-Semitic measures during 1938 was the writing on the wall for their intimacy. Helldorf had begun to think for himself. Goebbels' diaries for 1939 contain less mention of Helldorf, previously his closest friend, although the diaries also suggest that during 1940 and 1941, when a Nazi victory seemed imminent, their relationship to some extent revived.

Goebbels sought to recover his standing with Hitler by finding a way to accelerate the expulsion of Jewish Germans from the economy. He knew that Hitler shared his frustration at the slow pace of anti-Semitic measures. So Goebbels exploited the murder of a German diplomat in Paris by a Jewish refugee to launch the 'Crystal Night' Pogrom against the German Jews in November 1938, much as he had instigated Helldorf's Kudamm action against the Jews in 1931. Helldorf was on holiday during the pogrom. According to Gisevius, immediately after his return Helldorf summoned his officers and declared that if he had been in Berlin he would have commanded the police to shoot the rioters. Helldorf was a poacher turned gamekeeper. The anti-Semitic hooligan of 1931 was now President of Police. Violence against people and destruction of property in the streets of Berlin made Helldorf look ridiculous and undermined the prestige of his office. This explains his reaction to the pogrom, not any concern for the fate of the Jews. Furthermore, it was easy to be a bold gendarme after the mobs had dispersed. Helldorf's audience no doubt saw through his protestations. Helldorf did not become an opponent of Hitler because he had difficulties with anti-Semitism. Indeed, on the very day he reportedly denounced the pogrom Helldorf extorted an enormous bribe from a Jew desperate to emigrate.[52]

Helldorf's anti-Semitism undermined positive factors in his make-up such as his concern for the Protestant Church. His mansion at Wohlmirstedt had overshadowed the adjacent village church, exemplifying the protective relationship between squire and parson. During his later interrogation by the Gestapo, Helldorf protested that he had never understood why the issue of the Protestant Church was raised with such intensity. But as Police President of Berlin Helldorf placed such difficulties in the way of the 'Missionary Society for the Promotion of Christianity amongst the Jews' that the Reich Church Committee stopped its independent activity. Helldorf's benevolence extended only to a racially homogenous Protestant Church.[53]

At the height of his power in 1938, Helldorf epitomized the sleazy aspects of the Nazi Movement. He seemed the archetypal *Bonze*, the Party big-wig who exploited his position to live well. Like many other prominent Nazis, Helldorf led a life of luxury. In April 1938, shortly after the annexation of Austria, Hitler's architect Albert Speer went to Vienna to help stage Hitler's triumphal appearance. With the puritanism of the zealot, Speer was appalled to see how many Party bosses had arrived from Germany to exploit the well-stocked Viennese shops. In particular, Speer noticed Helldorf's descent on Vienna. During the war conspicuous consumption by prominent Nazis became a serious concern to the authorities. In March 1943 Goebbels asked Helldorf to produce a report on the Berlin grocer Noethling who supplied customers with fine wines, game and delicatessen in defiance of the rationing laws. Helldorf duly reported that a large proportion of those prominent in public life living in west Berlin had received great quantities of food from Noethling without using ration coupons. Helldorf stressed that Noethling did not deserve the main part of the blame, rather his customers should be punished more severely than Noethling himself. Helldorf's report and posturing were noteworthy for their hypocrisy. He prudently concealed the fact that he had bought spirits, wine and champagne from Noethling to the tune of about 3,100 *Reichsmark,* and had sent a police van several times to Noethling's premises to collect the bottles. In the aftermath of the July Plot the Gestapo found a grocery bill for over 2,700 RM among Helldorf's papers. The items listed included 1,500 cigarettes and four whole sheep at a time when meat was strictly rationed and Helldorf's responsibilities included the policing of Berlin's shops. The quantities involved are so big it seems likely that Helldorf was trading on the black market. Despite his financial difficulties during the 1930s, by 1944 Helldorf owned four homes. Such a rise to prosperity was scarcely possible on the basis of his official income. It seems that in extortion from Jews and the black market he had found lucrative additional earnings.[54]

The year 1938 had been the turning point for Helldorf's finances, when he had finally resolved his financial problems by extorting money from Jews desperate to emigrate. This brought in more income than even Helldorf could spend. It was also the year when he had cemented his grasp on the Police President's job by his deft handling of the Blomberg affair. But Helldorf was eager to rise further. His humiliating loss of the family estate as a young man had left him acutely ambitious, though his ambition was at odds with his natural sloth and carelessness. Helldorf's future career depended on Himmler's benevolence, as the latter determined senior police promotions. Yet the dentist episode suggested a lack of ideological punctiliousness on Helldorf's part. Even worse, with a striking lack of prudence in April 1938 he had warned Goebbels against the Security Service [SD] of the SS in the presence of an SD officer. Himmler had aided Helldorf with his debts in the past, and the pair addressed each other by the familiar 'Du', but Himmler doubted Helldorf's suitability for further promotion within the burgeoning SS empire. As discussed above, at one stage Himmler contemplated removing Helldorf as Police President of Berlin but concluded this would cause more trouble with Goebbels than the matter was worth. In any case, the undermining of such posts as the Police Presidency in the course of Himmler's restructuring of the German police meant that Helldorf could be left there and simply bypassed.

The key post in the future police structure was the 'Higher SS and Police Leader' established by a decree of Reich Minister of the Interior Wilhelm Frick in November 1937. In the event of war the Higher SS and Police Leader was to command all units subordinate to Himmler, whether police or SS, within a particular Army District. Himmler appointed *SS-Obergruppenfuehrer* Heissmeyer as Higher SS and Police Leader for the Berlin-Brandenburg District. On 2 September 1939 Helldorf was merely appointed to the subordinate post of Higher Police Leader for Greater Berlin. In addition to the units subordinate to him as Police President, Helldorf also gained some authority over the Berlin Fire Brigade. This was small consolation for Helldorf's failure to get the job that mattered, an embarrassingly clear signal that his career had stalled. He was now under Heissmeyer's jurisdiction. To rub salt in the wound, Helldorf's former secretary, Freiherr von Eberstein, was appointed Higher SS and Police Leader for Bavaria. As late as 1943 Heissmeyer remarked that 'despite my good working relationship with Count Helldorf I am convinced that the desires he has expressed [to become Higher SS and Police Leader] will never grow cold'. Himmler sought to deprive Helldorf of justification for his ambition by making sure he was kept fully informed. Nevertheless, Helldorf's failure to become Higher SS and Police Leader rankled so much that it proved a factor in prompting his resistance activity. He later told the Gestapo that, 'I saw in my subordination to an SS and Higher Police Leader [sic] for my Berlin area of jurisdiction a personal and undeserved slight.'[55]

After the failure of the July Plot, the Gestapo made Helldorf explain his attitude to the conspiracy. Helldorf replied that 'the causes which produced a change in my inner attitude to the Fuehrer and the Party date back months or years. It was a long process of development, often interrupted through new hopes and attempts to preserve my old belief ... I am not one of those people who can believe unconditionally, and because I could not force myself to unconditional faith, during the last years of the war I fell increasingly into a state of hopelessness and depression. I must also admit, that unlike many of my Party comrades I am not unconditionally devoted to the Fuehrer. Once I used to see in the Fuehrer the man who embodied everything I desired or hoped for my German people and Fatherland. Due to rational consideration this belief had begun to crumble from 1941 onwards, and my concern for my Fatherland became more important than the loyalty towards the Fuehrer which had previously been a matter of course. In face of the looming catastrophe and under the impact of the constant flow of bad news which was brought to me I hoped by whatever means to avert the great threatening danger through a change in the person of the head of state.' Helldorf further commented that 'my personal attitude remains today the same as ever, [namely] that I approve of National Socialism as it was understood and spread by us during the years of struggle ... [However] I can no longer approve of what is presented to me now as the realization of National Socialism.'[56] Helldorf's explanation of his attitudes has a careful and structured nature that makes it credible. It is not just an exculpation produced by duress.

Helldorf's first serious criticism of the regime came in a confidential official report on Berlin during October 1935. Helldorf drew attention to problems of supply, the cost of food, and rising unemployment. Although his officials no doubt provided the material for this report, by signing it Helldorf took overall responsibility for the contents. Goebbels was well aware of Helldorf's critical attitudes. In January 1936 he remarked on Helldorf's grousing, and in May 1937 he called him 'a born troublemaker'. Goebbels attributed Helldorf's critical attitude to a natural pessimism, but some of his later rage at Helldorf's role in the July Plot may have been due to a realization that he had been uncharacteristically obtuse in failing to perceive the scale of Helldorf's disillusionment. This discontent was about to be reinforced by regular contact with a perceptive critic of Nazism.[57]

In summer 1937 Fritz-Dietlof Graf von der Schulenburg, a vigorous defender of traditional Prussian standards in public service, was appointed Vice-President of the Berlin Police. The Reich Ministry of the Interior appointed Schulenburg to keep Helldorf in line. As discussed above, the Police President's indebtedness had concerned Grauert and his insubordination had provoked Daluege. Helldorf fought against Schulenburg's appointment for as long as he could. Yet when they eventually met, they hit it off immediately. Schulenburg wrote to his wife that Helldorf made 'an intelligent, witty impression. As far as his work is concerned he is absolutely a servant of the state and energetic defender of his position. I can't yet make out what is behind it all deep inside him, but anyway he makes an open and not a treacherous impression. I believe I will be able to work with him.' The historian Eberhard Zeller wrote that 'as the (Police) President emphasized the representational side of his work and building contacts and furthermore led a vigorous private life, the work was left to Schulenburg'. Some time later Helldorf met Schulenburg by prior arrangement at a Berlin swimming pool. With their voices masked by all the shrieking and splashing, they were able to exchange critical views about the Nazi regime.

At this early stage, both men still had hopes of a successful career within an increasingly powerful Nazi system, and Schulenburg was still thinking of reform rather than resistance. Schulenburg was particularly hostile to Nazi corruption, but he had little success in teaching Prussian austerity to Helldorf. The extent to which he propelled the Police Chief in the direction of resistance should not be exaggerated. In August 1939, at a time when Schulenburg himself was still in two minds about the regime, and so can scarcely have been putting a definite line to Helldorf, he was transferred from Berlin to Breslau and was no longer in daily contact with the Police President. Indeed, Schulenburg's own final conversion to anti-Nazi resistance came as late as the turn of 1942–43. Helldorf's former subordinate Gisevius had more influence in turning him against the SS in particular.[58]

By spring 1938 Helldorf had begun to establish links with critics of the regime outside his own immediate circle. He had a sense of loyalty towards the German Army and although the Blomberg affair had consolidated his own position, there is some evidence he came to feel Heydrich had used him during that episode. Blomberg's departure was quickly followed by that of General Werner von Fritsch, the Commander in Chief of the Army, on a trumped up charge of homosexuality. Hjalmar Schacht, Hitler's Minister of Economics who became an opponent of Nazism, recalled in his memoirs that Helldorf had told him the Gestapo had played a despicable part in the destruction of Blomberg and Fritsch. Helldorf felt particularly strongly about the intrigue against Fritsch. Homophobia had been mobilized to ruin Fritsch, just as it had provided a smokescreen for the murder of Roehm in 1934. For the Germans fret just as much about homosexual liaisons as the English do about affairs between men and women. Helldorf's indignation over the shabby and unjust way Fritsch had been treated was no doubt reinforced by his contacts in the army. On 28 February Helldorf vehemently denounced the intrigue against Fritsch to General Joachim von Stuelpnagel and in early March he made police documents relevant to the case available to Hans Oster, an officer in the Abwehr, the Secret Service of the German Armed Forces.[59]

The unsettling changes in Germany's military leadership gained greater significance in the light of the Czech crisis in late summer 1938, during which Hitler subjected Europe and the German people to a war of nerves. Helldorf became increasingly alarmed at the prospect of war. On 1 September 1938 Goebbels noted in his diary that 'Helldorf is a known pessimist. Now once more he is panicking at the prospect of war, spreading the craziest alarmist rumours and making himself the spokesman of sheer absurdities.' Hitler's adjutant and critic Fritz Wiedemann, who knew Helldorf, reported on the Count's alarm at foreign policy developments to General Ludwig Beck, the most prominent German opponent of Hitler's warmongering. After talking with Wiedemann on 29 July, Beck made a note that he should introduce Helldorf to General Erwin Witzleben, the Commander of Army District Three [Berlin]. Beck was relying on Witzleben to topple the Nazi regime in the event of war breaking out with Britain and France over Czechoslovakia. Gisevius was working closely with Witzleben, and claimed that in September 1938, 'Helldorf declared himself ready to fall in with us.' There is no other evidence to support Gisevius on this, but Helldorf may well have made a commitment at this stage. During the winter of 1938–39 he attended the retirement dinner of

General Witzleben, where he sat next to Wiedemann. The international situation seemed ominous to Wiedemann, so he commented to Helldorf: 'What do you think, what is to be done?' Helldorf replied: 'In the long run the only option will be for Hermann to mobilize his Goering regiment and close down your whole shop in the Wilhelmstrasse' [meaning the Reich Chancellery].

It is curious that even Helldorf, with his insider's knowledge of the Nazi Movement, was prey to the illusion of Goering as a conservative champion against Hitler. Wiedemann noted that Helldorf was on good terms with Goering. Certainly Helldorf could be sure of a place in a regime led by Goering, with whom he shared an unrelenting rapacity, whereas his prospects would be uncertain under a regime led by high-minded Christian officers. That the latter were willing to accept Helldorf as an ally, even with reservations, reflects the weakness of their support and probably owed something to their confidence in the influence of Helldorf's noble origins. Helldorf was returning to a class loyalty he had abandoned for Roehm in the 1920s. After Helldorf had thrown in his lot with the Nazis, he had been called a renegade by his noble relatives. By plotting against Hitler he could win the acceptance of some traditional Prussian aristocrats. Helldorf's noble status had helped to win patronage from Roehm, Goebbels and Goering. It had also provoked the hatred of figures like Roesner and Daluege, for whom Counts deserved no special place in the national community. As Helldorf's career stagnated from 1939 onwards, the slights he had endured in the Nazi Movement because he was a nobleman may have weighed more heavily with him than the early promotion he had enjoyed.[60]

Helldorf's contacts with the elite resistance in 1939 combined legitimate police business with opposition to the regime. On the eve of war, Helldorf was preoccupied with the prospect of unrest in the capital. On 24 August 1939 Helldorf expressed very great concern over the food supply to Admiral Canaris, the head of the Abwehr, and requested troops for Berlin, as there were not enough police. On 26 August Helldorf warned the Abwehr officer Helmuth Groscurth that the SS were planning a putsch against the Generals and wanted to instal Himmler as Reich Minister of the Interior with special plenipotentiary powers including influence on military appointments. Helldorf advised Groscurth 'that the Generals should do something immediately and demand the removal of the criminals who had got the Fuehrer and ourselves into this situation.

If the Fuehrer finally intervened, a stone would fall from the heart of the Wehrmacht.' Helldorf's warning about the danger of the SS to the army reached the Army Chief of Staff, General Ludwig Halder, who noted it in his diary. On 2 September 1939 Helldorf asked Groscurth for a liaison officer to the duty regiment in Berlin and three armoured cars. Groscurth went with Helldorf's request to Halder, who rejected it completely: 'What sort of impression would it make if armoured vehicles started rumbling around in Berlin now?' Groscurth noted in his diary: 'No military forces to be placed under the police! Halder does not believe there will be any disturbances at present.' Halder also made it clear that he did not trust Helldorf.[61]

During the 'Phoney War' of winter 1939–40 Helldorf maintained his resistance contacts. He passed to Canaris' private secretary, Hans von Dohnanyi, SD reports and SS films covering their massacres of Polish civilians. On 31 October 1939 Ulrich von Hassell, the former German Ambassador to Italy and an energetic opponent of Nazism, went to Horcher's, the most luxurious restaurant in Berlin. In one corner he spotted Helldorf together with Gisevius and Hans Oster, deputy to Canaris in the Abwehr and a central figure in the burgeoning elite resistance. When Gisevius visited Hassell a few days later, the latter remarked on Gisevius' evening with the Police President. Gisevius replied that he knew Helldorf from his time in the police and was 'completely sure that Helldorf thinks just as we do'. In Hassell's view Oster's presence at the Horcher meeting seemed to confirm this.[62]

On 5 January 1940 Helldorf met Oster again, this time in Abwehr headquarters. Helldorf had come to report to Groscurth on morale in Berlin and Oster sat in on the meeting. Helldorf began with some comments on the situation in the east, which he regarded as catastrophic. He reported a specific case in which the SS had shot Polish officers and expressed the fear that on their return to Germany the SS from Poland would no longer be able to rejoin civilian life, a phenomenon he himself knew only too well. After providing further material damning the SS, Helldorf discussed the situation in Berlin. The population were very mistrustful and sceptical, and morale would sink very quickly in the event of setbacks and losses. Helldorf thought that at most 40 per cent of people were in favour of the war and the Nazi Party. He reported that the active strength of the Berlin police was 6,000, of whom 2,000 were old and did office work. The attitude of the 4,000 men was good and they could never be used against the army. The tendency of Helldorf's report was very much to stiffen Hitler's military opponents by stressing the regime's atrocities in the east, its dwindling popular support at home and the goodwill of the police towards the army.[63]

Nazi Germany's astonishing victories during spring 1940 swept the ground from under the feet of the elite resistance. Popular morale soared and men of military age who had stayed at home now desperately sought to join up so they could share in the glory and loot. Helldorf had always been very interested in loot and his relations with Himmler had deteriorated again. After the German victory in Norway, he briefly attached himself to the army. He was present at the German offensive that led to the breach of the Maginot Line. The Gestapo later asserted that Helldorf's French campaign took place in a chauffeur-driven car with a valet in attendance.[64]

On his return to Berlin, Helldorf was involved in air raid precautions to deal with British bombing. As Police President, Helldorf had overall responsibility for the deployment of Berlin's fire-fighters and he also signed off the prodigiously detailed reports on air raid damage. In the winter of 1940–41 Berlin's air defences were inadequate and Helldorf doubted the city could withstand a serious onslaught. In spring he escaped to the army again. Goebbels noted that Helldorf 'is off to the front. The lucky man! In Berlin Himmler has taken all his powers away. After the war he [Helldorf] wants to resign.'[65]

Helldorf's return to the army was only temporary. As a minor political celebrity he was unsuitable for combat deployment and he did not have the training or knowledge of modern tactics for staff work. He was as embarrassingly redundant in the army as he was in the police, and soon found himself back in Berlin. As Hitler's strategy began to misfire from 1941 onwards, Helldorf intensified his contacts with the conservative opponents of Nazism. Helldorf told the People's Court that he had conversations with a series of men who increased his pessimism. He talked with Prussian Minister of Finance Johannes Popitz, and then had regular meetings every two months or so with General Friedrich Olbricht, head of the Army General Office, who explained military developments. Helldorf also frequently visited Ulrich-Wilhelm Count von Schwerin von Schwanenfeld, a resistance figure closely linked with Schulenburg. From February 1943 Count von Schwerin was on the staff of the Brandenburg Division, a commando-style outfit near Berlin that formed part of the Abwehr. Helldorf also had occasional meetings with General Fritz Fromm, the Commander in Chief of the Reserve Army, which mustered recruits for military service. Fromm told Helldorf that when he stood before his divisional commanders to give them a talk he had to speak as if wearing a mask in front of his face and afterwards felt like a liar. Fromm trusted Helldorf, and later told him that it would be best if Hitler took his own life.

Helldorf sought to escape from his own contradictions by returning to the army. In April 1943 he asked for Himmler's permission to serve at the front for several months. Helldorf's eldest two sons were both so severely wounded they could not return to the front for some time, and Helldorf told Himmler that 'I consider it appropriate in the present situation that at least one member of a large family should be serving at the front.' Himmler replied on 24 April that he could not spare Helldorf as Police Chief of Berlin as the city would probably be the target of further air raids. On 8 July 1943 Helldorf wrote to Himmler again saying that he had come to terms with his order. But he was becoming increasingly alarmed by Germany's military setbacks.[66]

During the year leading up to the 20 July attempt on Hitler's life, Helldorf's closest ally within the elite resistance was Gottfried von Bismarck, the Governor of Potsdam and an open Nazi like Helldorf. Princess Marie 'Missie' Vassiltchikov, who knew them both well, thought Bismarck liked and respected Helldorf. To her they seemed very close. During the late summer of 1943 Helldorf often came to Potsdam to visit Bismarck and they conferred late into the night. Princess Eleanore von Schoenburg-Hartenstein also took part in these discussions. However, many of the elite resistance tolerated Helldorf rather than welcomed him. As Berlin Police President he seemed too useful to exclude, but reservations remained. Princess Vassiltchikov noted in her diary that some anti-Nazi plotters were sceptical of Helldorf. Schulenburg later told the Gestapo that 'in our circles Helldorf was never in fact wholly trusted … I personally was the one who always maintained the view that Helldorf could be trusted completely, even if he did have certain peculiarities in his personal life.' After the coup the resistance planned to keep on Helldorf only for a limited period. According to Schulenburg, a permanent role for Helldorf was rejected, 'because it was believed that he was too tainted by his past'.[67]

The ambiguity of the July Plotters towards Helldorf comes across nicely from an account by a young artillery officer, Urban Thiersch.

In early July 1944 Thiersch visited Count Claus von Stauffenberg in the Bendlerstrasse building of the Army High Command. The previous month Stauffenberg had been promoted to Chief of Staff of Fromm's Reserve Army. He had also become the executive leader of the conspiracy. Oster could no longer play a co-ordinating role as he had fallen under suspicion. While Thiersch was waiting in the antechamber for Stauffenberg, an elegant senior officer in SS uniform arrived. Stauffenberg's adjutant, Bernhard von Haeften, groaned with a look up to heaven: 'How on earth can we get Helldorf to leave?' Haeften told Stauffenberg of Helldorf's arrival, whereupon Stauffenberg quickly appeared to accept Helldorf's congratulations on his recent appointment: 'Too kind, Mr President.' Stauffenberg considered Helldorf of such importance that during 1944 at times he personally maintained contact with the Police President, including two visits to his flat. Stauffenberg did not realize the extent to which Helldorf's titular power over the Berlin police no longer corresponded with reality. As Helldorf had suggested to Himmler in his letter of 19 April 1943, he was in fact dispensable as chief of police, 'because the police organization in Berlin had been split up into various groups of specialists and could no longer be led as a unit on the authority of the Police President.' In other words, Helldorf could not order about thousands of Berlin police as his title might imply.[68]

Another Nazi in the conspiracy, SS-General Arthur Nebe, had authority over the Criminal Police. In June 1944 Helldorf discussed with Nebe the occupation of the government district, the arrest of Dr Goebbels and Dr Ley, the dissolution of the Gestapo and the subordination of the SS to the Wehrmacht. Nebe promised Helldorf some Criminal Police officers to help in the Putsch. However, Nebe did not make these officers available on 20 July because Helldorf had not told him the Putsch would take place on that date. Before the coup, Helldorf advised the military plotters to replace Major Otto Ernst Remer, the commander of the battalion that guarded the government district. The plotters were relying on Remer to seal off the government buildings. Yet Helldorf had been assured by the Deputy Gauleiter of Berlin that Remer was a National Socialist of unquestionable loyalty. According to Gisevius, General Beck passed on Helldorf's warning to Stauffenberg, who refused to act on it. Princess Vassiltchikov confirmed that Helldorf suggested the removal of Remer, but that the military leaders ignored his warning.[69]

On 12 July 1944 Gisevius returned to Berlin from his Abwehr posting in Switzerland and telephoned Helldorf to check if it would be safe to come and see him. Helldorf replied 'with that cheek that was always so charming in him, that at that moment I could be safe with him from unwelcome bombings [ie the Gestapo]'. When Gisevius met Helldorf, the Police President outlined the plan for the coup. General Olbricht, now Fromm's deputy as commander of the Reserve Army, was to summon Helldorf and declare the Berlin police subject to the orders of the Wehrmacht. Helldorf would then seek to paralyze the police during the crucial first few hours of the coup. It is striking how vague the role Helldorf ascribed to himself was. Despite Stauffenberg's efforts to cultivate him, the Police President felt out of the loop. Gisevius thought Helldorf was ill at ease during their meeting on 12 July. Eventually the police chief complained that the old crew were no longer around and he didn't really have confidence in the young men. Stauffenberg denied him access to Beck and Olbricht and although Stauffenberg's messenger told him everything was perfectly prepared, Helldorf felt something was wrong. Stauffenberg had been very wary, not even revealing that he would personally assassinate Hitler at the Fuehrer's military headquarters in East Prussia.[70]

Helldorf's conduct on the actual day of the coup attempt was ambiguous and had little impact on events. According to Gisevius, he joined Helldorf in the Police Presidium at about eleven o'clock on 20 July 1944. Soon Gottfried von Bismarck arrived. Shortly after noon, a major came from Olbricht. The major was informed by Helldorf that it had been agreed the police would be held back during the initial hours of the coup. Once the Wehrmacht had occupied the key buildings, the police could start their work. Olbricht's messenger was baffled by this statement, and asked for Nebe's criminal police to carry out the arrests necessary. Helldorf said the detectives would only be available once the government buildings were secured. The major protested that the army were only meant to surround the buildings while Nebe's men did the rest. Although Helldorf calmly pointed out the errors in the major's understanding of the plan, clarification was of limited value at this critical moment. Gisevius' memory of this meeting suggests that the conspirators had not sorted out who was actually going to enter the government buildings first. Helldorf was determined that the police would not do this. He was distinctly reluctant to take part in the sharp end of the coup.[71]

As Olbricht's messenger left, Major Egbert Hayessen telephoned Helldorf from the Army High Command in the Bendlerstrasse, the rallying point for the military conspirators. Hayessen requested eight to ten Criminal Police officers who were familiar with the layout of the Ministries. From a safe distance on the telephone Helldorf was more co-operative, and declared that the police units in Berlin were at the disposal of the army. But he kept his involvement at the vague level of general goodwill, rather than taking specific actions that could not be denied later. Helldorf stressed to Hayessen that it was particularly important to capture Goebbels and the Reich Propaganda Ministry and to occupy the Gestapo Office. But he had not forewarned Nebe so no Criminal Police were to hand during the crucial hours of confusion in Berlin when Hitler's fate was uncertain. During this critical period it was certainly within the power of the conspirators to kill some of the prominent Nazis in the Reich capital. But on 20 July Helldorf did not order anyone to strike a blow in anger against the Nazi regime.

Late in the afternoon Helldorf was summoned to the Bendlerstrasse, where he arrived shortly before five o'clock. Gisevius and Bismarck were with him. According to Helldorf's testimony to the People's Court, he went straight up to Olbricht's office. The General told him that the Fuehrer was dead, the Wehrmacht had assumed power, orders had been given out to the troops and there was a state of emergency. Helldorf queried whether this was really true, ie was Hitler really dead, whereupon General Olbricht very seriously and solemnly assured him that it was true. He requested Helldorf to go the police and do what was necessary. Yet before Helldorf could reach the door, General Beck intervened and declared to the Police President that according to some reports Hitler might not be dead.[72] In fact, though Stauffenberg had placed his bomb near Hitler, the Fuehrer had indeed survived the explosion. Stauffenberg had seen the blast and returned to Berlin, thinking he had succeeded.

After the disconcerting news from Beck, Helldorf left the Bendlerstrasse and drove to his office. There he found a message from Goebbels or his Deputy Gauleiter that Helldorf should telephone. Bormann had alerted the Party's regional offices by teleprinter about the attempt on Hitler's life and had also hinted at the possibility of an army putsch. Thereupon a Berlin Party official had immediately tried to contact Helldorf but could not reach him. The cluster of Nazis around Goebbels in the Propaganda Ministry began to fear their old friend

Helldorf had been captured by the murderous rebels. Goebbels' press secretary, Wilfred von Oven, later recalled 'the notion that this holder of the Golden Party Badge was himself involved in the plot was so crazy that it occurred to no one'. Helldorf now responded to Goebbels' message that he should return his call. Helldorf had great difficulty in getting a connection, but he eventually succeeded and repeated to Goebbels what he had been told by Olbricht. Helldorf claimed to Goebbels that his actions thus far were prompted by loyalty to the regime. Helldorf then attended a meeting in the Police Presidium at which the Deputy Gauleiter was presiding. The Police President told the participants that he had to give them the terrible news that the Fuehrer was dead and that the Wehrmacht had assumed power. The Deputy Gauleiter declared that although he had no proof he felt the news was false and knew that the Fuehrer was not dead. This unthinking faith was highly praised by Freisler at Helldorf's trial, in contrast to the latter's intellectualism.

After his demonstration of loyalty the Deputy Gauleiter and the other participants in the meeting left the room and went to join Goebbels. Helldorf alone stayed behind in the Police Presidium and was later joined by Nebe and on two occasions by Gisevius. When Gisevius arrived for the second time he could tell immediately from the faces of the two men that all was lost. The turning point in the coup came when Goebbels persuaded Major Remer to speak to Hitler on the telephone. Remer accepted orders from Hitler to suppress the coup. If Helldorf's advice had been given any weight, both Goebbels and Remer would have been out of the way. Helldorf now declared that only brazen impudence could save Nebe, Gisevius and himself. They had to affect complete innocence and brazen it out. When Gisevius asked Helldorf whether he, Gisevius, was bound in honour to return to Beck in the Bendlerstrasse, Helldorf emphatically told him not to, as the Generals had shat all over them but achieved nothing. If his former subordinate Gisevius had been taken prisoner at the Bendlerstrasse, it would of course have made Helldorf's involvement even more obvious.[73]

By 23 July, three days after the failed coup, Gottfried von Bismarck was telling Princess Vassiltchikov that Helldorf was now the man in most danger. His role in the attempted coup had been too conspicuous and he would be unable to produce an alibi. Yet when Gisevius visited Helldorf the same day, the Police Chief radiated assurance in his fine uniform and showed off his latest medal, the Knight's Cross. Helldorf asserted that the regime would not dare to hang the Police President of Berlin. While the Count hoped for the best, Nebe planned to escape through a show of zeal and eagerly co-operated in uncovering the conspiracy. In particular, this meant turning in his friend Helldorf. When the Police President visited him on 24 July, Nebe detained Helldorf long enough for the Security Police to arrive and arrest him. Then Nebe himself fled. Before the coup, Helldorf had told Princess Schoenburg-Hartenstein that he was afraid he would break under torture. And indeed Helldorf made a confession. The execution of the diplomat Adam von Trott zu Solz was later postponed because he was believed to be withholding information; there was to be no reprieve for Helldorf. Gisevius believed the Count had kept silent under torture long enough to give his former subordinate a head start of about a week: if so, it was a brave achievement.[74]

Of all the participants in the July Plot, Helldorf's role produced the greatest fury amongst the Nazi elite, who saw him as the Brutus of the conspiracy. The rage of the Nazis showed itself first in the behaviour of the Gestapo officials who interrogated and brutally tortured the Count, and then later in the comments of the top leadership. As early as 27 July Gottfried von Bismarck had observed that Helldorf was doomed because Hitler was particularly incensed at him. When Helldorf confessed, an SS adjutant brought Hitler the report of the interrogation. Hitler read the document and commented: 'Yes, I wouldn't have thought that Helldorf was such a scoundrel. He's always been frivolous, it's true. At least four or five times I've paid his debts for him, and they were rarely less than 100,000 marks … I feel sorry for his wife and nice children, but this Augean stable has to be swept with an iron broom.'[75]

Helldorf's betrayal reflected more on Goebbels than anyone else in the Nazi elite, and he was correspondingly poisonous. Wilfred von Oven witnessed Goebbels' reaction to Helldorf's comment that he had become alienated from the Fuehrer: 'Alienated from the Fuehrer,' Goebbels repeated and drew his face into a sarcastic grimace. 'He was finished as far as the Fuehrer was concerned, completely finished, because of his quite unsavoury way of life [This from Goebbels]. I repeatedly protected and rehabilitated him as my old comrade in arms. More than that, I sorted out his debts, because it was gradually becoming a public scandal that the office of the Berlin President of Police was under constant siege by his creditors. My wife reproached me bitterly and said I might just as well have thrown the money straight out the window, as Helldorf was not worth a red farthing, never mind 100,000 marks ... I also bought him a small property of 500 acres from a special secret fund so that once again his feet would be on solid ground in the truest sense of the word. Finally I hung the Knight's Cross around his neck, which was certainly much less appropriate than the noose he'll soon be strung up with. He took presents and decorations and at the same time conspired with those who not only wanted to kill the Fuehrer but me as well ... Stauffenberg himself should not be judged as severely as Helldorf ... Stauffenberg was never a National Socialist like Helldorf and never benefited from the regime to the same unique extent that he did.'[76]

Both the bid to kill Hitler and the ensuing attempt at a military coup reflected very badly on Himmler as the overlord of Reich and Party security. Himmler's SS was expressly intended to protect Hitler, and had been found wanting. So Himmler was eager to deflect blame onto the quite unforeseeable treachery of Party veteran Helldorf. On 3 August 1944 Himmler gave a speech to a conference of the Nazi Gauleiter in Posen at which he discussed the participants in the July Plot at some length: 'Unfortunately an old Party Comrade, Count Helldorf, was one of the band. He took part in the treason fully and whole-heartedly ... It is an extraordinary paradox. He complained that the Party had supposedly become so corrupt. Thereupon one of our officials questioning him, *SS-Gruppenfuehrer* Mueller, immediately retorted: "May I point out that you are the most corrupt of all?" Mr. Helldorf of all people, whose debts Dr. Goebbels and I settled in the past certainly twice I believe if not three times.' Goebbels then interrupted Himmler to add: 'With 80,000 RM, and he now owns four homes in bombed-out Berlin!' Martin Bormann, head of the Party Chancellery, expelled Helldorf from the NSDAP two days later.[77]

The bitterness of the Nazi Movement against Helldorf was reflected in the sentencing of the People's Court. Its President, Roland Freisler, had once helped to prepare the defence against the charges arising from Helldorf's Kudamm Pogrom. On 15 August 1944 Freisler sentenced Helldorf to execution, dishonour and loss of property. After viciously condemning Adam von Trott, Freisler turned to Helldorf: 'One might think that in the context of such treachery an increase in horror and scorn was impossible. Nevertheless we believe the whole decent German people feels this way about the treachery of Wolf Heinrich Count Helldorf. The Fuehrer really ought to have been able to rely on him, to whom as an old comrade in arms he had entrusted the policing of the Reich capital. *Hohe Ehren hat er sich ... heuchlerisch erschlichen ...* He hypocritically slithered his way ... to high honours.' Freisler excelled himself in poisonous vituperation at Helldorf's expense, culminating in the reproach that 'he has no faith, indeed he is an intellectual!' It was meant as an insult, but Freisler was conceding that Helldorf had retained the capacity to think for himself, unlike the mindless Party hacks whose behaviour Freisler held up as exemplary. After Helldorf had been executed, one of his sons went unawares to Goebbels to ask for a reprieve. Goebbels refused to see Helldorf's son and did not even tell him that his father was already dead.[78]

One of Helldorf's old enemies in the Nazi Movement could not resist the opportunity to say 'I told you so'. On 25 August 1944 Gottlieb Roesner, whom Helldorf had destroyed more than a decade before, wrote to Hitler seeking his rehabilitation. Roesner declared that Helldorf had 'finally met the fate he deserved ... His carry-on has alienated countless people from Nazism, or at least made them disbelieve the doctrine of Nazism and the purity of the Party ... It was not an aberration which led Count Helldorf to the 20th July ... rather such aberrations ... run throughout his whole life like a red thread.'[79]

Nazi rage at Helldorf's behaviour was out of all proportion to his actual contribution to the July Plot. Helldorf had been in a position to provide the resistance with useful information and advice but his control over executive forces was less certain. His powers of command over the Berlin police had been eroded by Himmler's changes. The conspirators believed that by securing Helldorf's adherence they had won over a significant power factor in the Reich capital. This was not the case. Helldorf's involvement in the coup misled the elite resistance and gave it a false sense of strength. The situation in the police seems to have paralleled that in the army, where the adherence of a thin layer of officers to the conspiracy was not accompanied by active anti-Nazis in the lower ranks. There is little evidence that the Berlin police were behind Helldorf in opposition to Hitler, and it is significant that he was too shrewd ever to put the matter to the test. During the events of 20 July Helldorf merely confused the issue and failed to provide any practical help at all. It is impossible to say just how far Helldorf was hedging his bets on 20 July, but his behaviour is open to this interpretation. Prior to the coup he had indeed given excellent advice to the conspirators in recommending Remer's transfer, but this suggestion had been ignored.

It might be thought that for Helldorf and the other long-standing Nazis in the July Plot the path to resistance was particularly difficult because it required breaking old political loyalties. But for Helldorf at least, such ties were mitigated by the habit of rebellion. It was far easier for Helldorf to embark on a coup d'état than it was for the majority of the elite resistance. He had taken part in the Kapp Putsch in 1920, encouraged a Bavarian Putsch in 1923, and contemplated an SA Putsch in 1932. For Helldorf it was second nature to prepare a coup d'état if he believed the government was leading Germany into trouble. Furthermore, it is unlikely that breaking his oath to Hitler gave Helldorf any sleepless nights, unlike some of the military conspirators. Yet his participation in a coup was by no means a complete rejection of Nazism. Helldorf's grievances against the regime were that it had ignored his own merits, launched a reckless war and seemed likely to lose it. He claimed plausibly to the People's Court that he had not abandoned Nazi theory, but had become critical of its practice.

Helldorf's involvement in the July Plot was due to the fact that, despite his own excesses and crimes, he maintained a critical perspective on the regime. In particular, he never developed blind faith in Hitler. This was a characteristic he shared with Ernst Roehm. Helldorf took part in the conspiracy against Hitler partly because of a rebelliousness for which his patron Roehm had paid the price ten years earlier. Helldorf's participation in the July Plot was the last hurrah of the old SA leadership.

Chapter 3

New Beginning and Crucifix Struggles: Reviews

Waldemar von Knoeringen was an aristocratic resister of a very different stamp to Helldorf. An energetic and passionate idealist, Knoeringen guided the secret opposition of revolutionary cadres. Hartmut Mehringer's splendid biography [*Waldemar von Knoeringen: Eine politische Biographie*] gives a highly readable account of Knoeringen's political career of more than thirty eventful years within Bavarian Social Democracy. Having inherited the title of *Reichsfreiherr* [baronet], Knoeringen grew up near Rosenheim in Bavaria and made his mark in the SPD [Social Democratic Party of Germany] through his ability as a public speaker. Mehringer tells us how 'Knoeringen's substantial importance and effectiveness within the Party ... lay in his public speaking, in his conversation, in his personal ability to convince and in his own commitment, his power of enthusing and initiating.' During the final years of the Weimar Republic the SPD drew heavily on Knoeringen's abilities as a speaker. On 5 September 1932 Knoeringen wrote that, 'For fourteen days I spoke in a different place every day. On one Sunday ... I spoke for eight hours. Within three weeks I travelled 1600 km.' The Munich Gestapo later paid an involuntary tribute to Knoeringen's oratory: its application in 1938 to deprive Knoeringen and his wife Juliane of their German nationality claimed that Knoeringen had incited 'the masses with Marxist demagogy through the use of his compelling eloquence'; even as an émigré he was still 'amongst the most hostile opponents of the Third Reich'.

Knoeringen went into exile in March 1933 because he was one of the SPD politicians who had opposed the Nazis so vigorously that their lives were in peril. Hermann Esser, one of the Nazi leaders in Munich, threatened to kill Knoeringen if he could lay hands on him. Once safely abroad, Knoeringen watched the disintegration of the SPD with the mixed emotions typical of its young activists, who had regarded the 'bourgeois' Weimar Republic and even their own party with disdain. Once the Nazis had smashed the SPD machine, many young socialists felt relieved of so much ballast. Now they themselves could take the lead and shape things as they wished.

These activists were strongly attracted by the New Beginning organization, whose ideas were epitomized in a pamphlet of the same name published in October 1933. Its author, Walter Loewenheim, wanted to challenge Fascist rule by unifying the working classes in movements outside the existing Social Democrat and Communist parties. Loewenheim was particularly critical of the SPD, and argued that the future leadership of the working classes would have to come from a reinvigorated socialist core inside Germany. By autumn 1933 Knoeringen had been won over to New Beginning by Karl Frank, who was head of its Foreign Secretariat. At about the same time he was recruited by Hans Vogel of the Sopade [SPD in exile] to work for the latter organization. The SPD had managed to transfer assets abroad, and these resources gave it considerable power over impoverished exiles. The Sopade set up its base in Prague, as Czechoslovakia offered the best routes for smuggling underground literature into Germany. Border Secretaries were appointed to organize the distribution of literature, report on its impact and gather other information on the progress of the secret struggle. From autumn 1933 Knoeringen was Sopade Border Secretary for south Bavaria. Erich Rinner, who edited the information coming in to the Sopade and published it as *Deutschlandberichte* [Reports on Germany], knew that Knoeringen had close contacts with New Beginning: 'But as long as these Border Secretaries kept to the principles of reporting I had established, I saw no reason to dispense with their services, and Knoeringen was without doubt the best of our Border Reporters.' For his part Knoeringen gained from the Sopade an income, access to their information, and the opportunity to proselytize for New Beginning.

In addition to his abilities as a reporter, Knoeringen was also good at winning the confidence of the underground socialists who came to visit him at his base in Czechoslovakia. Energetic and straightforward, Knoeringen naturally sympathized with the majority of his visitors, who were youthful activists like himself. In contrast his relations with Hans

Dill, the Border Secretary for north Bavaria, were more difficult. After long years of party service Dill had eventually reached the Reichstag. He epitomized the SPD old guard, which the young activists detested. After meeting two such activists in May 1934, Dill reported with horror that 'after one year of Hitler's rule it was still more important for them that Otto Wels [SPD party leader] should disappear than Adolf Hitler'.

Knoeringen brought out the worst in Dill. Before leaving Germany, Knoeringen had fallen foul of Wilhelm Hoegner, a prominent figure in Bavarian Social Democracy. Dill now sought Hoegner's opinion of Knoeringen's character. Hoegner replied that, 'I do not consider him to be particularly heroic as after the first difficulties in March [1933] he ran away as fast as his legs could carry him.' After this reference any prospect of easy co-operation between Knoeringen and Dill vanished for good. Knoeringen was twenty years younger and far more successful at the work. Dill developed all kinds of complexes which found expression in vicious back-biting within the small world of the emigres. This kind of hostility on the part of older colleagues was to plague Knoeringen through much of his career, the high price he paid for his exuberant political talents.

Problems arose because both Knoeringen and Dill were trying to maintain contacts in Munich. Some comrades there were receiving duplicates of the SPD literature from the two separate sources. In this clash of jurisdiction Knoeringen succeeded in asserting himself. In his report for March 1934 Knoeringen told the Sopade that, 'Munich will now be provided with material exclusively by me.' This was just as well, as the police were on to Dill. From the following month the Bavarian Political Police were able to smash his entire network for the distribution of literature in north Bavaria. More than 150 people were arrested.

Knoeringen's constant vigilance for the security of his contacts was rewarded with the consolidation of his Bavarian networks. The most important of these were led by Bebo Wager in Augsburg and Hermann Frieb in Munich. Wager and Frieb led groups of like-minded people in their cities. The two eventually met in August 1936 and at the beginning of 1937 established contact with New Beginning groups over the Austrian frontier in Salzburg and the Tyrol. Knoeringen dealt with Frieb and Wager on New Beginning lines. They were to avoid direct action such as the distribution of literature. Instead, they were to carry out the ideological training of a cadre organization so it would be ready to act when the revolutionary crisis came. In his reports to the Sopade, Knoeringen sought to omit anything that might prompt a call for political action on the part of the underground, as he regarded his groups in south Bavaria as belonging first and foremost to New Beginning.

As Knoeringen began to leave the Sopade in the dark, they responded in kind. Erich Ollenhauer of the Sopade Executive later told Knoeringen and Franz Boegler, another Border Secretary loyal to New Beginning, that from the end of 1936 the Sopade was certain that 'we were to regard the pair of you as representatives of a competing organization, namely the group New Beginning'. Although the Sopade resented Knoeringen's disloyalty, his ability protected him from dismissal. In describing Knoeringen's activity for New Beginning and the Sopade, Mehringer provides a masterly account of the two organizations and the smouldering conflict between them.

While Knoeringen's standing in the Sopade waned, his influence in New Beginning grew. The Gestapo succeeded in eliminating New Beginning in Berlin, so Knoeringen's south Germans became more significant. In July 1937 Knoeringen became the executive head of New Beginning's Home Office, responsible for all the German operations of the group. All the same, he still believed that the movement's leadership had to come from the underground within Germany. He regarded himself merely as a factotum for jobs that could only be done abroad.

The disastrous Munich Agreement in September 1938 severely dislocated Socialist work from Czechoslovakia. The Sopade and New Beginning organizations for the most part moved to Paris, as did the Knoeringens. The trials of the last weeks in Prague and the transfer to Paris proved too much for Juliane Knoeringen. She had a miscarriage and nearly died. The Knoeringens were never to have any children. Knoeringen himself suffered from bouts of severe depression. It was not easy to resume work from the west, and Knoeringen was reproached by his colleagues. Most of the New Beginning office work was loaded onto him, as Franz Boegler, who was supposed to help out, proved a broken reed. In May 1939 Knoeringen wrote that Boegler 'feels that he has been pushed aside because of me and now displays a kind of love-hate, which makes working with him very difficult'. Juliane was more blunt and termed Boegler 'an utter shit'.

The strain of life in exile was beginning to tell. Knoeringen even began to contemplate getting an ordinary job, a desperate step for a professional revolutionary. As money worries mounted, Knoeringen wrote that 'at least I would like to have a trade which permits modest possibilities for earning money. Not being able to do anything at all except make revolutions is of limited use [when short of funds].' Juliane constantly worried 'whether Hitler would allow us enough time to get away from here … If we fall into the hands of evil it would be better to do away with ourselves.' Fortunately, before the outbreak of war the New Beginning Secretariat moved to London, and the Knoeringens went as well.

New Beginning lost its few remaining direct contacts with Germany after the Nazi occupation of western Europe. However, Knoeringen himself soon received a new opportunity to influence the revolutionary cadres he had helped to establish. He had found an influential patron in Richard Crossman of the Political Warfare Executive, who was organizing covert propaganda for Germany. Knoeringen later recalled that 'Crossman adopted my idea of transmitting independent Social Democrat radio broadcasts to Germany and championed the establishment of such broadcasts. Due to his efforts the Transmitter of European Revolution arose, whose programme I substantially developed myself.' This programme reflected the characteristics of New Beginning rather than the SPD. Its revolutionary propaganda was directed on New Beginning lines at the 'cell nuclei' of working-class opposition. Knoeringen also emphasized a New Beginning-style revolution from within. On 14 April 1941 he told his listeners that 'it will be the forces of resistance of the oppressed peoples, including the German people, which will subvert the Hitler dictatorship and overcome its rule'.

New Beginning's influence was also reflected in the Transmitter's goal of a united Europe. Comprehensive political and social revolution throughout the continent would lead to the voluntary union of all European peoples in a Socialist republic. Such aspirations show that Knoeringen and his associates had complete editorial independence. This was due to Crossman, who stopped other British agencies from interfering with the Transmitter of European Revolution. The broadcasting team, drawn largely from New Beginning, regarded Crossman not as a censor but as a friend and adviser. Knoeringen was the station's central figure and his good relationship with Crossman enabled the broadcasts to continue for nearly two years. They achieved some resonance within Germany. In various German big cities there were leaflets and wall inscriptions that referred to the Transmitter of European Revolution. The Revolutionary Socialists in south Germany listened to the station, identified Knoeringen and tried to contact him. Frieb eventually succeeded in getting a letter to Knoeringen, which he acknowledged in a broadcast.

The station's remarkable editorial freedom was too good to last. The final broadcast was made on 26 June 1942. It was the second of a two-part programme attacking British colonialism. Crossman then brought an ultimatum from the top that in future all manuscripts had to be censored. The broadcasting team thought about it for five minutes then packed their bags. The demise of the Transmitter of European Revolution was a heavy blow for Knoeringen. He later wrote that once the station had been lost, and 'it had finally become clear to us that fascism could not be overcome through internal forces, then I really reached my low point'. The basic concept of New Beginning was exposed as a fallacy, and the organization ceased to have any purpose.

Once again Richard Crossman came to the rescue. Under the aegis of the Political Intelligence Division [PID] of the Foreign Office, Crossman was now responsible for the political supervision of German prisoners of war [PoWs] in North Africa. Knoeringen later wrote that Crossman saw there was a new opportunity 'to resume the contact with German socialists and to provide proof that there really was another Germany, that resistance was going on there and that after Germany's defeat new people could be brought in'. Crossman persuaded Knoeringen to help him in the work with German PoWs. Before his departure Knoeringen discussed the matter with the SPD Party Executive in London. Having lost New Beginning's European revolution, Knoeringen was rebuilding his bridges to the old Party. He arrived in Algiers in February 1943.

After his nadir in the second half of 1942, Knoeringen's work with PoWs gave him new direction. Most of the prisoners were mistrustful, but Knoeringen realized that some of them might develop into future Social Democrats. It was only a matter of finding and developing them. Political education was to be the major theme of the remainder of Knoeringen's career, and it was an area in which he built lasting achievements.

His interest in political education was timely. In September 1944 the British government decided to introduce an official programme for re-educating German PoWs. Knoeringen eventually had an idea that transformed the rather condescending connotations of re-education.

His plan was the creation of a PoW university, in which re-education would be combined with political and historical study. During the months after the end of the war Knoeringen fought unceasingly for the establishment of such an institution and gradually the Foreign Office took notice.

In November 1945 the PID's PoW division, which still employed Knoeringen, established the Wilton Park Training Centre to supplement the general attempts at re-education in the PoW camps and provide their final culmination. It was intended to provide six to eight week courses for about three hundred students at a time. Knoeringen was closely involved in the planning of the courses and the actual teaching. In researching his book Mehringer questioned participants in the early courses, who all remembered Knoeringen as the moving spirit of Wilton Park. In a somewhat different form, the Wilton Park conferences continue to this day. They are a remarkable legacy from a political refugee of enemy nationality.

After the defeat of the Nazi regime, Knoeringen was eager to return to Germany. He did so as a Social Democrat. On 3 March 1946 Knoeringen wrote to Karl Frank that 'Social Democracy must have room for all strands of democratic socialism, and these must be openly visible. In this sense it was right to have dissolved New Beginning. We are going home as individuals and Party members.'

Knoeringen's priority after returning to Germany was to press on with his work of political education. On 26 September 1946 an 'SPD Central Office for Political Education' was established for Bavaria with Knoeringen in charge. The new office was to act in a variety of ways to improve the Party's intellectual and educational level. Knoeringen still had a radical agenda. In November 1946 he wrote to all the SPD branches in Bavaria stressing that the goal of Social Democracy was to occupy key positions and establish a socialist planned economy. In autumn 1947 Knoeringen was allocated a building for a training school and courses began the following summer. As at Wilton Park, he was the decisive influence. He shaped the programme of studies and was available to the school as a course leader and speaker.

Despite his commitment to political education, Knoeringen had not lost interest in the practice of politics. In December 1946 he was elected to the Bavarian parliament. Following the elections, the SPD formed a coalition government with the CSU. Knoeringen's old antagonist, Wilhelm Hoegner, became Prime Minister. The coalition was unpopular and Hoegner lost his grip on the Party. In May 1947 a conference of the Bavarian SPD elected Knoeringen to replace Hoegner as its Party Chairman. Another humiliation followed for Hoegner. On 13 September 1947 the SPD accepted Knoeringen's recommendation to leave the coalition despite Hoegner's appeals to stay in the Bavarian government. Mehringer shows that the decision to abandon the coalition was a serious mistake. The SPD lost influence on Bavarian policy-making and public appointments during the crucial years leading up to the establishment of the Federal Republic. In coalition with the SPD, the CSU had looked about to disintegrate; without the SPD, it got a new lease of life. In retrospect, every Social Democrat involved except Knoeringen admitted that it had been an error to leave the coalition.

Mehringer relates Knoeringen's life in an impressively fluent and clear style. Three themes particularly stand out: first, the recurrent malice that Knoeringen's exceptional talents provoked among some older colleagues in the competitive world of socialist politics, secondly, his interest in new ideas and particularly new approaches to socialism, and thirdly, his determination to educate an elite to spread radical socialism. In the 1930s Knoeringen sought to prepare revolutionary cadres to fight fascism. In the late 1940s he urged the training of SPD activists so that they would be able to implement a socialist society when their opportunity came. But it proved to be a long wait.

While the Social Democratic Party had been swept away by the Nazi seizure of power in 1933, the Catholic Church retained its essential structure and support from the Catholic laity. Bishops and priests could still speak openly to Catholics and seek to influence their attitudes to Nazi policies. The difficult questions were how much lay support the Church could expect if it was challenged by the regime and whether Catholic bishops and clergy should in fact mobilize the laity and expose them to danger. Such questions became acute when the Nazis unilaterally removed crucifixes from schoolrooms, as they did in the province of Oldenburg during late 1936.

There is much valuable material on church and laity during the Oldenburg crucifix struggle in a collection of essays edited by Joachim Kuropka (*Zur Sache – Das Kreuz!*). The disputes over crucifixes were concentrated in the districts of Vechta and Cloppenburg, which had belonged to Muenster until they became part of Oldenburg in 1803. The two districts remained part of the Muenster diocese and were known as the Oldenburg Muensterland. Clemens August von Galen, the Bishop of Muenster, usually delegated his routine duties in the Oldenburg region to an Agent based in the town of Vechta. Before the Nazi banning of political parties in 1933 Oldenburg had the highest percentage of Catholics voting for the Catholic Centre Party of any region in Germany. Most of the Oldenburg Catholics were concentrated in the south-west of the province, whereas the Oldenburg Protestants, who formed nearly three-quarters of the population, were concentrated in the north and east.

Father Franz Vorwerk, the Bishop's Agent, played a key role in the development of the crucifix struggle. Bishop Galen consecrated Vorwerk as his Agent in December 1933. Julius Pauly, the Oldenburg Minister of Churches and Schools, attended the ceremony and passed on the best wishes of Gauleiter Karl Roever. Pauly declared that Vorwerk was 'a man on whom one can rely in every respect'. Their good relationship did not last. During the following years Vorwerk wrote to Pauly again and again to protest against National Socialist school policy, but to little effect. Particularly contentious was Pauly's decree of 4 July 1936, which enacted fresh regulations for the Church's inspection of religious instruction. The parish clergy had previously assessed the progress of religious education on a regular basis, but Pauly's new measure restricted the frequency of assessments. The Catholic clergy were enraged by this change, and put pressure on Vorwerk to act. But he remained defensive, indeed almost despairing. In a sermon on 20 September 1936 he commented that, 'I am always being asked: why does the Church not take a stance on this or that ... How is the Church supposed to take a stance on all these many issues? The pulpit is there for preaching God's word.' Vorwerk's passive attitude was to change dramatically under the impact of Pauly's next decree.

On 4 November 1936 Pauly issued a decree that banned the religious consecration of school buildings and the placing of crucifixes and pictures of Luther in such buildings. Those already in place were to be removed. For Pauly this was just another step in forcing Christianity out of the Oldenburg schools. He had no appreciation of the symbolic importance of the cross. He later commented: 'After all, it is only a dead image.' To the Oldenburg Catholics the cross symbolized the Church's promise of salvation through Christ's resurrection. Its removal denied the essence of Christianity.

Vorwerk discussed Pauly's latest step with Bishop Galen and his advisers in Muenster. Here the decision was taken that Vorwerk should issue the clear public condemnation of Nazi school policy for which the clergy had been pressing for months. Vorwerk now changed from written protests to the regime to public appeals to the laity. He was encouraged in his resistance to the crucifix degree by a telephone call from the chairman of the Oldenburg branch of the Protestant Gustav Adolf Foundation, Dr Arend Ehlers. Ehlers requested Vorwerk to do something, 'as it is well known that the people in [Catholic] south Oldenburg can be mobilized better than those in the [Protestant] north'.

With this ecumenical moral support, Vorwerk appealed to the Catholic laity with a declaration that was distributed to the clergy by couriers and was read in all the churches on Sunday, 15 November 1936. In his declaration, which was agreed with the Bishop of Muenster, Vorwerk appealed for help from everyone: 'Stand up for the preservation of the cross in the schools!' Vorwerk reported to Galen that his declaration 'struck like a bolt of lightning, particularly where there was no knowledge of the matter'. Vorwerk had given the starting signal for a protest, for which he became the lynchpin.

The Nazi Party magnified the scale of its eventual defeat by a stubborn refusal to give way. On Tuesday, 17 November Gauleiter Roever claimed to a big rally that if he told Hess of Vorwerk's behaviour the Agent would end up in a concentration camp. Roever believed that he had won over his audience. In fact he had cowed them. He drew the mistaken conclusion that the way to deal with large angry crowds was to sway them with his oratory.

But Roever had met his match as a demagogue. The following day, Thursday 18 November, was set aside for the commemoration of the war dead, and a memorial service was held at Bethen, the Oldenburg pilgrimage shrine. Thousands of laity and war veterans attended. Father Franz Uptmoor delivered a masterpiece of rhetoric to the assembled crowd. He presented the faithful with the alternatives of 'either Christ or Satan ... living Christianity or Bolshevism ... And if they now want to tear from our hands the cross, the most sacred and precious thing we have, then in the fight for the cross we veterans will stand in the front line as in the old days'. Uptmoor's sermon helped to turn the outrage at Pauly's decree into a mass popular protest.

At this stage many Catholics still had misgivings because they feared reprisals by the regime. The overcoming of fear, as a necessary stage for most people before engaging in opposition to the regime, is skilfully brought out in a study of the community of Essen in the Cloppenburg district, which forms part of Kuropka's edition. Curate Niemann, who led the opposition in Essen, was nervous and worried, as indeed were many of his parishioners. One doctor refused to help and said 'let those who have children do it'. Nevertheless, on the day after Uptmoor's sermon, Thursday 19 November, the people of Essen forced the municipal council to hold a meeting. Several hundred men flocked into the municipal hall and demanded to know what the council thought of Pauly's decree. Both the Mayor and the Local Party Leader decided that they supported the retention of the cross in the schools. The Mayor declared to the angry crowd that he 'could not carry out this decree'.

Those present in the hall decided to send a delegation to Minister Pauly in Oldenburg to request the withdrawal of the decree. However, from the sixteen who originally agreed to take part in the delegation, only eight remained when they set off on Saturday, 21 November. When the delegation reached Oldenburg, three of its members were allowed to see Pauly, though no one wanted to go into the room first. All the same, they plucked up their courage and eventually demanded the withdrawal of the decree. Pauly became very annoyed and exclaimed: 'What are you suggesting! A ministerial decree!' One of the delegates tactfully remarked: 'Herr Minister, I am reminded of Bismarck, who even withdrew the *Kulturkampf* laws and nevertheless entered the history books as a famous man.' Even this flattering comparison failed to convince Pauly and the delegation returned to Essen with its goal unachieved. Their arrival home was greeted with great relief, as it was feared they might have been arrested. Indeed, if the Gestapo had arrested the Essen delegation on its arrival in Oldenburg, the opposition might have been nipped in the bud. Instead, the unsuccessful but unpunished protest of the Essen community gave a lead to the rest of the Muensterland.

Essen was the first community to send a delegation to Pauly. The news of their protest aroused great interest. On Sunday, 22 November people came to Essen from throughout the surrounding region to learn more about what had happened, and during the following days delegations poured in to Oldenburg to see Pauly. The delegation from Molbergen in the Cloppenburg district proved the final straw. The Molbergen delegation included not only its mayor, Heinrich Pruellage, but also the Local Party Leader, Josef Klinker. Klinker was an archetypal 'alter

Kaempfer' or Nazi veteran. Before the Nazi seizure of power he had been head of the Nazi Party throughout south Oldenburg and a frequent host to Gauleiter Roever. He was a holder of the Party's Golden Badge. He and Pruellage saw Pauly on Monday, 23 November. They expressed doubts that the decree was in line with Hitler's thinking. Both threatened that if the crucifix decree was carried out they would appeal to the Fuehrer directly and if necessary leave the Party. Pauly was put under such pressure that he finally declared that he was willing to cancel the decree for the community of Molbergen. However, the delegation from Molbergen refused to accept this solution. They declared that they would only be satisfied if the decree was cancelled for all communities. Though Paul would not go this far, his position had begun to crumble.

There was also pressure from the Protestant Church, and in particular the Gustav Adolf Foundation, whose purpose was to support German Protestant communities abroad. Its head wrote to Pauly on 22 November that, 'If in the motherland of the Reformation pictures of Luther and crucifixes are officially removed from the schools, then the impression on the German Protestant schools and churches abroad will be devastating.' On 26 November the Protestant Church in Wilhelmshaven wrote to Pauly insisting on the withdrawal of the decree because 'the cross is the chief symbol of the Christian Churches regardless of denomination'.

The articles in Kuropka's edition show that in November 1936 many mayors and Party members realized for the first time that their service to the regime clashed with their religion. Minor officials beseeched the Gauleiter to reverse Pauly's decree. For ten days Gauleiter Roever had watched the edifice of Nazi rule in Oldenburg disintegrate. Then on 24 November he finally realized he had to surrender. But he unwisely sought to transform the Party's climb-down into a propaganda triumph. He decided to announce the withdrawal of the decree at a mass rally in Cloppenburg on 25 November. A crowd of 7,000 gathered inside the *Muensterlandhalle* in Cloppenburg to hear Roever and there were a further 5,000 outside. Roever capriciously talked to the crowd about his experiences in Africa, where he claimed to have learned the importance of racial purity. He was interrupted by shouts of 'You should have stayed there … Get to the point, the cross.' When Roever finally announced the withdrawal of the decree the crowd stopped listening to him and pushed their way out. He had now provided thousands with the experience of taking part in mass opposition at a Nazi meeting for the first time since

1933, and quite needlessly given them the feeling that they had done so successfully and that it was their open dissent on this occasion that had forced Roever to withdraw the decree.

Galen sought to spread the news of the success in Oldenburg as widely as possible. He issued a pastoral letter on 27 November discussing the crucifix struggle. This was not only read in his Muenster diocese but also in the bishoprics of Speyer, Freiburg and Passau. Furthermore, Galen published the main documents relating to the struggle in a supplement to his diocesan gazette. Other German bishops also helped to spread this documentation.

Despite the achievements of the Oldenburg crucifix struggle, it soon became clear that the victory was only partial. In particular, the Protestant Church had a tough struggle to secure the replacement of Luther pictures in schools. In places where the pictures were not restored, it was up to the pastors to press stubbornly for their return. In Idafehn the Protestant pastor had to campaign for nearly eighteen months before the Luther picture was finally replaced in the school.

The Catholics were also disappointed as Pauly's decree was only partly withdrawn. While existing crosses could stay in the schools or be restored to their former places, it was forbidden in future for the Catholic Church to consecrate schools and decorate them with crosses. After Father Engles of Peheim consecrated its new school in spring 1937, he was arrested by the Gestapo and spent nearly six months in custody. In Molbergen, whose deputation had broken Pauly's resolve, a new man from the outside was appointed teacher and Local Party Leader. He ignored the decree restoring the crosses and took them out of his classrooms. Joseph Klinker, who had led the Molbergen delegation, was gradually deprived of his leadership role. Other prominent opponents of Pauly's decree were not treated so lightly. At least two were put in concentration camps. Gauleiter Roever's resentment at his humiliation poured out in comments to Vorwerk on 8 January 1937: 'This damned black Muensterland ... You are the lackeys of the traitor in Muenster ... But I'll grind you down, you can count on it ... My revenge is coming. You are the first.'

Roever sought to revenge himself on Vorwerk with propaganda intended to brand the Bishop's Agent a liar. But the Nazi regime also had a more effective reprisal to hand. The Church placed great value on the separate education of Catholics in their own schools. Bishop Galen admonished the parents in a pastoral letter of 18 May 1937 to 'Above all, preserve the Catholic schools for your children … It is your duty before God to stand up for the Catholic schools.' Galen's fears for the Catholic schools were borne out the following year when the Oldenburg government abolished them. On 26 April 1938 Vorwerk requested the Muensterland Catholics 'to demand the restoration of the confessional [Catholic or Protestant] schools … [This] is worse than the exclusion of the cross from the schools.'

In Goldenstedt in the Muensterland both Catholic and Protestant parents kept their children at home from 2 May 1938 to protest against the establishment of the so-called community schools to replace the previous confessional ones. However, the local Nazi regime had drawn the lesson from the crucifix affair that terror had to be used promptly to nip popular opposition in the bud. At least fourteen men were taken into protective custody, and twelve of them spent several months in a concentration camp. Instead of receiving deputations, Pauly announced that 'I will order the Gestapo to take into protective custody anyone who has not brought his children back to school by 7.30 am on 7 May 1938.' These words put an end to the school strike in Goldenstedt. The regime followed up this victory by expelling Vorwerk from the Muensterland on 30 June.

The regime's successful use of terror to attack the Church schools in the Muensterland after the Catholic triumph in the crucifix struggle illustrates how transient such victories could be. Indeed, Galen had already been forced to put up with the displacement of crucifixes under his nose in the province of Muenster, where Governor Klemm gave a secret order for Hitler's picture to be given the prominent position in school rooms. Galen was told of the change by teachers, and on 21 December 1936 he protested about the relegation of the cross into second place in favour of Hitler's picture: 'Are children, who are easily influenced, perhaps supposed to draw the conclusion from this that Jesus Christ, our God and Saviour, deserves less honour than a mortal human being, however worthy of honour he may be?' [Loeffler, *Galen. Akten, Briefe und Predigten*, 1988, vol. i, p. 476]. Galen's complaints were to no avail. Gradually the practice spread of transferring the cross from the head of the classroom to the side wall and putting Hitler's picture in the position formerly occupied by the cross. During 1937 such displacements also caused unrest in the Osnabrueck diocese. Eventually the Gestapo threatened that they would impose protective custody on local priests who appealed to the public on the crucifix issue. Bishop Berning gave way and on 10 March 1938 instructed the clergy to stop mentioning the re-hanging of the crosses. The Gestapo again made effective use of protective custody to win crucifix struggles for the regime in both Sieg in the Rhineland and at Frankenholz in the Saarland.

The Church's success in the Oldenburg crucifix struggle had helped to spark the attempts at opposition in many of these places. At Waibstadt in Baden the Oldenburg precedent not only encouraged Catholic protest but also made the local Nazi mayor determined to win. During October 1936 Eugen Laule, the Mayor of Waibstadt, gave instructions for all crosses to be removed from the primary and secondary schools. As Waibstadt was mostly Catholic, his action produced considerable resentment. On 12 January 1937 about two hundred people, including many schoolchildren, gathered in front of the town hall. The noisy crowd demanded the return of the crosses. About fifteen people forced their way into the town hall to lend emphasis to their demands. But Laule was a tougher customer than Pauly. He openly threatened those who had burst into the town hall: 'Unless you quieten down it will be the worse for you.' He eventually pacified the crowd and the following week seven men who had played a prominent part in the demonstration were arrested. As the prisoners were about to be driven off, a dozen or so people were standing near the town hall but no one dared to go up to the vehicle, or to make any critical comment. When the Church tried to secure the return of the crosses by negotiation, Laule told its representative that, 'I do not take back my decrees [a reference to Pauly], and as long as I am Mayor of Waibstadt I decide what is hung up in the schoolrooms.'

Kuropka's edition puts the Church's success at Oldenburg in a context of victories and defeats elsewhere. Nazi action against crucifixes in one or a few schools usually, though not always, succeeded. However simultaneous actions on a regional scale were an uncertain quantity for the Nazi regime. Although they failed spectacularly in Oldenburg and again in Bavaria during 1941, a regional action against crosses in a large proportion of the schools did succeed in the Prussian Rhine Province in April 1939, and, as we have seen, Galen had to tolerate the displacement of crucifixes under his own nose in the region around Muenster. Furthermore, Cardinal Adolf Bertram, the senior Catholic archbishop, refused to adopt a strategy of public confrontation. So the Oldenburg crucifix struggle did not become a model for nationwide Catholic opposition to Nazism.

Chapter 4

The Nazi Dissolution of the Monasteries: A Bavarian Case Study

During the later years of Hitler's regime Catholic opposition to National Socialism was hindered by divisions amongst the bishops.[1] Ulrich von Hassell, an influential member of the elite resistance, noted that the majority of the bishops, under Cardinal Adolf Bertram, were against an open struggle; Bishops Galen and Preysing, the representatives of the hard line, were in the minority. Hassell observed that 'people like Bertram will never achieve anything against people like Hitler and Himmler'.[2] Bertram, the Archbishop of Breslau, was Chairman of the Fulda Bishops' Conference, which spoke with the combined authority of all the German Catholic bishops. Bertram believed in negotiating formal Church–State agreements on the assumption that these would be kept. As relations deteriorated, Bertram reacted to Nazi aggression with memoranda that pointed out infringements to no effect. He also gave the impression to the outside world that Nazi encroachments were isolated blemishes on an otherwise satisfactory relationship.

Two factors help explain Bertram's conciliatory attitude to the Nazi regime. First, he believed that obedience to the state was ordained by God and Catholics should 'render to Caesar the things that are Caesar's'. After the Nazi occupation of the Sudetenland, Bertram welcomed back 30,000 Sudeten Germans to his diocese by reminding them of their duty to the state. The second factor prompting Bertram's conciliatory approach was his traumatic experience as a young theology student of the *Kulturkampf*, Bismarck's attempt to break the influence of the Catholic Church in Germany. In January 1938 Bertram remarked that he had lived through the *Kulturkampf* and could not allow things to go so far that Catholics would have to die without priests again. When Conrad Count von Preysing, the Catholic Bishop of Berlin, heard of Bertram's remark, he observed that 'the Cardinal's tactics could mean that it would certainly be possible for priests to be present, but the Faithful would die without priests, because they would not want them'.[3]

In contrast to Bertram, Preysing and his cousin, Clemens August Count von Galen, Bishop of Muenster, favoured a strategy of public confrontation with the Nazi regime. In particular, they wanted the German bishops as a group to mobilize Catholic opinion by using pastoral letters read in every parish church to inform the faithful in detail about each worsening of the Church struggle. The divisions over strategy amongst the bishops meant that for the Catholic, as for the Protestant Church, the 'Church Struggle' was not just a conflict with the Nazi regime, but also a struggle for influence within the Church itself. By August 1940 Pope Pius XII was so concerned about developments that he wrote to the German bishops stressing the importance of the 'spiritual solidarity of the episcopacy [and] its unity in intention and action'.[4]

Like the Catholic bishops, the Nazi elite was also divided in its strategy for Church–State relations, and this division was reinforced by the outbreak of war in 1939. While some leading Nazis like Himmler saw wartime conditions as the perfect opportunity to weaken the Catholic Church, other prominent Nazis worried that measures against the Church would cause disunity at home and endanger the war effort. This was the position of the Reich Minister for Church Affairs, Hans Kerrl, and of the Bavarian Governor, General Franz Ritter von Epp, and his State Secretary Hofmann. In early 1940 Hofmann wrote to Kerrl that 'we [Hofmann, Epp and Kerrl] are all of the same opinon with regard to the importance of the religious question and appropriate policy during the present war … for the fate of the people depends on the unity of the Home Front. The outcome of the last war proved this to us very clearly.'[5] Many Germans believed wrongly that their army had not been defeated in 1918, but had been 'stabbed in the back' by treacherous forces at home that had exploited divisions within the country to bring about Germany's collapse.

Unfortunately the desire of Kerrl and Epp for religious peace to prevent another '1918' did not extend to some of the most influential figures in the Nazi regime. As Hofmann pointed out to Kerrl in a letter of 8 February 1940, there was a 'very active minority which constantly seeks to terrorize the Party on these sensitive questions'.[6] This minority included Martin Bormann, from 1933 chief of staff to the Fuehrer's Deputy for Party Affairs, Rudolf Hess. After Hess' sudden flight to

Britain, Bormann was appointed to the headship of a newly established Nazi Party Chancellery in May 1941. This post gave Bormann a stronger hand in his active attempts to push back the influence of the Catholic Church. He saw it as a priority to explain the church issue to the Nazi Party. On 9 June 1941 he sent out a circular to the Gauleiter that emphasized 'the Church must never again be permitted to influence the guidance of the people'. Such influence had to be broken once and for all. The Reich Minister of Propaganda, Joseph Goebbels, shared Bormann's approach to the church question. In August 1940 Goebbels had told the Gauleiter to organize memorial ceremonies for the war dead in order to reduce the churches' influence in this sphere. While certain restraints had previously been necessary, now the war with France had been won so the offensive could be resumed.[7]

Hitler's own stance was characteristically shifty, so that both moderates and radicals were convinced that he shared their views. Hitler did indeed combine the radicals' ideological rejection of Christianity with the pragmatism of the moderates. He envisaged cutting the revenues of the Catholic Church drastically once the war was over, but until then caution was to be the order of the day. On 19 January 1940 he remarked that 'tough, political action [in religious matters] was naturally also thinkable, but only when Germany's position was completely secure. Otherwise the domestic strife which would break out would ruin us.'[8] Yet despite Hitler's awareness of the political dangers of an active anti-Christian policy, he only intermittently tried to impose restraint in church questions upon the radicals amongst the Nazi elite.

The dissolution of the German religious houses was one of the most damaging actions launched against the Catholic Church by the Nazi radicals in order to exploit the circumstances of the war. By summer 1941 at least 123 sizeable religious houses had been confiscated within Germany's borders before Hitler's annexations.[9] Between October 1938 and October 1941 the number of male religious houses within Germany fell by fifty-eight from 687 to 629, and the number of male religious, including those in training, from 16,596 to 11,891. Although during the same period the number of female religious also fell slightly, from 101,125 to 99,381, the houses for female religious actually rose from 7,785 to 7,906, suggesting a trend towards smaller communities.[10] The growth in the number of female religious houses would have been still greater but for the Nazi dissolutions. Although numerous female houses were dissolved during 1941, the Nazi seizure of male religious houses tended to attract more popular attention. The latter were usually larger and often played a conspicuous liturgical role. In addition to the widespread seizure of religious houses within Germany's 1937 borders, the Nazis also confiscated monasteries in Austria and in countries they occupied during the war, particularly Poland.

From the start the Nazis were motivated not just by ideological zeal, but also by greed for the Church's property. In addition to his duties as *Reichsfuehrer SS*, Heinrich Himmler was also Reich Commissioner for the Strengthening of the German Race, in which capacity he sought to resettle inside Nazi borders the ethnic Germans scattered throughout eastern Europe. On 30 December 1939 he empowered his resettlement agency, the *Volksdeutsche Mittelstelle [Vomi]* or Liaison Office for Ethnic Germans, to confiscate properties suitable for accommodating the large numbers of ethnic Germans returning to the Reich for resettlement. The Liaison Office used Himmler's authority to seize a whole variety of buildings, but monasteries proved particularly suitable.[11] The Liaison Office was particularly interested in monasteries comparatively near to the proposed resettlement areas, and consequently Bertram's archdiocese of Breslau, which corresponded to the Prussian province of Silesia, bore the initial brunt of the confiscations. The first Silesian victim was the Benedictine abbey of Gruessau, the majority of whose members were serving in the German armed forces. The SS confiscated Gruessau on 3 September 1940, provoking bitterness amongst the local population and indignation on the part of the army.[12]

On 9 November Cardinal Bertram wrote to the Liaison Office protesting that its officials had recently confiscated eleven religious houses at very short notice and without compensation. Bertram demanded an immediate suspension of the confiscations and sent a copy of his letter directly to Himmler and the Reich Chancellery. In February 1941 Himmler eventually wrote to Hans Lammers, the State Secretary responsible for supporting Hitler in his work as Reich Chancellor, but only to suggest that they should delay still further in replying to Bertram. Lammers finally replied to Bertram's complaints on 7 April 1941, saying that the confiscations were due to the necessities of war, which required unconditional priority.[13] The Archbishop of Breslau's letter to the regime completely failed to halt the Nazi confiscation of monasteries in his own Silesian diocese.

THE NAZI DISSOLUTION OF THE MONASTERIES

On 13 January 1941 Bormann instigated the most intensive phase in the Nazi dissolution of the monasteries in his capacity as Hess' chief of staff. He sent out a circular to the Gauleiter that claimed the people showed no dissent if monasteries were allocated to a purpose that seemed generally suitable, for example if they were transformed into hospitals, holiday camps, Adolf Hitler Schools or National Political Educational Institutes [*Napolas*], another type of Nazi school. Bormann instructed the Gauleiter to make more extensive use of such opportunities.[14] After Bormann's letter the Gauleiter knew that action against the monasteries was a yardstick for their performance.

The Nazi Party in Austrian Carinthia took the opportunity to seize three religious houses. At first the Reich Ministers of the Interior and of Finance thought the Reich should be the beneficiary of the seizures, whereupon the Deputy Gauleiter of Carinthia successfully appealed to Hitler. In February 1941 Bormann informed Lammers that Hitler had decided that the monasteries should become the property of the Carinthia *Reichsgau* and that he wanted the Reich Ministers of the Interior and Finance to be informed of this.[15] Other Gauleiters in Austria tried to match developments in Carinthia. Hitler gave permission to Gauleiter Eigruber of the Gau Upper Danube to seize the Upper Austrian monasteries of St Florian, Kremsmuenster and Wilhering together with the Sudetenland monastery of Hohenfurth. Hitler did not include in this list of permitted seizures Lambach Abbey near Linz, where he had frequently been swept off his feet as a boy by the 'solemn grandeur of the extremely splendid church rituals'.[16]

In addition to Carinthia and the Upper Danube region, Salzburg and Vienna were focal points of the confiscations in Austria. The fate of the Augustinian foundation of Klosterneuburg in Vienna exemplified the method used, with the Gestapo acting as the blunt instrument of the Gauleitung. When Gauleiter Baldur von Schirach received Bormann's letter of 13 January 1941, he told the Deputy Gauleiter that he wanted it to be implemented as quickly as possible. Vienna was in competition with Hamburg for a new Adolf Hitler School, and Schirach was determined that Vienna should win. The Deputy Gauleiter identified Klosterneuburg as the most suitable premises for an Adolf Hitler School and told the Governor, who headed the regional administration, to give this case his special attention. The Governor spoke to the Vienna Gestapo, who produced a variety of telling evidence against the monastery.

In particular, it was said the Abbot only displayed his picture of Hitler if he was expecting a party official. Finally, on 30 April the abbey was occupied by the Gestapo, who declared to the monks that it had been confiscated. Altogether twenty-six large Austrian monasteries were confiscated during the period of Nazi rule.[17]

During spring 1941 the seizures spread from Silesia and Austria into Bavaria and the Rhineland. The Bavarian bishops had encouraged the religious orders to provide space for evacuated children and Germans who were being resettled. In a letter of 30 November 1940 the Bavarian Minister of the Interior, Gauleiter Adolf Wagner, expressed his appreciation to the Archbishop of Munich, Cardinal Michael Faulhaber, 'for explaining to the monasteries the importance of the utilization', and because 'thanks to the supportive attitude of the Church, in almost no instances had a confiscation ... been necessary'. Furthermore, the Munich Senior Gestapo Office had requested the Archbishop to prevent the spread of rumours that were taking hold amongst the population about impending monastery dissolutions, and in his letter Wagner thanked Faulhaber for 'refuting the wild rumours'. On 19 February Faulhaber wrote to the Bavarian monasteries on behalf of the Bavarian Bishops' Conference, of which he was Chairman. He told them that they should be guided by the words of the Gospel: 'Therefore I tell you, do not be anxious about your life' [Matthew 6:25]. He continued: 'We expect of the Bavarian monasteries that they should not encourage a mood of panic amongst individual members by listening to wild rumours or by holding civilian clothes in readiness.'[18] Yet Faulhaber's exhortations were quickly overtaken by events, as the religious orders in Bavaria and elsewhere in Germany suffered a series of devastating blows.

As chairman of the national Fulda Conference, to which the members of the Bavarian Conference also belonged, Cardinal Bertram wrote to Lammers on 22 April 1941 protesting without avail that 'recently whole monasteries have been confiscated, the members of the order expelled and in this way the religious foundations concerned in practice dissolved ... These confiscations and seizures of property were implemented simply by Gestapo decrees.' Bertram listed eleven foundations that had just been confiscated. These included three houses of the St Ottilien Congregation of Missionary Benedictines, among them the senior abbey of St Ottilien in Upper Bavaria.[19] On 9 May 1941 the Gestapo and Security Service [*Sicherheitsdienst* or SD] dissolved the last surviving house of that Congregation, Muensterschwarzach

Abbey in Lower Franconia. Muensterschwarzach lay on the river Main, 12 miles east of Wuerzburg and 6 miles north of Kitzingen, the nearest town. It was a centre of both religious and economic life in the surrounding area, and its dissolution provoked great popular unrest. These protests at Muensterschwarzach highlight the possibilities and limitations of Catholic dissent on the monastery issue.

Muensterschwarzach was a tempting plum for a regime desperate to shelter ethnic Germans prior to their resettlement. The core of the abbey was a very large new building to which was joined a splendid modern church completed in 1938. The abbey's new building had the space to accommodate three hundred people. Furthermore, Muensterschwarzach was self-supporting in many respects. The abbey's home farm of about 135 hectares was generally regarded as the best agricultural concern in Lower Franconia. Its activity was supported by well-equipped technical workshops.[20]

For all the vigour of its economic activities, Muensterschwarzach's primary function was religious: it sought to recruit and train German Catholics for missionary work overseas, for example in East Africa and Korea, and to raise the funds to support the abbey and its missions. Although Muensterschwarzach was situated in the Wuerzburg diocese, it was exempt from the ecclesiastical control of the Bishop. As part of the St Ottilien Congregation it was under the nominal leadership of the arch-abbey of St Ottilien. When Burkard Utz was installed as Abbot of Muensterschwarzach in 1937, Arch-Abbot Chrysostomos of St Ottilien gave the sermon.[21]

Burkard's fellow monks saw him as a severe disciplinarian who demanded total obedience.[22] In return Burkard took complete responsibility for the welfare of his abbey and its monks. At the time of the abbey's dissolution, he presided over a community of fifty-five ordained priests or *patres* and 195 brothers. Although the brothers were not ordained, they had taken vows of poverty, chastity and obedience. In addition to its missionary activities, Muensterschwarzach also performed the religious functions common to most monastic houses. A primary concern of the abbey was prayer. As the Arch-Abbot told the congregation for Burkard's installation 'the monks' prayers brought God's blessing [and] God's blessing protects ... the people and the land on which they work'. Another function of the abbey was liturgical. Its new church was the largest built in Germany for Catholic use since the First

World War. The abbey's services were attended not just by the members of the monastery, but also by Catholic laity from the surrounding area, particularly on Sundays. The abbey also voluntarily made priests available to help the Wuerzburg diocese in its pastoral work.[23]

Relations were excellent between Abbot Burkard and Mathias Ehrenfried, the Bishop of Wuerzburg. Ehrenfried was one of the Catholic bishops most opposed to National Socialism. In September 1934 Dr Otto Hellmuth, the Nazi Gauleiter of Main [Lower] Franconia, which covered the same territory as the Wuerzburg diocese, referred to the 'known hostile attitude of the Bishop of Wuerzburg ... towards National Socialism'. Yet Hellmuth left Bishop Ehrenfried with little option but a policy of hostility. The Gauleiter exemplified at a regional level the anti-Church stance of national policy-makers like Bormann. Hellmuth was determined to break the moral hegemony of the Catholic Church in his region, and as a result the struggles between Party and Church there were of particular severity. Lower Franconia was a province of Bavaria. Nearly one third of the priests taken into protective custody in Bavaria during 1933 were from Lower Franconia, although Ehrenfried's clergy formed less than one seventh of the provincial total.[24]

National Socialists dubbed Ehrenfried 'Stoerenfried' or troublemaker. But his capacity to cause trouble was limited by the small size of his diocese and its limited economic and military significance. There was no big city, and only Schweinfurt had significant industries. Furthermore, while 81 per cent of Lower Franconia's population was Catholic, there was a significant Protestant minority of 18 per cent in the province, much of which lived in the Kitzingen district where Muensterschwarzach was situated. Less than half of the Kitzingen population was Catholic, though this percentage was far higher in the immediate vicinity of the abbey.[25] Even after the dissolution, Muensterschwarzach monks received support and assistance from Nazi officials amongst the local population. Father Gottfried Stuermer was regarded by the Gauleitung as a 'troublemaking preacher who never missed an opportunity to provoke unrest amongst the people'. Yet both the local peasant leader and the mayor of Muensterschwarzach were willing to give political testimonials on his behalf. In May 1939 the Kitzingen *Kreisleitung* or District Leadership of the Nazi Party complained that during recent visits by Bishop Ehrenfried even party officials had sometimes taken an active part in preparing decorations for him.[26]

Any indulgence towards the Catholic Church and Muensterschwarzach Abbey on the part of some local Nazi officials was more than compensated for by the unrelenting animosity of the Kitzingen Kreisleiter, Willy Heer. Heer was a decorated veteran who had served throughout the Great War, though he was never promoted above the rank of lance corporal. After the war Heer served in the Freikorps Epp, which helped to suppress a Communist revolution in Munich. He joined the NSDAP in March 1921 with the membership number of 1,100. In October 1922 he took part in the SA procession through Coburg that developed into a pitched battle with the local Socialists and Communists. To have marched in the Coburg Rally was a much-prized distinction in the Nazi Party. Heer dominated the Party in Kitzingen during the 1920s and 1930s, and in July 1932 became a Nazi Reichstag deputy. He had been brought up a Protestant by his mother, but left the Church in 1937.[27]

Heer saw Muensterschwarzach Abbey as a blot on the landscape. In January 1939 he reported on the introduction of new levels of civic tax in the Kitzingen District. He claimed that in Stadtschwarzach near the abbey there was considerable annoyance because the brothers did not have to pay tax. Heer reported that 'the local civic tax payer simply does not understand why these propagandists against National Socialism are free from this tax because they are allegedly "poor". Even if the members of the order do not possess any money themselves, the order itself in contrast is extraordinarily rich. After this Black [Catholic] brood have begged, stolen and twisted their way to their gigantic property and furthermore avoided work as much as possible and dodged their biological duty to the people and Reich, a double civic tax ought to be the lowest possible level for them.'[28]

In view of his animosity towards the abbey, Heer was no doubt particularly satisfied to receive a circular from the Gauleitung dated 24 April 1941. The surviving copy is addressed to the Kreisleiter of Marktheidenfeld, but the letter will have gone to all the Kreisleiter in Lower Franconia. On behalf of the Gauleiter, the circular requested a list of all local monasteries, together with a short description of their size, location and agricultural enterprises. The circular stressed that Reich offices were pressing for this to be done as soon as possible.[29] These Reich offices probably included the Reich Security Head Office [*Reichssicherheitshauptamt* or RSHA]. The RSHA's main agency in Lower Franconia was the Wuerzburg Gestapo, though it also made use of the Wuerzburg section of the SD. The Gestapo, SD and Nazi Party hunted like a pack to bring down their prey, Muensterschwarzach Abbey: their rows began over the division of the carcass.

The Wuerzburg Gestapo made the first direct move against Muensterschwarzach Abbey. On 5 May 1941 two Gestapo officials, Criminal Inspector Michael Voelkl and Criminal Secretary Franz Keil, appeared at the abbey. They declared to Abbot Burkard that on behalf of the Reich Security Head Office they had to secure 300,000 Reichsmark [RM] with immediate effect from the abbey's resources. At first Burkard refused to pay, so the officials threatened to confiscate the whole abbey except for the church. Burkard then asked what would be the position if he paid the money. Voelkl assured him that payment would settle the matter.[30] The Abbot had little choice but to comply. The following day, 6 May, he drove to Wuerzburg. There he met Franz Brand, the manager of the Wuerzburg branch of the Dresdner Bank. Brand was an old friend and adviser of the abbey, and willingly lent the Abbot the 300,000 RM he needed. But the Gestapo did not return for the money on 7 May as expected. Plans were now afoot to dissolve the abbey completely, and the Wuerzburg Gestapo was at the heart of these. However, a Gestapo official named Karl Immel warned Brand of the impending dissolution. Together with the legal officer of the Wuerzburg diocese, Dr Georg Angermaier, Brand drove out to Muensterwchwarzach late the same evening. Abbot Burkard was woken up and told that a force of about thirty to forty men from the Wuerzburg Gestapo would arrive the following morning at about eight o'clock to dissolve the abbey. Burkard believed the warning, as he knew Immel had provided Brand with reliable information on many previous occasions. The Abbot told the news to the other senior figures in the abbey and ordered the removal of documents from the premises. Various monks slipped away during the night either to monitor the dissolution from outside or to spread the news of what was happening.[31]

The following morning, 8 May 1941, a police formation led by Voelkl arrived at Muensterschwarzach. Altogether almost sixty people were mustered to deal with the abbey. There were about twelve officials from the Gestapo, ten from the Criminal Police and six from the SD. There was also a unit of constabulary about thirty strong. Whereas the Gestapo, Criminal Police and SD wore civilian clothes and only carried pistols, the constabulary wore uniforms including steel helmets and were armed with rifles and bayonets. They were ready for trouble. [32]

Burkard saw this small army arrive from his window, and asked Voelkl, 'Why have you brought so many people? I tell you that I am ready, under protest naturally, to pay the 300,000 RM and furthermore I am also in a position to do so.' In a very excited state, gesticulating and blowing great puffs of smoke from his cigar, Voelkl told the Abbot: 'I have a new commission: I have to carry out a search.' Thereupon Voelkl's officials began to search the cells of all the fathers and also the abbey's archive and library. In the library they found seven objectionable publications including a biography of Karl Marx, and in the abbey archive they found five illegal Communist brochures, one of which was a Stalin speech. These brochures had apparently been left behind by a Benedictine father who was abroad on missionary work. But the presence of the Marxist books in the library, which the Gestapo clearly regarded as the telling evidence of guilt, was extremely puzzling. The Catholic monks had no interest in the life of Karl Marx.[33]

The head of the Kitzingen SD was also in charge of air raid precautions for the area. During a recent air raid drill someone from Kitzingen had displayed a fire flag from one of the library's windows. During the fifteen minutes when the flag was flying the monks had no access to the library, so the SD had an excellent opportunity to add Marxist books to the shelves so that they could be 'discovered' on a later occasion. Keil, who was present during the search on 8 May, said afterwards to Frau Roellich, a Gestapo secretary: 'there's something fishy about the books. One of the SD people led us straight to where they were.' Abbot Burkard was now confronted with the books, but denied any knowledge of them. He asserted that even if the books were in the monastery, they did not constitute evidence of activity hostile to the state.[34]

Once the books had been discovered and recorded as evidence against the abbey, the Gestapo seemed at something of a loss, and waited several hours for further orders. Meanwhile, the focus of activity had moved outside the abbey. The parish priest of neighbouring Sommerach, Father August Falkenstein, was told during the afternoon that something was going on at Muensterschwarzach. As he later recalled: 'I immediately went to Muensterschwarzach with a large crowd of Sommerach youths, girls, men and women. When we got there, there was already a large crowd on the open square in front of the abbey. It was probably between four to five hundred people. The gates of the abbey were shut. Police in grey coats patrolled its surrounding wall ... Other policemen were milling before the gates or sitting in the Kieser public house opposite. The crowd was angry and shouted all sorts of things at the police.' While some people went home, others kept arriving. The mood of the crowd became increasingly excited. Between 7 and 8 pm someone suddenly found a way into the church via the garden gate. The throng pushed inside and on Father Falkenstein's suggestion said the Rosary. At about 10 pm the Benedictine Father Gottfried told them to go home, as nothing further would happen, and they dispersed.[35]

In fact that very evening the final nail had been struck in the abbey's coffin. The Gestapo had been waiting around for the RHSA to order the seizure of the abbey on the basis of the literature discovered. The key figure in persuading the RSHA to take action was the head of the Main Franconia Section of the SD, *SS-Sturmbannfuehrer* Friedrich Glitz, a former theology student who had joined the SS in November 1936. One of his former superiors commented in a personal appraisal that Glitz knew how to get his own way by one means or another. In addition to heading the Wuerzburg SD, he was also at this time the commander of a task force of Security Police and SD based at Muehlhausen in Alsace. Glitz was a formidable antagonist. The Gestapo official Karl Immel, who was present when Glitz eventually arrived at the abbey on 8 May, reported that the latter had clapped Voelkl on the shoulder and said: 'It's worked! They [the RSHA] didn't really want to at first, but I've put their minds at rest. Then Berlin agreed to the dissolution of the abbey.' Although the regime had now decided on complete dissolution, the formula of 'securing' the abbey was used initially for the sake of appearances.[36]

Abbot Burkard later recalled his meeting with Glitz: 'A man came who did not introduce himself to me despite my repeated requests. All the officials present seemed to be in great awe of him. In a deliberately quiet, not to say obsequious tone, which particularly struck me, he stated: "I am commissioned to carry out the securing of the abbey."' Burkard asked what Glitz meant by this, whereupon he declared it meant the monks could not dispose of things in the abbey. Burkard protested that he did not have the authority to set aside the rights of the abbey in such a way; rather this was a matter for the monks' chapter [Konvent]. Glitz then reluctantly accompanied the Abbot to where the monks were waiting and announced that he was securing the abbey. Voelkl added that all unrest was to be avoided. At about 9 pm the Gestapo and other officials left the abbey, except for three Gestapo officials who stayed overnight.[37]

For Glitz, securing the abbey was merely a preliminary to its confiscation. But before it could be seized, he needed to find someone to manage it afterwards. For this purpose Glitz seems to have contacted Gauleiter Hellmuth. The Gauleiter had a greedy eye on the abbey's property, as he was strapped for cash. In 1937 he had approached the Nazi Party Treasurer for 22,246 RM to buy a Mercedes, but was turned down, not least because his Gau was short of money.[38] Muensterschwarzach might do the Gau finances a power of good. During the night of 8–9 May Hellmuth was visited by several men who are described in the only account of the meeting as being from the Reich Security Head Office. They were probably Glitz and some SD colleagues.[39] Describing them as men from the RSHA seems to have been an attempt to camouflage the central role in the affair played by the local SD.

Glitz was looking for someone to run the abbey. Hellmuth thought of Dr Oskar Dengel, the Wuerzburg City Treasurer. Dengel did not belong to a church, and the Wuerzburg Kreisleitung described him as a 'hater of the Blacks'. From October 1939 until March 1940 he had been Government Commissioner of Warsaw. One Polish historian writes of Dengel that 'his period of office ... was the most difficult for the leadership of the Polish city administration': when he left Warsaw he took with him part of the Town Hall furniture. Dengel was a man Gauleiter Hellmuth could work with.[40] At about 2.30 am on 9 May the latter telephoned Dengel and requested him to come to his flat immediately. When Dengel arrived, he found Hellmuth with several men. These were introduced as being from the RSHA, which probably meant, as noted above, that they were SD men, including Glitz, acting on its behalf. Hellmuth told Dengel that Muensterschwarzach was to be confiscated suddenly the next day, and that the RSHA men were looking for an experienced person to act as 'temporary administrator of the abbey'. Dengel agreed to take on the job. As he explained after the war, his purpose was to prevent someone of dubious character getting the post.[41]

The Gestapo prepared for the seizure of Muensterschwarzach by getting Abbot Burkard out of the way. At 9 am on 9 May the Gestapo telephoned the abbey to summon the Abbot and Father Barnabas, his right-hand man, to come to Wuerzburg immediately. There they were received by the head of the Wuerzburg Gestapo, Criminal Commissioner

Ernst Gramowski, and by Voelkl. Gramowski told them that their order was dissolved and said to Burkard: 'You as abbot have control there, so now go out and tell your fathers that they are to pack up quietly. They are being moved to Kreuzberg [Abbey] and can carry on their lives there.' Burkard refused to go out to the abbey to tell his fathers to leave: 'If Muensterschwarzach is to be killed, then you are the one who works for the Gestapo, not me.' Having refused their co-operation, Burkard and Barnabas were held in solitary confinement to keep them out of the way while the dissolution was taking place.[42]

Later on 9 May Voelkl and his officials drove out to Muensterschwarzach. Voelkl assembled all the fathers in one room to inform them of the dissolution. However, a Benedictine priest on leave from the army, Father Hahner, repeatedly sought to disrupt proceedings. When Voelkl tried to make him leave, Hahner drew his bayonet. He was immediately overpowered and dragged out, dazed and bleeding, to a Gestapo car standing in the square in front of the monastery. On the way he shouted loudly so that the people standing around should see what was happening to him.[43]

Hahner had a considerable audience of at least 160 people, including both men and women and many children. A total of 160 people can be counted on a surviving photograph of the demonstration taken some time after Hahner's arrest, by which time the crowd had probably diminished.[44] The people demonstrated vociferously, though without violence, against the Gestapo's dissolution of the monastery. The people had been summoned by the bells of the abbey church and those of the parish church in neighbouring Stadtschwarzach. The bells had begun to ring towards 3 pm when the Gestapo arrived. One eyewitness, a curate from Wuerzburg, commented that 'When I crossed the Main bridge near Muensterschwarzach I heard [bells ringing] ... I could also see that people were leaving their tools standing or lying in the fields and were running to Muensterschwarzach. Then I cycled there too. Many people were already standing in front of the abbey. Some farmers were ... cursing.' One farmer had brought his medals from the First World War and threw them away. Some of the crowd sang hymns and said the rosary. The tension mounted until the moment when the fathers were driven off in Gestapo cars to another monastery. The Wuerzburg curate recalled that, as the fathers left, 'all kinds of shouting broke out together, such as "Hail, Jesus Christ, Fare Well" ... The names of fathers were also called out. It may be that "Pfui" [shame] was called out as well.' Once the fathers had been taken away, the crowd gradually dispersed.[45]

It is surprising that the Nazi authorities tolerated the second demonstration on 9 May after it had already endured the first demonstration the previous day. It is even more remarkable that there was a third demonstration on 11 May. About five hundred people came to attend high mass in the abbey church at 9 am as usual, even though a notice had been posted on the church wall stating that entry was barred to outsiders. The 11 May demonstrators consisted of men, women and children. They were mostly from the surrounding villages, but some had come from Wuerzburg. When the demonstrators arrived at the abbey church, they were pushed in the direction of the local pub by a squad of police. So they proceeded to hold a lay mass with prayers and hymns in front of the pub.[46]

The head of the Kitzingen Police was commanding the police operation. He reported to the Landrat [District Official] of Kitzingen that 'the demonstration was carried out according to a plan. Its purpose was to compel the government ... to make the abbey church available to the church-goers. It was decided not to use force against the demonstrators because direct resistance was not offered and we were supposed to avoid too drastic measures.'[47] 'Softly softly' was regarded as the best way to police events in front of the abbey in order to defuse the situation.

What was the wider significance of these demonstrations? Did they help to draw popular attention to the dissolution of Muensterschwarzach? Indeed, how extensive was knowledge of the event? There was no mention of the dissolution or demonstrations in any newspapers. The regime believed that silence was the best policy and tried to keep the Muensterschwarzach affair as quiet as possible. By contrast, there were persistent attempts on the Catholic side to publicize the closure. Various different clandestine leaflets, two of which were widely circulated, drew attention to the events at Muensterschwarzach. The first of these was drawn up by a Muensterschwarzach Benedictine, Father Sales Hess. He later explained that he had wanted publicity for three reasons. First, it was necessary to prevent donations from benefactors reaching the abbey and enriching the Nazis. Secondly, many of the abbey's friends criticized the regime in their letters and these friends had to be warned not to write. Thirdly, as Father Sales put it, 'the Catholic people had a right to know what had happened to its monasteries'.[48]

When the abbey's dissolution was pending, Sales asked one of the brothers to prepare an addressed envelope for each name on the abbey's mailing list. In all, 16,000 envelopes were made ready. Having been tipped off via Immel that the Gestapo were about to act, Sales left the monastery early on 8 May. At 7 pm the following day he learned that the dissolution had taken place. In addition to the buildings at the main abbey complex, Muensterschwarzach owned other property, including a college in Wuerzburg, St Benedikt, which was intended for members of the order studying at the University. Despite its proximity to their office, the Wuerzburg Gestapo failed to seize St Benedikt immediately, so Father Sales was able to use the college as the base for his propaganda action. He drew up a circular that gave a brief factual report of the monastery's fate and concluded: 'we express our thanks for your previous generous support, but request that in future you send neither letters nor money to Muensterschwarzach.' The letter was signed by 'your devoted loyal expelled Benedictine missionaries of Muensterschwarzach'.[49]

About thirty to forty assistants, mostly boys and women, gathered in St Benedikt to copy Father Sales' letter and put it in the prepared envelopes. They began at 8 pm on 9 May, and by 3 am the following day the final letters were ready. Sales himself posted about 2,000 letters in Nuremberg and another bundle in Fuerth. Other batches were posted in Munich, Wuerzburg and Bamberg. The letters were posted in small quantities so as not to attract attention. All the same, 4,320 letters were intercepted and sent to the Wuerzburg Gestapo. This still left nearly 12,000 unaccounted for, and a large number reached their destinations. A few hours after the final letters were produced, the Gestapo seized St Benedikt. The trail of the circulars soon led to Sales, who was arrested and taken to the Wuerzburg Gestapo. As he later recalled, 'Voelkl emerged and placed himself in front of me like an insulted god ... I had ruined everything and would have to take the consequences.' Sales confessed his own involvement, but refused to name any of those who had helped him. He succeeded in protecting his assistants, but because of his silence spent the rest of the war in Dachau concentration camp.[50]

Besides Father Sales' letter, a partisan account of the dissolution also circulated as a leaflet. The unknown author concentrates on the events of 8, 9 and 11 May. The description is very emotive. The author writes of the 'disgusting cowardice' of the police and goes to town on the treatment meted out to Father Hahner, who lay 'covered in blood on the ground' and was 'beaten worse than a dog'. This second anonymous leaflet surfaced in the Rhine Palatinate.[51] As we have seen, Father Sales' letter also circulated outside Lower Franconia, and there were furthermore at least three different types of leaflet found in varying numbers within Lower Franconia.[52]

These various leaflets circulated illegally and had the appeal of forbidden fruit. Their impact was complemented by an official statement from the Bishop of Wuerzburg. Ehrenfried made the dissolution of Muensterschwarzach Abbey the theme of a pastoral letter to be read from all the pulpits in the diocese on Whit Sunday. He was the first German bishop to devote a pastoral letter to the closure of a monastery. Kerrl, the Minister of Church Affairs, considered Ehrenfried's pastoral letter about Muensterschwarzach of sufficient importance to deserve mention in a letter to Himmler on 11 June.[53]

The demonstrations, leaflets and Ehrenfried's pastoral letter publicized the dissolution of Muensterschwarzach throughout Lower Franconia. Even before the reading of Ehrenfried's letter in the churches, a female apprentice in Kitzingen had told the police: 'I would like to stress that people everywhere are talking about the events in Muensterschwarzach.' Popular reaction in the province was overwhelmingly negative. The president of the Wuerzburg court reported that 'even in circles with a thoroughly positive attitude to National Socialism, the measures ... were condemned because they were likely to cause unnecessary unrest amongst the population at a time when everything had to be done to preserve unity'.[54]

The combination of intense popular interest in Muensterschwarzach and the media blackout inevitably led to the proliferation of rumours. These were invariably to the discredit of the Nazi regime, though not its leader. Ian Kershaw has shown that Hitler was usually seen as the protector of traditional religion against the attacks of Party radicals.[55] The rumours following the dissolution of Muensterschwarzach that mentioned Hitler conform to this pattern, with the Fuehrer cast in the role of a *deus ex machina* who puts everything back to rights. In contrast, the rumours tended to criticize Gauleiter Hellmuth. One rumour claimed that Bishop Ehrenfried had reported the dissolution to the Pope, who had told the Duce, who in turn informed Hitler. Gauleiter Hellmuth had then fled. In one variation of this rumour the Fuehrer had been in Wuerzburg one night and called the Gauleiter to account for closing the monastery. In another variation, Gauleiter Hellmuth had been caught on the Swiss frontier with a waitress and a quarter of a million marks, presumably looted from Muensterschwarzach. The police investigating the Pope, Duce and Hitler story eventually stopped questioning further witnesses in despair, 'as it would produce a whole chain of people spreading the rumour which would run on for ever'. By the time news of the events at Muensterschwarzach had reached Karlsbad in Bohemia, it had been transformed into a story that an attempt to close a monastery in Wuerzburg had been prevented by farmers bearing flails.[56]

The widespread rumours about Muensterschwarzach and the accounts circulated by the Catholic Church meant that most people in Lower Franconia probably knew that something untoward had taken place at the abbey. Outside Lower Franconia it was a different matter, and in other regions of Germany probably only a large number of Catholic clergy, a smaller number of lay patrons of the abbey and a limited number of Nazi officials knew about the dissolution. The events at Muensterschwarzach did not become a *cause celèbre* throughout Catholic Germany in the same way as the Oldenburg crucifix struggle. Whereas the Oldenburg demonstrations succeeded in reversing Nazi policy, the protests at Muensterschwarzach Abbey did not.[57]

Another reason for the comparatively limited resonance of the Muensterschwarzach affair was the skilful way in which the Gestapo handled the aftermath. During May 1941 the Gestapo ruled out any question of putting the monks on trial because of their possession of seditious publications. This avoided a court case that could provoke the local population. Furthermore, the Gestapo donned velvet gloves for its handling of the Catholics who were involved in the popular agitation. When the abbey bells were rung to signify the arrival of the Gestapo, a teenager from neighbouring Stadtschwarzach had run to his village church and rung the bells there. The teenager escaped with a warning. The Wuerzburg Gestapo noted that 'further measures were not taken against him for reasons of expediency'. The farmer who threw away his medals also only received a warning. The wife of a Nazi Party member said during the tumult in front of the abbey on 9 May that 'she would write to her husband in the army that he should now turn around his rifle and fight against his own comrades'. The Gestapo recorded that no measures were taken against the woman 'in view of the annoyance prevalent at the time amongst many women from the vicinity of Muensterschwarzach'.

As the Nazis did not believe women belonged in politics, their dissent mattered less.[58]

Local Nazis were not always as cautious as the Gestapo in the aftermath. Party members felt threatened by the popular criticism, and to defend themselves they made the most far-fetched assertions about the monks. For example, a teacher in the district of Bad Neustadt an der Saale told his pupils that Muensterschwarzach had been dissolved because the monks were spying for England. The Gestapo official who reported on this claim considered the teacher's remarks 'inappropriate, as they did not correspond to the facts ... Such inappropriate remarks ... repeatedly produce counter-declarations from the clergy or their sympathizers, so that the discussion over Muensterschwarzach never ends and a complete pacification never takes place.'[59]

The negative reaction to the dissolution made the fate of the abbey's property all the more important for the Nazi Party in Lower Franconia. In January 1942 the Gau economic adviser, Dr Vogel, wrote that 'we want to avoid being reproached some day for not having administered the people's property at least as well as the Blacks'. In addition to this political motive for careful management, the Gauleitung had another reason, as it regarded the stolen abbey very much as its own property. Of course, the Reich Security Head Office in Berlin had taken the responsibility of ordering the abbey's dissolution. In October the same year an RSHA official visited Muensterschwarzach and picked out three hundred books from the library. But he was not allowed to take them away. Vogel noted that, 'I have told Gramowski [the head of the Wuerzburg Gestapo] that books must not be removed from the library without the approval of the Gauleiter.' Vogel's firmness on this point suggests an awareness that the Gauleitung had support at the Reich level for such a stance. On 19 April 1941 Bormann had written to Reichsleiter Alfred Rosenberg that 'the libraries and works of art in the monasteries confiscated in the Reich are to remain for the time being in those monasteries unless the Gauleiter determine otherwise ... On no account should there be a centralization of all the libraries, which the Fuehrer has repeatedly rejected.' One Gestapo official later stole a set of Goethe from the Muensterschwarzach library. With this exception, the Gestapo and SS which had played the main part in dissolving the abbey received none of the very considerable spoils.[60]

After achieving the abbey's dissolution, Gauleiter Hellmuth's first instinct was to sell it. This offered two advantages. First, it would give a major boost to the shaky Gau finances. Second, if the abbey complex were used for a completely new purpose by an outside agency, it would make comparisons with the Benedictine administration difficult. On 1 July 1941 four officials from the *Intendantur Ley* inspected Muensterschwarzach. As Organization Leader of the NSDAP, Robert Ley was partly responsible for the Adolf Hitler Schools. Having seen the abbey, his officials decided it was suitable for such an institution. Similarly, SS General Heissmeyer, who was responsible for the *Napolas*, wanted the abbey complex for one of his schools. In early July 1941 Gramowski visited Deputy-Gauleiter Kuehnreich [Hellmuth was away at a spa] to emphasize Heissmeyer's interest in the abbey. Gramowski claimed that when he had mentioned this project to Hellmuth, the latter had made no objections. Just as with the abbey's books, the head of the local Gestapo was brushed off in his attempt to assert SS interests in the use of the whole complex. Kuehnreich told him that the Gauleiter had meant to raise no objection in principle to the use of the abbey for educational purposes, but not specifically to agree to the establishment of a *Napola* there. Besides Ley and Heissmeyer, the Reich Colonial League was also interested in Muensterschwarzach. On 24 September 1941 its chief executive wrote to Gauleiter Hellmuth saying that he was convinced the League should acquire the entire property for training purposes. Yet the chief executive admitted that it was scarcely possible for the League to acquire the abbey from its own resources.[61]

Fifteen years of working with the most vicious political machine in German history had given Hellmuth all the training he needed to become an estate agent. As there was a question mark over the finances of the Reich Colonial League, Heissmeyer now seemed the most promising customer. On 26 September the Gauleiter wrote to Heissmeyer, pointedly mentioning the League's interest in the property. He also listed many attractive features of the abbey complex: indeed Hellmuth had the shamelessness to praise the architecture of the abbey church. The entire property could be Heissmeyer's for a very reasonable 3½ million RM.[62] Hellmuth prudently omitted to mention to his potential clients the fact that he was not the legal owner of the abbey and so could not transfer the official title to it. As mentioned above, in March 1941 Hitler had ruled that the property of enemies of the people and state was to be confiscated, not for the benefit of the Reich, but for that of the particular Gau in which the property was located. If the property was located in several

Gaue, it was to be divided sensibly amongst them. But the division of these scattered properties proved very difficult in practice. So on 25 May 1941 Hitler decreed that property belonging to enemies of the Reich was to be confiscated initially in favour of the Reich. This was intended solely as a technical instrument: on 22 April 1942 Bormann issued a circular that stressed Hitler still wanted the confiscated property to benefit the Gaue. In theory the Reich's involvement was merely to divide the property fairly. In practice the Reich's legal ownership of confiscated property like Muensterschwarzach was to prove a formidable obstacle to its sale by the Gauleitung.[63]

After a brief period as administrator of Muensterschwarzach Abbey, Oskar Dengel had been with the German forces on the Russian Front. He was rescued by Hellmuth and appointed to a senior administrative role as Deputy President of Lower Franconia. On 30 January 1942 Dengel wrote in his new capacity to inform Abbot Burkard that he was confiscating the entire property of the abbey in accordance with the Fuehrer's decree of 25 May 1941. The next day he also wrote to the Reich Minister of the Interior, asking him to transfer ownership of the abbey free of charge to the Main Franconian District Association, an agency of Hellmuth's Gauleitung.[64] This initiative made efforts to sell the abbey inopportune. On 3 February one of Dengel's assistants noted that his master now wanted all sales negotiations to be wound down. Otherwise there was a danger that the Ministry of the Interior would insist on disposing of the property itself. In the event the Ministry, despite repeated requests, never replied to Dengel's request to transfer legal ownership of the abbey. Consequently the Gauleitung never gained a clear title to it, and could sell neither the whole property nor even part of it. Thus it had to manage the abbey as a unit from the time of the dissolution until the Americans arrived in 1945.[65]

The Nazi administration of Muensterschwarzach was very successful financially. Dengel had only run things on the spot for a short period from 9 May until 20 June 1941. But once installed as Deputy President he represented the abbey's legal owner, as the Lower Franconian regional administration was the local agency of the Reich Ministry of the Interior. Gauleiter Hellmuth, the nominal head of the regional administration, left supervision of the routine economic management of the abbey to Dengel and Vogel. Dengel abolished the previously separate economic administrations of the abbey's Wuerzburg college, St Benedikt, and of

St Ludwig, a dependent priory the Benedictines had run 10 miles to the north of the abbey. Dengel united the management of these two auxiliary houses with that of the abbey itself. The advantages of this centralization proved so great it was kept after the war.

The most immediate problem facing the Nazi administration was how to keep Muensterschwarzach solvent. Father Sales' letter stopped the flow of donations from outside benefactors on which the abbey's finances depended. From being the crock of gold the Gauleitung hoped for, the abbey threatened to become a crippling liability that could not be shaken off because of the uncertain legal position. On 6 September 1941 Vogel noted that 'there must be a thorough examination of how the abbey is to survive, now the donations are no longer coming in'. On 11 September he recorded the abbey's debts as 113,000 RM.[66] Dengel, Vogel and a succession of administrators on the spot ensured the economic survival of the property by letting the buildings to various agencies and, most importantly, by enforcing the collection of rent. For example, the Liaison Office for Ethnic Germans had occupied part of Muensterschwarzach since 1 October 1940 but had never paid any rent. Following an approach from the Gauleitung, in January 1942 the office of the Reich Commissioner for the Strengthening of the German Race, which had responsibility for the Liaison Office, agreed to pay 900 RM a month for the accommodation its agency was using. As the Liaison Office was an SS agency, this meant that in practice the SS lost financially from its role in dissolving the abbey. The Liaison Office had signed a rent agreement with the previous Benedictine administration, but had never bothered to pay up.[67]

The most lucrative of the new letting arrangements was with the army. In the late summer of 1941 the Nazi administration of Muensterschwarzach negotiated an agreement with the army, which agreed to pay 4,500 RM a month to locate a hospital for wounded soldiers in the abbey. These substantial arrangements with the army and SS were complemented by numerous smaller letting arrangements with local government and private business. The Nazi administration used some of the income generated to make improvements to the property. But the rent income was eventually so great that a large surplus remained. Abbot Burkard found it waiting for him on his return in 1945. The Nazis' energetic management of the abbey's resources provided the funds for Muensterschwarzach's missionary activity after the war.[68]

Throughout his years of exile, Burkard never accepted the dissolution of his abbey as final. Following his release by the Gestapo shortly after the confiscation, he sought to maintain and even strengthen the remaining Benedictine presence in the abbey while at the same time challenging the dissolution through official channels. Burkard's strategy of keeping Benedictines as far as possible in the abbey received an early boost when Oskar Dengel, the first administrator of Muensterschwarzach, left in June 1941. As he went during the period of the Gauleiter's visit to a health resort, it was up to Deputy Gauleiter Kuehnreich to find a successor. Having consulted Dengel, on 28 June Kuehnreich appointed Raimund Rueth, the Landrat of Kitzingen. When Hellmuth learned of the appointment he commented: 'I very much doubt whether Party Member Rueth is generally up to dealing with these scoundrels. Rueth will be taken in good and proper.'[69]

Rueth was a Catholic by birth, but had joined the SA in 1922 and the Nazi Party itself in March 1926 with the membership number of 33,034. For a period in 1932 he had held office as a Nazi Kreisleiter. A decorated veteran of the Great War, Rueth's overall credentials for preferment in the Third Reich were not much inferior to those of Kreisleiter Heer.[70] But his attitude to Muensterschwarzach was the exact opposite. On the day the abbey was dissolved, the Benedictines noticed how depressed Rueth was looking.[71] He soon gave offence to the Nazi elite in Lower Franconia. In particular he let numerous Benedictines return to the abbey. When the abbey was dissolved, most of the priests had been expelled, but the lay brothers had been allowed to stay as their labour was needed to work the land. Then in June 1941 Dengel expelled the brothers who were too old to work, a cruel decision dressed up as a rationalization measure. Having spent most of their lives in the abbey, they were now thrown out in their old age. Abbot Burkard was understandably very concerned about these older lay brothers, and once the military hospital had been opened in Muensterschwarzach he saw an opportunity for their return to the abbey. In July 1941 he had a meeting with Rueth in Wuerzburg and pointed out that the old brothers could help the hospital by doing light work. Rueth proved receptive to this suggestion, and during July most of the elderly brothers were summoned back to the abbey.[72]

On 16 July 1941 Hasenschwanz and Schuebel, the two SS officials in charge of the Liaison Office in the abbey, wrote to Kreisleiter Heer complaining about the return of these brothers. They pointed out that with the return of former members of the monastery it was rumoured far and wide that the dissolution had taken place without the knowledge or permission of the Fuehrer: 'it is generally believed that the Fuehrer himself has ordered the recall of these unjustly expelled monastics.' The two SS officials also complained that when Dengel left, the atmosphere in the abbey changed: 'As long as Dr Dengel was the officially appointed administrator of this abbey, it was obvious the Black monastery inmates were being given real discipline. In contrast, recently we get the almost tangible sense that these people feel they are the lords and rulers of the monastery again.' Hasenschwanz and Schuebel cited various instances of the monks' intolerable behaviour, but the one they felt most deeply was the matter of the doughnuts. About ten days earlier the 'Black gentry' had baked doughnuts, but had not given any to the SS officials. Schuebel had been so concerned about a possible offence against the rationing regulations that he had telephoned Landrat Rueth to tell him about the doughnuts, which really ought to be reported to the *Reichsfuehrer SS*. Rueth had merely declared that Schuebel 'should not be so nasty and petty'.[73]

Kreisleiter Heer took the complaint from Hasenschwanz and Schuebel very seriously. On 18 July 1941 the Kitzingen Kreisleiter wrote to Deputy Gauleiter Kuehnreich enclosing a copy of a letter from the two SS officials and expressing his support for their statements: 'Landrat Rueth ... does not have the guts to stand up to the fathers and brothers left in the monastery ... I would like to propose the removal of Party Member Rueth from the leadership of the administration of Muensterschwarzach Abbey ... The people assume the Party bears the main guilt for the dissolution of the monastery. There is no point in keeping this secret [i.e. by having a state rather than a Party official as head of the monastery].'[74]

The Gauleitung was convinced by these arguments and replaced Rueth as abbey administrator with the Local Nazi Party leader of Gerolzhofen, one of Kreisleiter Heer's subordinates. The new administrator maintained a correct attitude in business matters and let the monks alone in other respects. Everyday life within the monastery was not Nazified. When Gau Economic Adviser Vogel visited Muensterschwarzach in January 1943 he noted with horror that no one said 'Heil Hitler' either on his arrival or on his departure and that the fathers were still wearing the robes of the order. He concluded that 'the inmates of the monastery today still consciously feel themselves to be members of the order and behave accordingly'. Owing to Rueth's management of the monastery during a decisive phase, the realism of his successors, and the tenacity of the monks themselves, Muensterschwarzach Abbey retained not only a physical Benedictine presence, but also a Benedictine mentality.[75]

Besides his efforts to sustain Benedictine influence within the abbey, Burkard also sought to have its dissolution reversed. For this he needed the support of the church authorities in Berlin, Papal Nuncio Orsenigo and Bishop Heinrich Wienken, who represented the German Catholic bishops vis-à-vis the Reich Security Head Office. Unfortunately Orsenigo and Wienken were among the least resolute of the Catholic leaders. Orsenigo thought there were 'priests who criticized [the Nazi regime] but also good priests and curates, who said nothing'. Bishop Wienken was preoccupied with such issues as whether Catholic priests in the medical corps should take part in the disinfection of military brothels.[76]

Dr Georg Angermaier, the legal adviser to the Wuerzburg diocese, visited Berlin during the final week of May 1941. He saw both Orsenigo and Wienken. Wienken told him that it was urgently necessary for Abbot Burkard to visit the Reich Security Head Office. Briefed by Angermaier, Burkard took Wienken's advice and visited the RSHA on 14 June 1941. There an official told him that 'unfortunately the Muensterschwarzach documents cannot be found ... but one thing is certain: if a penalty was imposed on your Abbey, then there must also have been reasons for it'. Burkard pointed out that when he had asked the Wuerzburg Gestapo about the reasons for the dissolution they had referred him to Berlin: 'Now I am here to learn the complete explanation for a measure which seems to me completely unjustified and incomprehensible and regret it extremely that you do not have the documents to hand.'[77] As Bishop Wienken's suggestion had proved fruitless, the Abbot went to see Nuncio Orsenigo later the same day. Burkard sought to persuade the latter to advocate Muensterschwarzach's case to the RSHA. But Orsenigo refused to contact the latter, and Burkard concluded in retrospect that 'in my case he [the Nuncio] inclined more to the side of the RSHA'.[78]

In contrast to Wienken and Orsenigo, Bishop Ehrenfried of Wuerzburg provided significant help to the Abbot. He appointed Burkard a diocesan councillor to prevent him being called up by the Wehrmacht. Besides his pastoral letter on Muensterschwarzach, Ehrenfried also sent a letter of protest on 20 May 1941 to Lammers, Kerrl, the High Command of the Wehrmacht, the Reich Ministers of the Interior and of Justice, the Bavarian Ministry of Education and the Wuerzburg Gestapo. Ehrenfried requested that the confiscation of Muensterschwarzach Abbey should be reversed. He stressed that 'the abbey was taken away without any orderly legal procedure', whereas 'the abbey as a corporation of public law and its members as citizens of the German Reich have a right to be treated according to the recognized principles of the law'. Ehrenfried's protest was largely ignored. A Reich Chancellery official noted its receipt at the Fuehrer's headquarters on 25 May. He also observed that various other agencies had received the same appeal: 'therefore there is probably no need to do anything'. Lammers wrote to Ehrenfried confirming the receipt of his letter and swept it under the carpet.[79] Ehrenfried might have been wiser to concentrate his fire on one authority: his wide spread of letters made it easier for individual agencies to ignore him. After all, he was only the head of a small and relatively insignificant diocese. When nothing was done at the Reich level, Ehrenfried let the matter drop. Despite the regional popular outrage and Ehrenfried's protest to the national authorities, the events at Muensterschwarzach did not influence Nazi policy towards the monasteries at a higher level.

The German espiscopate as a group was no more effective than Ehrenfried. The Fulda Conference of all Germany's Catholic bishops, including those of Austria, met from 24 to 26 June 1941. They agreed to a joint pastoral letter referring to the dissolution of the monasteries that was to be read from every pulpit on 6 July. This was the first joint pastoral letter since 1938, and was in line with the Preysing–Galen strategy of public confrontation with the regime. But though the technique was confrontational, the price of obtaining general consent was a text that suffered from contradictions and vagueness. The bishops on the one hand proclaimed that the survival of Christianity and the Church in Germany was at stake, yet on the other hand assured Catholic soldiers that they were 'serving not only the Fatherland, but also at the same time the sacred will of God'. No doubt the bishops were thinking of the Nazi invasion of the anti-Christian Soviet Union, which had begun a few days previously. They expressed 'deep sympathy with the members of orders who have been driven from their monastic homes ... The Catholic people ... will not leave these loyal sons and daughters ... in the lurch.' But those responsible for closing the monasteries were not identified. The thirty bishops and diocesan representatives gathered around the grave of St Boniface refrained from criticizing specific agencies of the regime.[80]

On 1 July 1941 the seven Austrian bishops acted on their own and wrote to the Reich Ministry of the Interior protesting far more specifically about the dissolution of the Austrian monasteries. The first line of their letter identified the Gestapo as the responsible agency, and the Austrian bishops also criticized the grounds on which the monasteries were seized. They declared that the confiscations were not carried out to punish failings, nor just to get hold of monastic property, the economic importance of which was exaggerated anyway; it was rather that 'here a deliberate planned fight against the orders as such is being waged with the intention of hitting the Church in the branch of its institutions which are meant to lead to the highest development of Christian life'. Although the letter of the Austrian bishops was more forthright than the Fulda pastoral, it too included conciliatory material, as the seven appealed for the justice which 'would give us bishops and the whole Catholic people in the Ostmark [Austria] the certainty that our Faith and Church are not outlawed, but have a true home in the greater united German Fatherland, to which our Catholic Ostmark soldiers dedicate their health and lives with heroic commitment'.[81]

Both the pastoral letter of the Fulda Bishops' Conference and that of the Austrian bishops tempered objections with patriotism. Despite their protests the dissolution of the monasteries continued unabated. Two-thirds of the confiscations in the Cologne diocese took place after the public reading of the Fulda pastoral letter on 6 July.[82] During the second week of July the Gestapo also carried out extensive seizures in the Muenster diocese of Bishop Galen, which bordered on Cologne. Galen presided over a vigorous Catholic community. In 1941 there were 1,833,258 Catholics in his diocese, who formed 59.5 per cent of the local population. Of these, 50.3 per cent went to church, the sixth highest proportion of any German diocese, and on average there were fourteen communions per Catholic a year, the sixth highest rate in Germany.[83]

Just as the Gestapo began to suppress the religious orders, the city of Muenster itself was shattered by British bombing. In the context of this terrifying visitation from the air, Bishop Galen rose to the Gestapo challenge with a series of impassioned sermons. On 13 July Galen declared that 'while the whole of Muenster still reels under the impact of the terrible devastation which the external enemy ... has brought upon us this week: at such a time, yesterday, 12 July, the Gestapo confiscated the two Jesuit houses ... in our city ... We must brace ourselves for a spread of such terrible news during the next few days, that here too one monastery after another is to be confiscated by the Gestapo and its inmates, our brothers and sisters ... are to be thrown onto the streets like helots without rights and hunted from the region like criminals.' As the British bombing was making many ordinary people homeless, it was easy for Galen's listeners to appreciate how the expelled members of religious orders felt, although the local Gauleitung shrewdly worked against such sympathy by earmarking the confiscated religious property for the use of air-raid victims. In his sermon Galen proceeded from a criticism of the Gestapo's treatment of the religious orders to a more general condemnation of the secret police. Overall his comments constituted by far the most devastating Catholic attack on the closure of the monasteries.[84]

The day after his emphatic sermon, Galen sent a telegram to the Reich Chancellery in which he referred to the Gestapo's confiscation of the monasteries and religious houses in Muenster and the expulsion of their inmates. He continued: 'I request the Fuehrer and Reich Chancellor in the interest of justice and the solidarity of the Home Front to protect the freedom and property of these honourable German people against the arbitrary measures of the Gestapo and against robbery for the benefit of the Gauleitung.' Galen read out this telegram in church during his sermon on the following Sunday. From the tone of his next communication to the Reich Chancellery it seems likely that he received a brush-off from Lammers along the lines that the Fuehrer was too busy with urgent matters to consider Galen's request. On 22 July the latter wrote to Lammers with a brusque denial of the regime's mythical image of Hitler, asserting that, 'Adolf Hitler is not a divine being, raised above every natural limitation, who is able to keep an eye on and direct everything at the same time ... When ... the unrestrained Gestapo shatters the Home Front ... then I know [I am called upon] ... to raise my voice loudly [so as to bring the matter to Hitler's attention]'. Galen enclosed for Lammers' consideration copies of the sermons that he had given on 13 and 20 May.[85]

Galen's most devastating sermon was delivered on 3 August. In this he returned once again to the regime's dissolution of the monasteries, reporting that during the past week the Gestapo had continued its work of destruction against the Catholic orders. But most of this sermon consisted of a blistering attack on Nazi euthanasia, the regime's systematic secret murder of the mentally ill and incurably sick. During these weeks Galen had been profoundly troubled both by the regime's closure of monasteries and its euthanasia campaign. Indeed, his worry over the religious houses may have detonated his public onslaught on euthanasia. On 3 August Galen announced that he had pressed charges against those responsible for the killings, and concluded: 'Let us pray for the poor sick people threatened by death, for our religious orders in exile, for all those suffering, for our soldiers, for our people and Fatherland and Fuehrer.'[86]

Some historians who discuss Galen's protest against euthanasia see this in isolation.[87] Yet in reality, Galen's most important sermon against euthanasia on 3 August was the result of a growing anger with the regime due to more than one cause, just as the sermon itself dealt with more than one issue. The concurrent Nazi measures against the monasteries and the mentally ill enraged Galen so much that he threw caution to the wind and put the regime to flight on both issues. His sermon on 3 August contributed directly to the ending of the 'T4' euthanasia action, though some euthanasia murders continued to take place.[88] Similarly, his attacks on the dissolution of the monasteries on 13 and 20 July almost certainly influenced Hitler's cancellation of this policy. The Committee for the Religious Orders, established by the German bishops in the summer of 1941 to monitor Nazi policies against the regular clergy, repeatedly emphasized the central role of Galen's sermons in producing a stop decree from Hitler. Pope Pius XII also attributed 'the cancellation of measures against the Church' to the 'brave action of Bishop von Galen'.[89]

There is no specific documentary evidence linking Galen's protests with Hitler's cancellation of the monastery action. However, on 29 July Hitler discussed with Lammers two eloquent letters from Bishop Bornewasser of Trier requesting an end to the dissolutions. In connection with this matter they also talked about another unnamed subject, perhaps Galen's forthright protests. On 31 July, even before Galen's most famous sermon, Bormann, as head of the Party Chancellery, wrote from the Fuehrer's headquarters in East Prussia to the Gauleiter: 'The Fuehrer has decreed that seizures of church and monastic property are to stop immediately until further notice. Independent measures by the Gauleiter must not take place under any circumstances.' Bormann now had to stifle the action he had fostered six months previously. Similarly, on 5 August the Inspectors of the Security Police and SD passed on to the Gestapo offices the following instruction from the Fuehrer: 'With immediate effect no further actions may be undertaken against monasteries.'[90]

Just as the regime had tried to carry out the destruction of the monasteries in silence, so too its halting of the action was not publicized. Even Kerrl, the Minister for Church Affairs, was not told initially. On 14 August Lammers wrote to Bormann that 'I leave it to your judgement as to how Reich Minister Kerrl should learn of the Fuehrer's decision.'[91] Kerrl was kept in the dark to deprive him of a sense of victory over Bormann and Himmler. Even though the decisive blow was struck by Galen, throughout the summer Kerrl too had protested against the dissolutions. On 11 June he informed Himmler that 'in principle I oppose monasteries and religious orders and ... welcome a disappearance of this obsolete form of church life. However I consider the way in which the dissolution of the monasteries is being carried out now during the war as very questionable for domestic and foreign policy reasons.'[92]

Kerrl continued his campaign against the dissolutions even after Hitler had issued his stop degree because no one told the Reich Minister of Church Affairs. On 2 August Kerrl wrote to Lammers stating that, 'I can scarcely believe that the way in which the removal of the monasteries is being carried out now during the war corresponds to the will of the Fuehrer.' By 4 September Kerrl had finally learned of the stop decree, and from it he drew the conclusion that Hitler did not approve of the confiscations, just as Kerrl had always said.[93]

Hitler's stop decree brought the main thrust of the Nazi dissolution of the monasteries to a halt. On 28 August 1941 Bishop Preysing noted that recently there seemed to have been no further dissolutions.[94] On 28 January 1942 Himmler wrote in response to an enquiry from Lammers that there was 'extensive incriminating evidence' concerning Beuron Abbey in Wuerttemberg which would justify its dissolution, but that action had to be postponed because of the Fuehrer's order to stop further confiscations of church property. On 14 August 1943 the Bishops' Committee for the Religious Orders reported that 'the Fuehrer's stop decree ... produced by the sermons of His Grace the Bishop of Muenster has for the most part been observed'.[95]

Although Hitler's decree did end the mass open onslaught on the German monasteries, they were still perceived in some quarters as an

Rudolf Hess, Hitler's Deputy
for Nazi Party Affairs
(Bundesarchiv, Bild 146II-849 /
CC-BY-SA 3.0)

Count Wolf-Heinrich von Helldorf
in 1933 (Bundesarchiv Bild
W0623-501)

Above: Helldorf giving the Hitler salute with his wife Ingeborg, 13 February 1938 (Bundesarchiv Bild 183-H01857)

Below: Helldorf bowing to his patron Joseph Goebbels, Reich Propaganda Minister and Nazi Gauleiter for Berlin, 29th October 1938 (Bundesarchiv Bild 183-H14225)

Helldorf wearing his
Knight's Cross decoration
(Bundesarchiv Bild
183-J09181)

Helldorf during his show
trial before the People's
Court (Bundesarchiv Bild
151-45-16)

Clemens August Count von Galen, Bishop of Muenster (Bildersammlung des Bistumsarchivs Münster, des Erbnehmers der Urheberrechte)

Franz Vorwerk, Galen's representative in Oldenburg

Muensterschwarzach
Abbey (Photoarchiv
Muensterschwarzach)

Burkard Utz OSB, Abbot
of Muensterschwarzach
(1937–59) (Photoarchiv
Muensterschwarzach)

Above: Popular demonstration
against the dissolution
of Muensterschwarzach
(StA Wue Gestapo 3693 Bl. 3)

Left: Hugh Trevor-Roper,
MI6 officer and Christ
Church historian (copyright
Dacre Trustees)

Above left and above right: Nazi Armaments Minister Albert Speer (Wikipedia) and Hitler's doctor Theodor Morell, two of many witnesses questioned in person by Trevor-Roper after the war

Below: Hitler amid wartime staff (Bundesarchiv, Bild 183-R99057 / Unknown / CC-BY-SA 3.0)

A view outside Hitler's bunker, with an entrance to the left (Wikipedia)

inviting target. When two religious houses in Silesia were requisitioned in early 1943, Cardinal Bertram sent a protest memorandum to the Reich Chancellery. Bormann thereupon instructed the local Gauleiter to return the two religious houses and issued a circular to the Nazi Party on 26 April 1943 that emphasized the stop decree was still in force. Now that the fortunes of war had turned against the Nazi regime, Bertram's memoranda were taken more seriously.[96] Hitler's own comments about the monasteries suggest that his stop decree was purely tactical. On 7 April 1942 he remarked that 'It is gratifying that through the dissolution of the monasteries many men willing and able to work could be given back their freedom. The dissolution of the monasteries does not present ... any great difficulties.'[97] It seems that the stop decree meant only a temporary respite, and that after victory those monasteries that had escaped the onslaught of 1940 and 1941 were to be swept away in their turn.

Some overall points concerning the Nazi regime and the Catholic Church emerge from a consideration of the dissolution of the monasteries in general and that of Muensterschwarzach Abbey in particular. Like the immorality trials of clergy in 1936–37, and some of the regional actions against crucifixes, the dissolution of the monasteries was halted before its conclusion. In the case of Muensterschwarzach, the SD, Gestapo and Gauleitung co-operated closely to bring down the abbey. The leading role was played by the local SD, which both smuggled the incriminating evidence into the abbey and persuaded the RSHA to take action. The Gestapo provided the blunt instrument in the closure of Muensterschwarzach, but dealt with the series of popular demonstrations with flexibility and surprising leniency.

The Church only exploited the resentment over the closure of Muensterschwarzach to a limited extent. Perhaps Bishop Ehrenfried could have gone to the abbey himself in its hour of need. Bishop Galen went to at least three small urban religious houses while they were being confiscated and berated the Gestapo officials as they went about their work.[98] The Bishop of Wuerzburg was a loyal supporter of Abbot Burkard, but Ehrenfried's diocese was too insignificant and his own political skills too limited to make an impression on Lammers and through him on Hitler. It was a different story with Galen, who presided over a large and important diocese that gave him both influence and protection. On 13 August 1941 Goebbels commented that if anything was done against Galen the populations of Muenster and the rest of Westphalia could be written off for the rest of the war.[99] Galen showed what could be achieved by a public appeal to lay Catholic opinion, which was not channelled effectively on the monasteries issue until he intervened at a late stage.

Why were some other Catholic bishops such as Bertram apparently reluctant to confront the regime in public over the dissolution of the monasteries? As traditional patriots they were reluctant to do anything that might undermine Germany's war effort, which from 22 June 1941 was directed in the main against the abhorrent Soviet Union. Church leaders were furthermore determined to avoid any behaviour that could provide the Nazis with a basis for alleging a 'stab in the back' on the part of the Church. The Catholic bishops were also concerned not to provide material for enemy propaganda against Germany. Galen's sermons had done exactly that. Brigadier R.L. Sedgwick of the Political Warfare Executive [PWE], the British organization for psychological warfare, wrote after the war that 'the Bishop of Muenster had provided the British propagandists with most powerful material … every department of PWE pounced avidly upon it'. Indeed, the Royal Air Force dropped Galen's sermon of 3 August over Germany as a propaganda leaflet. Galen paid a price for putting religious and moral criteria before Germany's war effort. Other bishops were reluctant to do this.[100]

A comparison with Poland shows the limited nature of the Nazi attack on the monasteries in Germany. Although the Nazi treatment of the Catholic foundations in Germany was vindictive and damaging, it lacked the unrelenting ferocity of the attack on the religious orders in Poland. There, the absence of any restraint on the SS and Nazi officials like Dengel meant that the Polish orders were routinely exposed to a murderous brutality that their German counterparts were usually spared. In the western dioceses of Poland virtually all monasteries and religious houses were closed and their inmates condemned to forced labour or driven away; almost all Jesuits were imprisoned or put in concentration camps. A special concentration camp for Catholic nuns was established at Bojanowo in the Wartheland, the territory around Poznan directly annexed to the Reich. In the Government General, the area of German-occupied Poland not incorporated into the Reich, monks were more likely than other clergy to suffer imprisonment. However, many members of the Polish religious orders were simply murdered outright. The German regular clergy were usually spared such treatment. The national identity they shared with their oppressors protected them from the worst excesses of Nazi persecution.[101]

Chapter 5

Hugh Trevor-Roper and
The Last Days of Hitler

Hugh Trevor-Roper's study of Hitler's death was published to remarkable acclaim. Lewis Namier, at that time the most distinguished historian in Britain, wrote to Trevor-Roper that 'I read your book, if I may say so, with the greatest interest and admiration. You have made a truly excellent job of it and combined very thorough scholarship with a lightness of touch and a style which I am glad to see is not yet extinct at Oxford.' A.J.P. Taylor reviewed *The Last Days* as 'an incomparable book, by far the best book written on any aspect of the second German war: a book sound in its scholarship, brilliant in presentation, a delight for historian and layman alike. No words of praise are too strong for it.' And *The Last Days* has remained a standard work. In the best recent study of Hitler's death, *Inside the Bunker*, Joachim Fest praised 'Hugh Trevor-Roper's superb overview, his sound judgement, and his splendid style'.[1] How did Trevor-Roper produce this modern classic? What were contemporary reactions to the book and to what extent has Trevor-Roper's analysis of Hitler's regime indeed stood the test of time? These questions can now be answered by drawing both on public sources and on Trevor-Roper's remarkably extensive and carefully maintained personal archive.

Trevor-Roper achieved fame as a historian, but he began his Oxford career with the study of Classics. As he wanted to read the classical scholar Wilamowitz in German, during March 1935 he went to Freiburg to improve his grasp of the language. He would recall that his landlady's son was devoted to Hitler: 'I was made to witness processions and marches, fluttering swastika flags, harangues by party bigwigs. I was disgusted by this inflammatory oratory; disgusted also by the abject conformity of the German people.' When he returned to Oxford, Trevor-Roper drew up a balance sheet for his visit to Germany, and decided it was in deficit. Although Trevor-Roper had mastered German, now that he could read Wilamowitz he concluded that the famous scholar was actually a silly fellow, so that all the effort had been for nothing.[2]

Only the Munich Agreement of September 1938 redirected Trevor-Roper's attention to Germany. He was particularly impressed by the insight of the British historian Robert Ensor, who had predicted in 1935 that Hitler would annex Austria in spring 1938 and in the autumn of the same year would either provoke a European war or force the capitulation of Europe to avoid war over Czechoslovakia. So Trevor-Roper studied Ensor's pamphlets about Hitler and Nazism. Because Ensor stressed that reading Hitler's *Mein Kampf* was the precondition for understanding international affairs, Trevor-Roper read the book in German and concluded that Hitler was a man with ideas and goals. Trevor-Roper's knowledge of German was to provide the basis of a remarkable career in British Intelligence. After the outbreak of the Second World War he joined the Radio Security Service and in early 1940 broke a hand cipher used by the German Secret Service. This success pointed the way for British professional code-breakers, who then decoded substantial quantities of Abwehr [German Military Intelligence] messages.[3]

In 1941 Trevor-Roper became a member of the British Secret Intelligence Service [SIS, also known as MI6] and developed into its leading expert on German secret wireless. Inside SIS he became fascinated by Hitler's court. He studied the transcripts of conversations recorded without their knowledge between two German generals captured in North Africa, Ludwig Cruewell and Ritter von Thoma. Trevor-Roper noted privately that, 'Even the politicians aren't safe from von Thoma's merciless tongue. Hess ... will only eat vegetables planted at full-moon; Hitler ... can't sleep ... and has ever wilder attacks of rage, in Munich they call him *Teppich-beisser*, carpet biter ... Thoma goes on, it's quite true, he lies on the floor, and snaps around like a mad dog ... But best of all is Thoma's description of Goering ... He was dressed completely in white silk – a white silk shirt such as the Doges used to wear, with big puffed sleeves ... On his head he wore St. Hubert's stag, with a swastika of gleaming pearls set between the antlers.'[4] From 1943 Trevor-Roper headed a section in SIS that produced research papers on the Abwehr of the German Armed Forces and the Security Service of the SS and highlighted the competition between the two organizations. As Trevor-Roper studied the politics of intelligence within Nazi Germany he became familiar with Admiral Wilhelm Canaris, the head of the Abwehr, and Heinrich Himmler, the *Reichsfuehrer SS*.

Why did Trevor-Roper's major work on the Third Reich focus on the death throes of Hitler's regime? His interest in Nazi Germany was channelled this way by Cold War politics. The chaos and destruction that attended the fall of Berlin made the circumstances of Hitler's death mysterious. Uncertainty could only distract the German population from reconstruction. It was politically necessary to solve the mystery of Hitler's fate. Brigadier Dick White, head of the Counter-Intelligence Bureau in the British Zone of occupation, later recalled that 'this seemed to me important at the time for the general security and stability of the occupied zones ... The idea of an enquiry into Hitler's fate was wholly mine. I explained it to [Field Marshal] Montgomery [Commander in Chief of British Forces of Occupation in Germany] who suggested that I should begin by seeing the Russians and he immediately signalled [Marshal] Zhukov [Soviet Commander in Germany] proposing this. I visited Berlin ... and [was]... entertained to lunch by a Russian General – a cheery, knock about and rather boozy occasion. He assured me Hitler and Goebbels had committed suicide in the Chancellery and their bodies burned. He produced Hitler's identified false teeth in evidence.'[5]

But while his general was reassuring Dick White, Stalin decided to muddy the waters. On 1 May he had been informed of Hitler's death, and on 5 May officers from Soviet Military Counter-Espionage [Smersh] had dug up Hitler's corpse. On 11 May the technician who had made Hitler's dentures confirmed that the body was indeed the Fuehrer's. Hitler's false teeth were subsequently passed to Dick White's Russian general. On 31 May Laventi Beria, the head of the Soviet secret police, was told about this important dental evidence and ordered the information to be given to Stalin.[6] Yet the Soviet dictator defied this positive evidence because an undead Hitler concealed by the West could prove a valuable propaganda asset.

On 6 June 1945 Stalin told President Truman's envoy Harry Hopkins that 'he was sure Hitler was still alive'. On 9 June Marshal Zhukov was asked at a press conference what had happened to Hitler. Zhukov replied that 'we have not discovered any corpse which could be identified as that of Hitler. He could have left Berlin by air at the last moment.' The Soviet Commandant of Berlin added that in his opinion Hitler had gone into hiding, possibly with Franco. Next the Soviet news agency Tass announced that Hitler had been seen in Dublin, where he had cleverly disguised himself in women's clothes, though the toothbrush moustache rather gave the game away. It was also rumoured that Hitler had become President de Valera's butler. More pointedly, the Russians accused the British of concealing Eva Braun and Hitler in their zone. This allegation made it all the more necessary for British Intelligence to collect the available evidence about Hitler's fate and establish the truth.[7]

But to whom should Dick White entrust the enquiry? He regarded Hugh Trevor-Roper as the foremost German expert in British Intelligence. Although other officers had spent more time in Germany, none could match him for sharpness, determination or expertise. In March 1943 White had minuted that 'I can think of no single officer, either in MI5 [the British Security Service] or MI6, who possesses a more comprehensive knowledge of the Abwehr organization, particularly on its communication side, than Capt. Trevor-Roper.' Trevor-Roper later recalled the occasion in September 1945 when Dick White sounded him out: 'it was when I was drinking hock with Dick White … in Bad Oeynhausen [headquarters of the British 21st Army Group] that my researches were first instituted … over the third bottle of hock … Dick … asked me if I would accept the job, and of course I said yes'.[8]

Before Trevor-Roper could start, White had to prise him out of his current work in the War Room of Allied Counter-Intelligence in London. The War Room was an intelligence centre for collating incoming material on German Intelligence and initiating further action. The initiative to set up such a centre had come from Major General K.W.D. Strong, intelligence chief at the Supreme Headquarters Allied Expeditionary Force [SHAEF]. On 10 November 1944 Strong wrote to Sir David Petrie, head of MI5, that 'an adequate sized and comprehensive German War Room is necessary and … It should contain all the best personnel which the Special Agencies can make available for the task.' An accompanying note stressed that 'CI [Counter Intelligence] Staffs in the field require … one comprehensive organisation, constituted as their expert advising staff on all questions of German clandestine activity.' As MI5 realized, the great advantage of the arrangement was 'that information from all sources would for the first time be effectively brought together'.[9]

The War Room was active from 1 March 1945 under the direction of MI5's Colonel T.A. 'Tar' Robertson. It provided Allied armies in the field with advice and information on the organization, operations and personalities of German Intelligence. It included a publications section, which was a misnomer as its reports on German Intelligence were classified secret and circulated only to relevant officers within Allied Intelligence, whose attention was drawn to particular gaps in Allied knowledge and the methods by which they might be filled. The publications section consisted of three officers brought in from SIS, namely Trevor-Roper, Stuart Hampshire and Charles Stuart. While in SIS the three officers had studied the radio traffic and other material of German Intelligence and issued regular reports. So much of their basic work stayed the same. But now they had considerably more information. Their section had access to all the evidence that flowed through the War Room, such as decrypts of the German enigma machine, captured documents and records of prisoner of war interrogations.[10]

War Room staff advised Allied officers who were questioning captured intelligence functionaries and also took part in interrogations themselves. So his work in the War Room developed Trevor-Roper's interrogation skills and knowledge of the German opponent. His section was particularly concerned with gaps in existing knowledge and these did not come any bigger than the mystery of Hitler's death. Yet, as always with bureaucracies, Trevor-Roper's paperwork had acquired a momentum and rationale of its own.[11]

He was rescued from this treadmill by White, who on 10 September 1945 wrote to Trevor-Roper's boss, T.A. Robertson, pointing to 'a considerable amount of comment in the Press on the subject of whether or not HITLER is still living ... the chap who has kept the closest tabs on the matter appears to be Trevor-Roper. I am, therefore, anxious that he should prepare a brief ... subject to your agreement ... a job like this, unless it is done now, will never get done and unless it is done by a first-rate chap, won't be worth having ... it should I think be a work of some considerable historic interest.' This last comment was remarkably prescient. Robertson replied that 'I agree with you entirely that the idea of clearing up this business about Hitler is essential and that it should be done now. The only thing that worries me slightly is that you should have picked upon Trevor-Roper to undertake this task, as, although he may not think so, he has a fairly formidable job in front of him writing two papers: one on Economic Espionage and the other on Successes and Failures of the German Intelligence Service, before he can really be turned on to any other work.' Although on 10 September it was decided to close the War Room from 1 November, the planned reports still had to be finished. Fortunately Trevor-Roper succeeded in convincing the reluctant Robertson that White's task should take priority and that the other jobs could be done later.[12]

How did Trevor-Roper carry out his enquiry? His position as a British intelligence officer gave him considerable advantages. He could call on the assistance of British Army intelligence staff, the Field Security Police and the administration of Prisoner of War camps. He had access to much captured documentation, such as the papers of the Doenitz government, which briefly followed that of Hitler, and the diaries of the Luftwaffe Chief of Staff Karl Koller and Hitler's Finance Minister, Lutz Graf Schwerin von Krosigk. The American occupation authorities at Frankfurt also put their material at his disposal and he was helped by the American Counter-Intelligence Corps. Much relevant evidence from British and American interrogations or bugging of prisoners was circulated to the War Room in London or the British Counter-Intelligence Bureau in Germany and routinely passed on to Trevor-Roper. He could request British and American agencies to carry out enquiries or interrogations on his behalf like a team of research assistants armed with powers of arrest. Although the witnesses did not usually want to be found, if they drew British or American attention Trevor-Roper could get access to them. Yet he suffered from the major handicap that although the Russians promised White their co-operation, this was not forthcoming. This excluded various key witnesses, some of whom Trevor-Roper finally interviewed when they were released from Soviet captivity in 1955.[13]

The search for Trevor-Roper's witnesses in the British zone was orchestrated by Major Peter Ramsbotham, who worked on the intelligence staff at British Army of the Rhine Headquarters. On 18 September 1945 Ramsbotham wrote to the intelligence staff at the three British Army Corps in Germany and at Berlin Army Headquarters. He told them that 'an exhaustive enquiry is being undertaken by this Headquarters into the circumstances surrounding Hitler's death, in order that it can be established definitely whether or not he actually died, and under what circumstances his death occurred'. Ramsbotham requested any information held about witnesses on a list of thirty-three names that he enclosed.[14]

Trevor-Roper concentrated on finding witnesses for what he called the 'dark period' between 22 April, when much of the Nazi elite left Berlin, and 2 May, when the Russians reached Hitler's Bunker: 'seven witnesses of the dark period, from different and independent groups, had been located and interrogated ... by 1st November 1945, when the report of my conclusions was due'. The seven witnesses included a detective from Hitler's security, Bormann's secretary, and the Fuehrer's chauffeur. The questions Trevor-Roper put to witnesses were brief and specific, usually focusing on events and whom the witness saw on a particular occasion. He treated the evidence with scepticism, as he explained later in a letter of 6 February 1946: 'It is quite impossible to arrive at a complete estimate of events if one begins by accepting any individual statement as accurate throughout. All witnesses in the present case are fallible, as is only to be expected at this distance of time. They are particularly fallible in the matter of dates: they could not possibly be otherwise, living as they did, perpetually underground, not distinguishing night from day, in circumstances of siege and bombardment, and only asked to remember the details at least five months later ... All the dates which I have given are based on external evidence.'[15]

In his eventual report Trevor-Roper admitted that 'the only conclusive evidence that Hitler is dead would be in the discovery, and certain identification, of the body'. Nevertheless he felt that the evidence for Hitler's death was 'positive, circumstantial, consistent and independent. There is no evidence whatever to support any of the theories ... which presuppose that Hitler is still alive ... It is considered quite impossible that the versions of the various eyewitnesses can represent a concerted cover-story; they were all too busy planning their own safety ... to learn an elaborate charade which they could still maintain after five months of isolation from each other and under detailed and persistent cross-examination.' On 10 November 1945 Trevor-Roper presented his report in person to the Quadripartitite Intelligence Committee of the four Allied Powers in Berlin. An appendix to the report asked whether any of the powers held eight further witnesses from the Bunker and asked the Russians to make a statement on the body recognized as Hitler's by the teeth. But 'very interesting' was the only comment the Russians would make.[16]

Trevor-Roper's report only proved inaccurate in one significant respect. He stated Hitler married Eva Braun on 30 April. In fact the wedding took place a day earlier. This detail emerged from the discovery of Hitler's marriage certificate and wills. Trevor-Roper would recall that 'at the end of November 1945 a document purporting to be Hitler's will was discovered in the coat-lining of a suspect [Heinz Lorenz] detained by the British authorities at Hannover and I was asked to return to Germany and investigate this matter too'. Lorenz was being held in a prison camp for using false papers when a sergeant of the guard told him to move on. Not satisfied with Lorenz's reaction, the sergeant grabbed the prisoner by the shoulder, and pushed him in the right direction. In doing so he felt paper in Lorenz's shoulder pad. When the jacket was searched, Hitler's will was discovered.[17]

Lorenz had in his possession Hitler's personal and political testaments with an appendix to the latter by Goebbels. Lorenz had been a senior editor at the German News Service. He was responsible for collecting typescripts of broadcast news and bringing them to the Bunker. On 29 April 1945 Bormann gave him the wills, which he was to take to Munich. According to Lorenz, Wilhelm Zander, an official of the Nazi Party Chancellery, was also given copies of the personal and political testaments, which he was to take to Hitler's appointed successor, Grand Admiral Doenitz. Major Wilhelm Johannmeier, assistant to Hitler's Chief Wehrmacht Adjutant, was given the political testament to take to Field Marshal Schoerner, Commander of Army Group Centre in Bohemia. In his will Hitler appointed Schoerner Commander in Chief of the Army. Although the three messengers succeeded in escaping from Berlin, they realized their missions were hopeless and abandoned them.[18]

On 14 December 1945 Trevor-Roper left for Germany on his new quest, and stayed for three weeks. Lorenz and his documents were in British hands. Trevor-Roper set out to locate Zander and Johannmeier and find their documents. Johannmeier was living in the British Zone, but claimed he was merely escorting the other two messengers. Trevor-Roper was not wholly convinced, as Johannmeier was a veteran of the Eastern Front. He reasoned that 'If Johannmeier was considered a more experienced and determined man than the others, and one who could be relied on to get them through the Russian lines ... it would seem natural and obvious to use him not solely as an escort, but also as a bearer. Equally it seems eccentric that Johannmeier, if he were merely escorting the bearers of vital documents, should have no instructions as to what he should do if ... the bearers met with an accident or were killed on the way.'[19]

As Johannmeier was obdurate, on 18 December 1945 Trevor-Roper interrogated Lorenz, who protested that he had seen Hitler's political testament in Johannmeier's hand. However, before returning to Johannmeier, Trevor-Roper began the search for Zander. When questioned by the British Field Security Police in Hanover, Frau Zander claimed that 'she had last heard from her husband on April 12th 1945. She said she was herself anxious for news, and gave many details which seemed evidence of her sincerity, including photographs and the names and addresses of Zander's mothers and brothers in Saarbruecken. In fact ... these details were intended as smoke in our eyes.' Zander's wife had spun such a convincing tale that even his mother believed he was dead. The story unravelled after an American intelligence officer learned that Zander had been treated under an assumed name in a hospital near Munich for injuries sustained walking from Hannover to Bavaria.[20]

With the help of the American Counter Intelligence Corps, on 26 December 1945 Trevor-Roper interrogated contacts of Zander's near Munich, one of whom revealed his friend's false identity. This enabled Trevor-Roper to track Zander down to an address near Passau, as he later recalled: 'having motored all day and all night in a jeep, through mud and sleet and snow, I stood, at 3.0 in the morning, in the village of Aidenbach, near the Austrian frontier, and posting a man with a revolver at each corner of the crucial house, since no one answered on knocking, I sent a German policeman to climb through a window and open the door. Then I went in and broke into a bedroom; and from the bed saw emerging ... a giant nose, the unmistakeable nose of Bormann's assistant, SS Standartenfuehrer Wilhelm Zander.' On interrogation Zander confirmed much of what Trevor-Roper already knew about Hitler's last days, and admitted that he had been given copies of both Hitler's wills and two other documents, namely the Hitlers' marriage certificate and a note from Bormann to Doenitz. These documents now came into the possession of American Counter-Intelligence.[21]

Zander confirmed that Johannmeier had also been given a copy of Hitler's political testament. On 1 January 1946 Trevor-Roper re-interrogated Johannmeier, yet in the face of all the evidence the Wehrmacht veteran stuck fast to his story. As he did not have any documents he could not produce them. So Trevor-Roper appealed to Johannmeier's reason, saying that the others had already given the game away and all the relevant information was against his story. The British had no interest in holding him captive but had to do so as long as there was this discrepancy. For two hours Johannmeier resisted firmly. Then Trevor-Roper took a break from his interrogation, and during this interval Johannmeier caught up with the argument and realized the futility of his silence. As the two Nazi officials had already spilled the beans, it was absurd to suffer further in the cause they had abandoned. When the interrogation resumed, Johannmeier first sought assurance that he would not be punished. Then he finally admitted: 'Ich habe die Papiere.' He led Trevor-Roper to a corner of his garden in Iserlohn and dug up a bottle containing, as his interrogator expected, Hitler's political testament and a covering note from the Chief Wehrmacht Adjutant to Schoerner.[22]

The tracking down of Hitler's wills was Trevor-Roper's finest hour as a British intelligence officer. Afterwards Peter Ramsbotham wrote that 'everyone ... is full of admiration for the speed and efficiency with which your investigations were concluded'. Trevor-Roper's triumph in locating the wills was only made possible by Stalin's silence. As early as 17 May 1945, Hitler's personal adjutant Otto Guensche had stated to Red Army Intelligence that Johannmeier, Lorenz and Zander had received copies of Hitler's will, but this information was kept secret. In any event, Trevor-Roper's success quickly turned sour. As he was leaving Munich, he asked his American counterpart to keep the discoveries quiet until there could be an agreed Anglo–American statement. He was assured that the documents were locked up in the safe of General Lucian Truscott, Commander of the United States Third Army, where they would stay pending an agreed statement. But next day, when Trevor-Roper had reached Frankfurt, he was shown a copy of *Stars and Stripes*, an American armed forces' paper, which had banner headlines about the great coup of Third Army, personally communicated by General Truscott. There was no reference at all to any British participation. So Trevor-Roper drove on to British Headquarters, where he held a press conference giving details of the documents taken from Lorenz.[23]

Shortly after his press conference Trevor-Roper received a telephone call from Colonel Sands of American Intelligence in Frankfurt, who asked: 'Did you, on your recent visit to the U.S. Zone, discover any documents other than those handed to Third Army HQ?' The implication was that the Lorenz documents had in fact come from the US Zone. Trevor-Roper denied any further discoveries, and gave Sands a guarantee that he had not taken any documents out of the American Zone.

Despite his protestation, from January 1946 Trevor-Roper was for a time *persona non grata* in the US Zone. So Sands promised that he would arrange any future interrogations Trevor-Roper required along the lines he wanted. Trevor-Roper recalled that this 'was not very satisfactory, as the interrogators did not have the necessary background to pursue such topics as might emerge during interrogation, or to detect possible errors or lies at the time'. Trevor-Roper's forced absence was a handicap in respect of various prisoners, in particular Artur Axmann, head of the Hitler Youth, captured by the Americans in December 1945. In retrospect, Trevor-Roper felt that General Truscott had double-crossed him twice, first by prematurely publishing the story and taking all the credit, and second, by twisting Trevor-Roper's press conference over the Lorenz papers to blacken his name falsely as a document thief and so justify having rushed into print. Truscott's bad case of Hitler fever marred Trevor-Roper's remarkable triumph in finding the wills.[24]

***

The historical possibilities of the enquiry had struck the history graduate Dick White from the beginning. While he was carrying out the enquiry Trevor-Roper had no plans to write about it for the public, as he thought this would not be allowed. In January 1946 Trevor-Roper took up a teaching appointment at Christ Church Oxford. Then White proposed that Trevor-Roper should write up his research as a book, which would need to be authorized by the British Joint Intelligence Committee [JIC], the body that co-ordinated British security and espionage. White advised Trevor-Roper not to submit a proposal to the JIC: 'No government agency will ever sanction a proposal of which they cannot foresee the effect … But if you were to write it first, and take the risk of their decision, and submit the text to them, then they would at least see the limits of what they were allowing.'[25]

Reassured by White, Trevor-Roper found the idea of a book very appealing: 'above all, I was attracted by the unique opportunity to write a book of contemporary history which I believed, if done carefully, would stand the test of time.' Normally works of contemporary history quickly become obsolete due to the release of new documents: 'but in this case the circumstances were unusual, even unique. Hitler spent his last days enclosed under siege in a subterranean bunker. The number of witnesses was limited, and there were very few primary sources. Everything suggested that the facts could be reconstructed without any fear of later contradiction ... I was vain and young enough to believe that I could write a book which combined immediacy and historical value. So even though the events were so close and dramatic I decided to consider them from a distant historical perspective.'[26]

Trevor-Roper would remember that he wrote *The Last Days* during 'the spring and summer of 1946, in the evenings, during the term'. Dates on the manuscript itself suggest he may have written most of the text even more quickly than this. Dates are rubber stamped in red on some of the pages, and suggest an astonishing tempo. It seems he wrote more than two-thirds of the book in less than a month between 18 February and 15 March 1946, for example about 12,000 words during four days in late February. This impetus would certainly help to explain the fluency and consistency of style in *The Last Days*. Once he had fixed the topic in his mind he wrote it out very quickly. The main text was finished by 22 May and entitled *Hitler's End*.[27]

Trevor-Roper had written to White on 12 March asking him to read the book. On 18 March White replied enthusiastically that 'I think the whole world ought to be told your story and I don't doubt that your elegant pen has done justice to it. Incidentally I read your writing easily so please send me the MS as soon as possible. I am all eagerness.' White also pressed on with obtaining official approval for publication. On 16 May he discussed the book with Harold Caccia, a senior British diplomat and chairman of the Joint Intelligence Committee [JIC]. Caccia told White that the Foreign Office was responsible for the policy aspect, namely any international implications, and the JIC should give a ruling on the security aspect.[28]

Next White submitted a minute about the book to the JIC, which discussed the matter at its meeting on 14 June 1946. Colonel I.I. 'Tim' Milne of SIS pointed out that 'whereas Mr Roper was in SIS at the time, the material for his book had not been obtained as a result of his SIS work ... [So] 'C' [General Sir Stewart Menzies, Chief of SIS] ... had no objection to one of his officers publishing such a book after demobilisation.' Other committee members mentioned the 'positive advantage in publishing this book, to which view the Foreign Office gave their full support. The book had as its object the preventing of the creation of a Hitler "myth", and in its detailed and readable form was likely to appeal to a wide public. Further, the Foreign Office might be invited to consider the translation of the book into Foreign Languages, including German, for dissemination as propaganda.' However, the committee considered that 'there might be objections to publication before the War Crimes Trials at Nuremburg had ended'. The point was also made that 'in view of the propaganda value of the book, added weight might be given if a foreword to the book was written by a responsible Commander in authority at the time of the incidents described. The foreword ... would thereby gain the support of a famous man to the publication. Mr. Roper might like to approach, for example, Lord Montgomery or Lord Tedder' [Deputy Commander, Allied Expeditionary Force, 1944–45]. Lastly, the JIC invited the Foreign Office to undertake the final clearance of the book for publication. This was more of a formality than anything else, as White told Trevor-Roper in a letter that enclosed the relevant section of the JIC minutes.[29]

Trevor-Roper was content for the Foreign Office to consider the issue of translation into German. As he told White on 19 June, 'I should certainly be glad if some such authority would take the decision (at least as regards translation into German), as at present I find it difficult to decide myself. The book is intended as history rather than propaganda: I think the facts are true as given; and I have been more concerned to understand the events and their causes and relations, than to push a point of view.' Trevor-Roper also promised to wait until the conclusion of the Nuremburg Trials before publication. The reason for this was, as Caccia pointed out at a later JIC meeting, 'to publish the book before might embarrass the Court and the British President, who would deliver the principal judgement. This was in no way acceptable.' Trevor-Roper further set about recruiting a great man to write the foreword, telling his friend Solly Zuckerman that 'of the two names mentioned, I would greatly prefer Tedder. Do you think he would consider writing such a foreword if asked? (that means, if asked by you?) ... I do not think that I want a foreword by anyone else.' On 4 July Zuckerman reported that, 'I have seen Tedder and shown him your draft introduction and synopsis of contents. He is definitely interested.' In due course Tedder completed the foreword on 21 October 1946.[30]

While Zuckerman was recruiting Tedder to write the foreword, Dick White had passed the manuscript to Harold Caccia. On 4 July he wrote to Trevor-Roper that 'Harold Caccia is still reading your book but hopes to let me have it back at the end of the week. Incidentally he describes it as "enthralling" and is most complimentary about it.' However, Caccia felt that any intelligent reader was bound to ask himself how this collection of monkeys had been able to control Germany and thought Trevor-Roper might like to put in an extra page on this aspect. Trevor-Roper replied to White on 6 July that 'I agree entirely with Harold Caccia's point about the necessity for some explanation, and am in fact finishing the book with an epilogue which will try to answer the question.' When he eventually saw the epilogue, Caccia felt that it 'certainly gives me an adequate answer to the points which I raised, and, like all the rest of his writing, is lucid and coherent. But who am I to set myself up as a critic of so excellent a work?' All the same, the JIC had asked the Foreign Office to undertake the final clearance of the book, so on 27 September Trevor-Roper called on Caccia to enquire whether any further formality was required before publication. Caccia declared that no further authorization was necessary. So he missed an opportunity to raise the question of the German translation for propaganda purposes which the JIC had explicitly invited Caccia to consider, and disregarded a remarkable propaganda opportunity for influencing the German public.[31]

While the book was going through its Foreign Office vetting, Trevor-Roper's publisher was waiting eagerly. Initially he had flirted with the publisher Hamish Hamilton, feeling that Macmillan, who had published his first book on Archbishop Laud, were 'mugwumpish'. Nevertheless, in the event he stayed with Macmillan, whose representative Lovat Dickson wrote to him on 14 June 1946 asking, 'Have you any news yet? We are anxious to have the MS as soon as possible.' On 8 July Dickson wrote to acknowledge receipt of the manuscript and the signed contract. Dickson also acted as a channel for communication between Trevor-Roper and Macmillan's American company. In a letter of 8 August Trevor-Roper queried why the title had been changed for the American contract. On 17 September Dickson wrote that, 'The American Company are very anxious to call the book *The Last Days of Hitler*. This seems to us a much better title than *Hitler's End*, and as I think you said at one stage you did not mind ... we should now settle on that.' So the idea for the particularly apt title came from an anonymous American editor.[32]

Trevor-Roper agreed to the new title but the change made him suspicious. When Macmillan offered to correct the proofs to save time, Trevor-Roper declined. Dickson then complained that 'there has been further delay at the blockmakers owing to the fact that you made corrections on the drawings in red ink, instead of making them on the margins. These corrections have had to be carefully erased.' But in December Dickson wrote with the news that the Book Society was going to make *The Last Days of Hitler* its March choice and would take at least 15,000 copies. Macmillan now ordered an initial imprint of 30,000 copies, twice as many as their next largest for a new book in December 1946. Although the book's subject and topicality meant it was bound to do well, Macmillan's shrewd alteration of the title vindicated Trevor-Roper's decision to stay with them.[33]

****

The Last Days of Hitler was published in March 1947. It attracted great public interest. Much of the attention was very favourable, though sometimes praise was tempered by criticism. The Cambridge reviewer David Thomson, while admitting that Trevor-Roper had done an admirable job in piecing together the evidence, observed that with his 'sweeping generalizations about the character of the Nazi regime and some of its leaders ... Mr Trevor-Roper treads on thinner ice ... in a way all too common among Oxford historians'.[34]

Trevor-Roper's general comments about the Nazi regime may have been sweeping, but they were also compelling: 'we must recognise that Hitler was not a pawn; that the Nazi state was not (in any significant use of the word) totalitarian; and that its leading politicians were not a government but a court ... In Nazi Germany neither war production, nor manpower, nor administration, nor intelligence, was rationally centralised ... The structure of German politics and administration, instead of being, as the Nazis claimed, "pyramidal" and "monolithic", was in fact a confusion of private empires, private armies, and private intelligence services.' Hitler's clear mastery over the National Socialists was not matched by clarity in the exercise of power within the Nazi regime, which disintegrated into manageable empires in the hands of the dictator's subordinates, as 'the rule of a court conceals a political anarchy ... [of] jealous feudatories, with their private armies and reservations of public resources'.[35]

Trevor-Roper was not the first to deny that Nazi Germany was totalitarian. Franz Neumann's *Behemoth*, published in 1942, had emphasized that the Nazi ruling class was a fragmented assortment of powerful groups. Neumann argued that the Nazi state was far from homogenous and that no one organ monopolized political power. But Trevor-Roper's argument was based on more extensive evidence and expressed with characteristic vigour and clarity. His perceptive account of institutions competing for power in a way that was partly independent of Hitler was confirmed by later historians such as Martin Broszat.[36]

Trevor-Roper drew controversial material for *The Last Days* from Hermann Rauschning, a former Nazi president of the Danzig senate who had fled abroad in 1935. Once in exile, Rauschning became a critic of Nazism and in 1938 he published *Die Revolution des Nihilismus*. The following year this thoughtful book came out in English as *Germany's Revolution of Destruction*. In 1939 Rauschning also published another book, *Hitler Speaks*, which purported to be a collection of conversations with Hitler from the period 1932 to 1934 when Rauschning was supposedly one of Hitler's intimate circle. In early 1940 Goebbels noted in his diary that Rauschning was 'the most cutting propagandist on the other side. His book *Hitler Speaks* is exceptionally skilfully written and a huge danger for us.' Rauschning was difficult to refute due to his great skill in blending fact and fiction.[37]

Trevor-Roper's use of *Hitler Speaks* prompted some criticism. Namier, who thought so highly of *The Last Days*, told Trevor-Roper that 'one thing about which I cannot quite agree with you is the valuation you put on Rauschning ... like a real German he rides every point to death, and the general style of his "Hitler Speaks" with its imaginary ending does not give me sufficient confidence in the man ever to quote any passage from that book as authoritative'.[38]

In a Historical Association pamphlet published in 1943, the Byzantine historian Norman Baynes had observed that the conversations recorded by Rauschning 'took place in the years 1932 to 1934; the book was published in 1939. The form in which these conversations are here presented, it must be confessed, awakes suspicion. We are told that 'the writer jotted [these conversations] down under the immediate influence of what he had heard. Much may be regarded as practically a verbatim record.' The question of course is 'How much?' The student would have welcomed a reproduction of the contemporary "jottings".'[39]

In *The Last Days* Trevor-Roper took issue with Baynes and wrote that 'the vast mass of intimate matter since available has shown Rauschning to be completely reliable'. Trevor-Roper repeatedly quoted from *Hitler*

Speaks in *The Last Days*. He later championed *Hitler Speaks* in his introduction to *Hitler's Table-Talk*. Trevor-Roper felt that Rauschning's predictions had been vindicated, and as he told Namier, 'it seems to me more reasonable to suppose that Rauschning was reporting the truth than that he accidentally invented what turned out afterwards to be true'. Rauschning's book was also drawn on by Alan Bullock in his classic biography of Hitler, and applauded by A.J.P Taylor. Then, in 1971, Rauschning admitted that *Hitler Speaks* was not a publication of his original notes: 'instead I wove together an overall picture of Hitler from notes, memory and indeed information from others about Hitler'.[40]

Ten years later, Rauschning's press agent Emery Reeves explained to the Swiss historian Wolfgang Haenel how Rauschning came to write *Hitler Speaks*. In 1939 Rauschning had found himself in Paris with high medical bills, an expensive flat and five children to support. Reeves told Rauschning to write up his experiences and conversations with Hitler in the form of quotations so as to interest the public, and gave him the largest advance payment ever made in France. In fact, Rauschning had only met Hitler four times. Even with Hitler's propensity to monologue, these meetings scarcely sufficed for a book of more than three hundred pages. So *Hitler Speaks* is not the verbatim record of conversations with Hitler that it appears to be, though fragments of the book may indeed be authentic scraps from the four meetings. But for the most part Rauschning simply recycled material from his *Revolution of Destruction* and various contemporary publications, including Hitler speeches and *Mein Kampf*. Trevor-Roper's personal copy of Haenel's booklet shows that the Oxford historian carefully worked through the pages marking particularly telling passages. By 1990 he had concluded that he had given Rauschning too much credit: 'Wolfgang Haenel has convinced me I should have been more careful in this respect.' But the error should not be exaggerated, as *Hitler Speaks* is consistent with more authentic records of Hitler's opinions.[41]

Hitler Speaks offered a beguiling trap, not least because Rauschning's earlier publication, *Revolution of Destruction,* was so thoughtful and fluent. For his book Trevor-Roper also used the *Revolution of Destruction*, which offered a wide-ranging analysis of Nazism. Rauschning's discussion was not flawless. Its main weakness was his refusal to credit Nazism with ideas. He argued that Nazism had left behind its racialist origins and by 1938 was merely using it 'as a necessary element in propaganda. Racialism is its make-believe' and 'Intensive settlement in the east of Europe in territory won for Germany is no longer the central aim of National Socialist foreign policy ... it is no longer of any importance.' Rauschning considered Hitler an opportunist, not a man with goals: 'There was and is no aim that National Socialism has not been ready for the sake of the movement to abandon or to proclaim at any time.' As its title suggests, the main themes of Rauschning's book were revolution and destruction: 'the revolutionary elite can maintain itself in power in its permanently critical situation only by continually pushing on with the revolutionary process ... When the political structure of the country has been razed to the ground, the elite will march over the frontier, to upset the existing international order.'[42]

Trevor-Roper chose wisely in his use of *Revolution of Destruction*. He kept its perceptive emphasis on nihilism but departed from Rauschning in also giving weight to Hitler's other ideas. Trevor-Roper identified the purpose of the Nazi system as 'World power or Ruin'. 'World power' meant 'the conquest of Russia, the extermination of the Slavs, and the colonisation of the East'. If the quest for world power failed, the alternative was ruin or nihilism. Rauschning's influence is discernible in Trevor-Roper's statement that 'nihilism ... had inspired the Nazi Movement in its early days ... in the last days ... it was to this nihilism that it returned as its ultimate philosophy and valediction'. Nearly sixty years later Joachim Fest supported Trevor-Roper's emphasis on the essentially destructive nature of Nazism when he wrote: 'the intent to demolish had always been Hitler's first and preferred course of action, an expression of his true voice, which now [1945] could be heard once more'.[43]

Trevor-Roper believed that the isolation of Hitler's Bunker and the limited evidence about its circumstances guaranteed that his account would remain valid and protected from subsequent revision. Yet as well as Hitler's last days he also discussed the general development of Nazi Germany. This wider vision gave his book much of its depth and explanatory power but also allowed errors to creep in. The position of Albert Speer, Hitler's Minister of Armaments and War Production, illustrates Trevor-Roper's inability to restrict his analysis to the Bunker. Speer particularly caught Trevor-Roper's attention, but Speer was not a Bunker inmate, he only paid occasional visits, and otherwise travelled widely around Germany. Trevor-Roper was too indulgent towards Speer. In 1946 he wrote that 'Speer was not an artist, nor a politician. He had no common interests or ambitions with the rest of the court. He observed their antics, but did not compete in their field ... Speer was a technocrat and nourished a technocrat's philosophy. To the technocrat, as to the Marxist, politics are irrelevant.' Trevor-Roper's account of Speer stressed his attempts to frustrate Hitler's scorched earth policy inside Germany at the end of the war and his plan to assassinate Hitler in his bunker. Nevertheless, in his epilogue Trevor-Roper characterized Speer as 'the real criminal of Nazi Germany', because Speer supposed politics to be irrelevant.[44]

His treatment of Speer, like his use of Rauschning, raised questions among his readership. J.K. Galbraith, the American economist, wrote to Trevor-Roper in July 1947 complimenting him on 'an exceedingly fine and wonderfully restrained exercise in history'. Yet Galbraith saw Speer differently. As a director of the American Strategic Bombing Survey he had questioned Speer and 'after the first few days of interrogation I found myself concluding that, among his other notable qualities, he was a really superb actor ... He was aware, in those early days, that his colleagues were putting on a rather bad show. To be, as later Goering became, the unregenerate Nazi was unwise as well as unbecoming ... [Speer] chose, instead, the mantle of the aloof observer and made this convincing by holding forth on his personal loyalty to Hitler. Then, since he is both a man of personal courage and also aware that no one respects a coward, he assumed an attitude of complete indifference as to his personal fate. The whole, I conceive, to have been an admirably devised and executed scheme for survival ... here is a truly first-class rascal, ... who played with the gang, cherished his success, and in the end had a somewhat better alibi and a much better story than his companions ... Not one man in a million could have handled himself so well in a crisis.'[45]

Later research has supported Galbraith by showing that Speer was a superlative politician who took to the power struggles of the Third Reich with consummate ease. Speer's qualms came after the war. In 1939 he contentedly kept in line with Nazi racialism as his office redistributed stolen Jewish property in Berlin.[46] In 1945 Speer sought to keep Germany fighting by putting the interests of the Armed Forces and war manufacture before those of civilian survival. On 15 March he circulated a Hitler decree that on Speer's suggestion ordered that priority for transport was to be determined 'only by its immediate value for the conduct of the war'. The operational needs of the Wehrmacht were given priority over refugees trying to escape, many of whom were overtaken by the Red Army. Speer never asked Hitler to surrender. Indeed, in a memorandum of 18 March he urged drastic measures to defend the Reich at the rivers Oder and Rhine. He had no scruples about the deploying of Hitler Youth and old men as cannon fodder. Instead he wanted 'to win the enemy's respect' in a final battle and so achieve a favourable conclusion, very much the illusion from which Hitler was also suffering.[47]

Looking back on *The Last Days* more than forty years later, Trevor-Roper honestly conceded that he had been misled by Speer. He had despised most of the Nazis he questioned. They had lost all dignity in defeat. By contrast, Speer neither cringed nor tried to deny his past: 'Speer attracted me through his apparent ability to look honestly at events and himself and to judge his own responsibility and admit it – or at least a great part of it. Later, as the evidence grew, and I got to know Speer better, I was compelled to modify my view of him. Now I regard him as a highly intelligent man in whom the sense of right and wrong was undermined by the experience of power … Conversations with him after his release from Spandau confirmed this. How, I asked myself, had this cultivated man been able to share the podium at the Berlin Sports Palace on 28 February 1943 with Goebbels and applaud his dreadful tirade of hate against the Jews? … After I had spent a day with him in Munich, I went to the Institute for Contemporary History and read [the speech] … I felt sick.'[48]

If Trevor-Roper overestimated Speer, he gave a vivid and accurate portrayal of less subtle members of the Nazi elite. Trevor-Roper delighted in Goering's grotesque luxuries, first discovered when he listened to the surreptitious recordings of General von Thoma. Material from Thoma is reproduced in *The Last Days*. Trevor-Roper also showed a good understanding of the power struggle between Himmler and Bormann. In *The Last Days* Trevor-Roper emphasized the superstitious and credulous weaknesses of Himmler, but also brought out his efficiency as an administrator and in particular his gift for choosing able subordinates. He traced the growing power of the SS during the war, its successful encroachments on the Armed Forces, and Himmler's appointment as Reich Minister of the Interior in 1943. Himmler's SS came increasingly into conflicts of jurisdiction with the Gauleiter or Regional Leaders of the Party who were backed by Martin Bormann, the head of the Party Chancellery. Bormann successfully asserted the role of the Gauleiter in the face of the SS, and in early 1945 crowned his victory by securing the appointment of Himmler, a former sergeant major, to the hopeless task of commanding Army Group Vistula in the fight against the Red Army. Recent scholarship bears out Trevor-Roper's theme of the increasing power of the Nazi Party in the final year of the war.[49]

The most controversial aspect of *The Last Days* was provided by Trevor-Roper's observations on Christianity. He wrote that Hitler 'had no trouble from the Churches'. Dr Johann Neuhaeusler, suffragan Bishop of Munich, took issue with this statement, writing to Trevor-Roper that 'in my opinion you could only have reached this judgement in ignorance of the facts'. Neuhaeusler drew Trevor-Roper's attention to his own book on the topic and the English book *The Nazi Persecution of the Churches* based on Neuhaeusler's evidence. The Bishop failed to convince Trevor-Roper, who replied that 'after careful consideration I am convinced that although individuals – priests, pastors and devout Christians – fought actively against Nazism ... the Churches themselves as organised institutions did not plan actions against the regime or carry them out, neither the Protestant nor the Catholic Church. On the whole I share your opinion that the Church was indeed persecuted, and also that you tried to defend your areas of jurisdiction. But I can find no evidence of other opposition.' Trevor-Roper retained the offending sentence in later editions.[50]

Trevor-Roper's references to the Catholic Church produced even more annoyance than his general dismissal of Church opposition to Hitler. These comments were not intrinsic to the argument or evidence in *The Last Days* but were rather comparisons drawn in order to explain Goebbels and Himmler. To illustrate Goebbels' propaganda he chose the Jesuits and to clarify Himmler's mentality he selected a Catholic saint. These were not, perhaps, the most tactful of comparisons. Trevor-Roper wrote that 'Joseph Goebbels was ... the prize-pupil of a Jesuit seminary, [and] he retained to the end the distinctive character of his education: he could always prove what he wanted ... As the Jesuit persuades his penitent that all is well, that he had not really sinned at all, and that the obstacles to belief are really much less formidable than they appear, so Goebbels persuaded the Germans that their defeats were really victories ... As the Jesuits created a system of education aimed at preventing knowledge, so Goebbels created a system of propaganda, ironically styled "public enlightenment", which successfully persuaded a people to believe that black was white.'[51]

Father Brodrick, a Jesuit reviewer in *The Tablet*, the English Catholic weekly, was incensed by this passage and commented: 'could Joseph Goebbels himself, with all his Latin and Jesuitical snakiness ... have hinted more evil of people whom he disliked in as brief a space ... there is no proof whatever that Goebbels received his early education from the Jesuits. They had been driven from Germany by Bismarck and did not return until 1919 ... To pass to another point, how on earth does he know what Jesuit confessors say to their penitents in the confessional? Is he God's spy or has his brief connection with the Secret Service given him delusions of omniscience? ... As for the Jesuits having created a system of education "aimed at preventing knowledge", I defy anybody, including Mr Trevor-Roper himself, to explain what that means.' Brodrick referred to the many Jesuits murdered by the Nazis and expressed his resentment at 'any furtive and despicable attempt, worthy of Goebbels at his worst, to plant swastikas on their graves'.[52]

Brodrick also resented Trevor-Roper's explanation of Himmler's combination of private virtue with mass murder by comparing him with a Grand Inquisitor. Trevor-Roper had written that, 'The Grand Inquisitors of history were not cruel or self-indulgent men. They were often painfully conscientious and austere in their personal lives. They were often scrupulously kind to animals, like the blessed Robert Bellarmine, who refused to disturb the fleas in his clothes. Since they could not hope for theological bliss (he said), it would be uncharitable to deny them that carnal refreshment to which alone they could aspire. But for men who, having opportunities of worshipping aright, chose wrong, no remedy was too drastic.' Brodrick objected that Bellarmine was never an Inquisitor, and that he was attended not by fleas but by flies that landed on the Saint's large nose.[53]

In addition to outraged clergy, Trevor-Roper also received a considerable correspondence from Catholic laity, including the novelist Evelyn Waugh, who wrote in an open letter that 'you give the unwary reader the impression that Bellarmine was Grand Inquisitor – a purely Spanish function. He was "consultor" to the Holy Office in Rome. I do not know of any instance of his being zealous in securing death penalties. Do you? Can it be that you are one of those who believe Galileo was burned? The whole passage rather reminded me of the Englishman who, being told that the Americans have never forgiven the burning of Washington in 1812, said "I never knew we caught the fellow" ... I wish you would direct me to the Jesuit confessor who would try and persuade me I am sinless. I find they take quite a different line.'[54]

Trevor-Roper fended off the torrent of criticism from Catholic clergy and laity with a mixture of resistance and retreat. He was not convinced by the advocates of Bellarmine. In the second edition of *The Last Days* published in 1950 he retained the offending passage and defended it against Brodrick in a footnote, drawing on a contemporary biography by Jacopus Fuligatus to insist that the insects in question were fleas not flies. On a more substantial point, he cited Bellarmine's opinion that it was an act of charity to liquidate heretics, 'since if they live longer they will only conceive more heresies, and deceive others, and thereby intensify their damnation'. Although Trevor-Roper defended his comparison of Himmler with Bellarmine, he abandoned his parallel between Goebbels and the Jesuits. This had produced more protests than any other aspect of *The Last Days*, and Trevor-Roper discovered that he was in error. Father Bernard Bassett SJ, who knew Trevor-Roper from Oxford, assured him that Goebbels was never at a Jesuit school. Trevor-Roper had already turned to the biographer of Goebbels, F.W. Pick, from whose book he had drawn the information, only for Pick to discover from further enquiries that he was mistaken. Goebbels' old teacher informed Pick that there had been no Jesuit teachers at either of the schools Goebbels attended in Rheydt. So Trevor-Roper conceded his error in the introduction to the English second edition and removed four references to the Jesuits in the paragraph introducing Goebbels, though this offending material enjoyed a renaissance in the German edition of 1965.[55]

***

Whatever the shortcomings of individual passages, Trevor-Roper's book tore aside the pretensions of the Nazi regime as seldom before. So it quickly assumed political importance. On 13 July 1947 the Prime Minister's private secretary informed the private secretary of the Chancellor of the Duchy of Lancaster that 'the Prime Minister [Clement Attlee] has recently been reading H.R. Trevor-Roper's "The Last Days of Hitler" and feels that this damning exposure of the character and intrigues of the Nazi Leaders ought to be distributed in Germany as widely as possible. He has, therefore, asked me to enquire whether it has yet been translated with a view to publication in Germany, or whether any steps are contemplated to that end.'[56]

At the time of Attlee's enquiry, the British Element in the Allied Control Commission for Germany based in Berlin had already realized that plans for publishing the book in Germany had gone badly astray. In November 1946 Trevor-Roper's publisher, Macmillan, had offered the newspaper serialization rights in the German language to the Control Commission. On 10 December came the reply that the leading papers in Vienna and in the British zone of Germany did not think the time suitable: 'The policy at present is not to devote too much attention to the past, but to concentrate on the positive tasks of reconstruction.' Next Macmillan offered the German language book rights to the Control Commission, but once again received a rebuff. The official concerned failed to grasp the political value of the book and missed an excellent opportunity. Macmillan also separately approached the American Military Government to no avail. Trevor-Roper suggested his publisher try Switzerland, and Macmillan sold the book rights in German to the Swiss publisher Amstutz and Herdeg on 26 February 1947.[57] During March extracts from the book amounting to 10,000 words appeared in *Die Welt*, a German newspaper published with British sponsorship.[58]

The British edition of *The Last Days of Hitler* was published on 18 March 1947. Yet there was still no German book version in prospect for the British and American zones, although Michael Balfour and Robert Birley of the Control Commission felt that 'this is the kind of book which the Germans ought to read'. David Whyte of the Foreign Office wrote to the Control Commission that 'it is certainly a very unfortunate chain of events which have led to our not being able to secure the German rights of this book ... Macmillan are doing everything they can to help us and to bring pressure to bear on the Swiss publisher.' Meanwhile, in July 1947 Spiegel Press did bring out a German translation of *The Last Days*. This edition appeared in a rudimentary binding with a cyclostyled text, and there were only eight hundred copies.[59]

Trevor-Roper's book needed a mass edition for the German market, but the Foreign Office was stymied by the Swiss publisher. Whyte wrote to Amstutz on 6 September offering him the paltry sum of £100 for a licence to produce a German edition of 20,000 copies. Amstutz replied that '£100 is so inadequate that it would hardly be worthwhile for any publisher to consider it'. On 3 December Amstutz came to the Foreign Office and Whyte 'exercised all powers of persuasion possible, emphasising that we wanted to get a German edition of "L.D. of H." out quickly and the interest that was being taken in this case by the P.M.'s office' but to no avail. He concluded that Amstutz was 'a very self-willed man and extremely obstinate ... in principle opposed to accepting any sterling offer we can make him. He is interested only in operating a branch of his publishing house in Germany.' In February 1948 Amstutz wrote again informing Whyte that the Swiss edition was due to appear in March in case he wished to buy any. After Amstutz belatedly got access to the German market, he complained to Macmillan that his edition of *The Last Days* had not done well there, selling only seventy-three copies in the whole of 1951.[60]

In the late 1940s most Germans who wanted to read Trevor-Roper in full had to work through the English edition of his book. On 23 February 1948 the British Information Control Branch asked its Information Centres throughout the British Zone for German reactions to *The Last Days*. The Centres were almost unanimous in recording a great demand. For instance, the Neumuenster Information Centre reported that 'everyone who can read English asks for this book'. German readers felt Trevor-Roper was objective in his judgements. According to the Information Centre in Schleswig, 'Readers say that the book is written in a fair way. The author has tried to see things in a dispassionate way.' The Gelsenkirchen Centre reported that *The Last Days* was 'one of the most widely read books in our library', though it added that 'people are very cautious in making comments in the presence of the staff'. Another reporter stated that 'this book is generally returned without comment. If a reader does make a remark, it is to the effect that "Hitler deserved this fate".'[61]

Although Whyte ordered ninety copies of the Swiss edition for the Information Centres, the initial absence of a substantial German edition limited the readership. How much greater would have been the book's impact in Germany if the British Government had required the German translation rights as a quid pro quo for approving a book that, after all, had been researched at their expense? The JIC had sanctioned the book not least with a view to a German translation, but the Foreign Office failed to ensure this was done in a way that would best serve British [and indeed German] interests. So the full intended value was not gained from Trevor-Roper's enquiry and the subsequent publication of his book.[62]

In conclusion, we should return to the questions posed at the beginning. Trevor-Roper came to write *The Last Days* because he was ideally qualified to do so. He had visited Nazi Germany in the 1930s, gained a mastery of the German language, and used this to good effect while working for British Intelligence during the war, all the while further enhancing his knowledge of the Nazi regime. It was his obvious interest in Hitler's fate that led to him being chosen to carry out the official enquiry that was the basis of his book. And as a professional historian with a uniquely appealing style of presentation, no one was better suited to turning the original enquiry into contemporary history. His penetrating explanation of Hitler and Nazism was largely confirmed by later historians, as was his emphasis on the late resurrection of the Nazi Party under Martin Bormann. Certainly Trevor-Roper was taken in by Hitler's persuasive Armaments Minister Albert Speer. Nevertheless, his book remains a compelling and invaluable study of Hitler's fall. He planned a book that would stand the test of time, and he succeeded. Anton Joachimtaler's modern study identifies relatively few errors of detail in Trevor-Roper's account of Hitler's death. The virtues of his book continue to outweigh its defects. Although Trevor-Roper engaged in furious controversy with A.J.P. Taylor over Hitler, no one praised *The Last Days* more than Taylor, who wrote in 1968 that Trevor-Roper's 'brilliant book demonstrated how a great historian can arrive at the truth even when much of the evidence is lacking or, as in this case, deliberately kept from him ... This was all the doing of one incomparable scholar.'[63]

* This essay was first published in the *Vierteljahrshefte fuer Zeitgeschichte* 57/1 (January 2009). I would like to thank Renate Bihl, Judith Curthoys, Richard Davenport-Hines, Hermann Graml, Roy Hughes, Elizabeth James, Jeremy Noakes, Alysoun Saunders, Adam Sisman, Nathan Winter and Blair Worden for their assistance with the original article. Blair Worden also made many helpful suggestions for the English version.

Chapter 6

Hugh Trevor-Roper's
Special Missions in Germany*

In autumn 1945 the British historian and intelligence officer Hugh
Trevor-Roper carried out an investigation into the fate of Adolf Hitler
and concluded that the Nazi dictator had killed himself. Soon afterwards
he made a supplementary enquiry into the problem of Hitler's wills.
Subsequently he wrote a book, *The Last Days of Hitler*, which attracted
much praise, some corrections and controversy, and lasting public
interest.[1] Indeed the book still remains in print seventy years later, and
Trevor-Roper's analysis of the Nazi regime has largely stood the test of
time.

After the war Trevor-Roper taught at Oxford University, and was
appointed Regius Professor of Modern History in 1957. He was
raised to the British peerage as Baron Dacre of Glanton in 1979
and the following year became the head of Peterhouse at Cambridge
University. An eminent authority on both the early modern period and
Nazi Germany, in 1983 Trevor-Roper proclaimed authentic 'Hitler'
diaries that were actually compiled by the forger Konrad Kujau. Having
first declared the diaries and other documents stored with them as 'an
archive of great historical significance', within weeks Trevor-Roper
was admitting that 'I made a grave error.'[2] He faced the subsequent
ordeal stoically and continued with his academic responsibilities
undeterred. Since Trevor-Roper's death in 2003 there has been renewed
interest in his work due to the publication of an outstanding biography
and seven further books of his writings. These posthumous books are
largely based on manuscripts from Trevor-Roper's very substantial
private archive. [3]

Reappraisal of Trevor-Roper's Investigation

Trevor-Roper's personal papers have not only made it possible to publish more of his writings, they have also facilitated study of his research methods. In particular, since my own essay reproduced as Chapter Five,[4] Trevor-Roper's investigation into the death of Hitler has been examined not only by his biographer but also in an article by Geoffrey Parker and Sarah Douglas and a more recent essay by Richard Overy.[5] Professor Parker poses the question 'could a single person, even one as energetic and shrewd as Trevor-Roper, have interrogated numerous "potential witnesses" single-handed, sifted through their evidence, and separated truth from falsehood in less than six weeks? It seemed highly improbable.'[6] Parker writes that 'both in Germany and back in England he apparently spent most of his time reading and annotating the transcripts of interrogations carried out by others and made available to him on the orders of his colleague, Peter Ramsbotham'.[7] Parker mentions that when he was teaching at the University of St Andrews in the 1970s, Professor Norman Gash, his head of department, claimed that 'in 1945 he and many other Intelligence Officers had been "involved with Trevor-Roper in the investigation into the death of Hitler"'. Parker asks, 'Why did Trevor-Roper choose to present *The Last Days* as entirely his own work?'[8] In similar vein, Professor Overy writes that Trevor-Roper 'gave scant acknowledgement to the large number of intelligence officers and interrogators who helped to piece the story together'.[9]

Professor Parker's co-author, Sarah K. Douglas, draws attention to the British intelligence officer Captain Humphrey Searle, who compiled a timetable of events in Hitler's Bunker. Douglas writes that Trevor-Roper 'along with Ramsbotham, Searle, and the countless other interrogators from all over Europe, established a credible account of Adolf Hitler's final days in the *Fuehrerbunker*. It was this collective effort that became *The Last Days of Hitler*.' Douglas also asserts that 'the actual text of the book remains the same through every edition'.[10]

How accurate is the account by Parker and Douglas of Trevor-Roper's investigation into Hitler's fate and the genesis of *The Last Days of Hitler*? Did Trevor-Roper mostly read interrogations done by others during his trips around Germany? What materials did he actually draw on for his book? This essay will show that, although Parker and Douglas have provided a lively impetus to research in this area, they present an account of Trevor-Roper's work that suffers from a surprising number of inaccuracies. Not least, they underestimate Trevor-Roper's achievement as an interrogator, as does Professor Overy.

The Reasons for Trevor-Roper's Enquiry

Why did British intelligence have to investigate the circumstances of Hitler's death at all? Despite Hitler's unique notoriety, in summer 1945 his fate was uncertain. In a reply to a parliamentary question on 15 May as to whether 'the death of Hitler has now been established beyond all shadow of doubt', the British Prime Minister Winston Churchill admitted that 'I know no more than any other member of the House who reads the newspapers.'[11]

The Russian leader Josef Stalin was better informed than Churchill. On 1 May he had been informed of Hitler's death, and on 5 May Soviet Military Counter-Espionage [Smersh] had dug up Hitler's corpse. Yet the Russians were still not quite sure. On 9 May Field Marshal Wilhelm Keitel, Chief of the Wehrmacht High Command, was asked by Soviet officers whether Hitler was really dead. They claimed that his body had not been found.[12] During the following weeks the Soviets made important progress, as Hitler's dental nurse confirmed that gold bridges and teeth shown to her by Smersh had belonged to the dictator. Soviet Intelligence concluded that 'there is no doubt that the supposed corpse of Hitler is really his'.[13] But their western allies remained in the dark.

The uncertainty over Hitler troubled Brigadier Dick White, a senior counter-intelligence officer attached to the British Forces in Germany, who decided on his own initiative to clear up the matter. He visited Berlin and, as he wrote decades later, 'a Russian General ... assured me that Hitler & Goebbels had committed suicide in the Chancellery & their bodies burned. He produced Hitler's identified false teeth in evidence but no documents.'[14] Nor did the Russian general make any witnesses available, so it was a helpful rather than a conclusive interview.

The British War Office was also interested in the dental evidence for Hitler's death. In June 1945 the War Office received from the British Secret Intelligence Service [SIS] a detailed description of Hitler's 'dentition', originally provided to the Americans by his dentist, Professor Hugo Blaschke. Major Norman Gash, who worked in sub-section 14(d) of War Office Military Intelligence, realized the potential significance of Blaschke's information. As he informed a colleague in a different sub-section, 'the Russians have apparently been trying to identify Hitler's body from his dental records'. Gash repeated the description of Hitler's teeth and suggested the information should be passed on to the Russians. However, a War Office colleague torpedoed this suggestion, pointing out that the Russians would probably demand to interrogate Blaschke, and it would be awkward if the Russians told the Americans what they had learned.[15]

By the following month the Russians were playing down the dental evidence. On 16 July 1945 the senior British and Russian security staff in Berlin met at the latter's headquarters. According to Colonel E.A. Howard, staff officer responsible for British military intelligence in Berlin, 'The Russians were asked if they had any information concerning the bodies of Hitler and Eva Braun. They said that two bodies were found buried ... at the exit of the Chancellery air-raid shelter, but were in such a condition that they could not be identified, even to the extent of telling whether they were of a man or a woman. A dentist had said that the teeth were those of Hitler but the Russians said the evidence was not convincing.'[16]

Rumours of Hitler's survival proliferated, and there was endless speculation as to how he might have escaped. White realized that his meeting with the Russian general was not enough to settle the issue. Instead of investigating further himself, White brought in Hugh Trevor-Roper, who was an expert on the Abwehr, the German Secret Service. For much of the war Trevor-Roper had led a small team in SIS that studied the Abwehr's deciphered radio messages. Trevor-Roper wished to extract the maximum advantage from Abwehr decrypts by discussing the messages with intelligence staff outside SIS. His emphasis on exchanging and discussing information was not welcomed by his SIS superiors, who were concerned for the security of the material. Nevertheless Trevor-Roper fought with increasing success to circulate his material to other departments.[17] Trevor-Roper's wartime struggles in London complemented his German expertise. Dick White knew that Trevor-Roper was not just a clever don, but also an aggressive battler, someone who would finish the job even if he had to defy senior officers.

By 1945 Trevor-Roper was working in the War Room of Allied Counter-Intelligence in London. He was a member of its publications section, which saw the extensive intelligence flowing through the War Room and compiled reports on German Intelligence for the use of British and American Forces. While working in the War Room, Trevor-Roper also took part in the preliminary interrogation of *SS Brigadefuehrer* Walter Schellenberg, formerly chief of Nazi foreign intelligence.[18]

In early September 1945 Dick White instructed Trevor-Roper to 'assemble and review all the evidence' relating to the death of Hitler.[19] Although White entrusted the mission to Trevor-Roper alone, he did not work in a vacuum, but could draw on many assistants. Trevor-Roper provided the crucial brain power behind the investigation, but much spade work was done by others, as he explained: 'In this investigation no other person was joined with me, but I was given authority to use the resources of [the British] 21st Army Group and to call on the help of British intelligence units, Field Security Police [FSP], and Prisoner-of-War camps as I might need. The American authorities at Frankfurt (USFET – [United States Forces European Theatre]) were asked if they planned any such enquiry. They replied that they did not, and orders were given to American units to co-operate with me in the same way. I carried out my investigation by collecting available documents … and by identifying and (where possible) locating persons who might have been witnesses of the events in Berlin at the end of April. Some of these witnesses were found in Allied (i.e. British or American) PoW camps. Others I traced myself by following up the results of interrogation, and caused to be arrested by the FSP or (in the US zone) the CIC [Counter Intelligence Corps]. In general, I interrogated them myself, but sometimes, when more convenient, I had them interrogated by the British or US camp authorities.'[20]

Trevor-Roper's Autumn Interrogations

The hunt for witnesses to Hitler's fate was orchestrated in the British Zone by Major Peter Ramsbotham, who worked on the intelligence staff at the British Army of the Rhine [BAOR], formed from the British 21st Army Group in August 1945.[21] How much did Trevor-Roper himself have to do with these witnesses? Professor Parker questions whether Trevor-Roper could have 'interrogated numerous "potential witnesses" single-handed'? Indeed he could. During his autumn enquiry it seems that Trevor-Roper personally questioned at least eighteen witnesses or persons with leads to witnesses, and in eleven of these cases a significant interrogation took place.[22] He returned to question again one of the persons with leads and also re-interrogated one of the witnesses. After the initial enquiry was concluded, during December 1945 and 1946 Trevor-Roper interviewed eleven more witnesses or persons with leads; eight of these people were interrogated by him, one of them twice. In 1955–56 he visited Germany twice to interview three witnesses previously held captive by the Russians.

Trevor-Roper's zeal in carrying out interrogations himself undermines the notion that he spent most of his time in Germany reading the transcripts of interrogations done by others. Of course, Trevor-Roper did work through many such documents, but why go to all the bother of travelling around Germany just to study material he could have read far more conveniently in London? In fact, Trevor-Roper was making these journeys to carry out enquiries and interrogations in person. How then did Trevor-Roper carry out interrogations and who did he interrogate personally?

Trevor-Roper enjoyed distinct advantages over many Allied interrogators. He knew the context of the Third Reich extremely well and did not need an interpreter. Certainly Trevor-Roper was not someone to trifle with: a major in British uniform was an intimidating figure to disorientated Germans, and furthermore could recommend the incarceration of recalcitrant witnesses or the liberation of prisoners who were helpful. The questionnaires Trevor-Roper drafted for other officers suggest that he kept very much to the point with a relentless sequence of factual questions. This method is confirmed by Bernd Freiherr Freytag von Loringhoven, formerly adjutant to Chief of Army General Staff, whom Trevor-Roper interrogated at Bad Nenndorf near Hanover.[23]

Trevor-Roper began with Albert Speer, formerly Hitler's armaments minister, who was being held at 'Dustbin', an interrogation centre for VIP technicians at Schloss Kransberg near Frankfurt am Main.[24] Speer was regarded in the British Foreign Office as 'head and shoulders above our other captives'.[25] Trevor-Roper questioned Speer on 11 September 1945 about his experiences between 20 April 1945 and the capitulation. Speer told his interrogator about his two visits to Berlin. During his second visit Martin Bormann, head of the Nazi Party Chancellery, asked him for support in advocating flight, but Speer joined Propaganda Minister Joseph Goebbels and Eva Braun in urging Hitler to stay in Berlin.[26]

According to Douglas, Trevor-Roper went 'to interview Albert Speer in Frankfurt' but 'Speer never mentioned meeting Trevor-Roper'.[27] Yet in his published diaries Speer recorded that Trevor-Roper had visited him in Schloss Kransberg, and that his questions revealed a thorough grasp of his brief. Speer was so eager to help that the following day he wrote to the Schloss commandant 'as a supplement to my questioning on 11th September' with the names of three more people present in the Fuehrer Bunker on the night of 23–24 April.[28] Later in September Trevor-Roper wrote to Major P.M. Wilson, of the Enemy Personnel Exploitation Section, noting that 'Attached are five copies of the special interrogation of Albert Speer which I carried out with your permission on 11th September, 1945.'[29]

On 13 September Trevor-Roper questioned Dr Theodor Morell, Hitler's doctor, who was being held by the Americans, 'on the subject of his last experience in Berlin. Morell seemed physically decayed and mentally gaga; he was unsure of most of the facts he gave, and probably genuinely unsure.'[30] Douglas refers to this interview in a footnote, but did not realize it was carried out by Trevor-Roper. She writes that 'Trevor-Roper arrived in Germany on 24 September to help with the gathering of information for his report.'[31] By then he had in fact already personally questioned Speer and Morell, and was planning a series of further interrogations. These began at Camp 030 in Ploen, Schleswig-Holstein.[32]

On 25 September Trevor-Roper interrogated Bormann's secretary, Else Krueger, one of the most informative witnesses he encountered. Krueger told Trevor-Roper about Hitler's marriage and reported an atmosphere of gloom and depression at his wedding feast.[33] Early the following day Trevor-Roper interrogated two more witnesses at Camp 030. First he interviewed *SS Obersturmbannfuehrer* Werner Grothmann, former military adjutant to *Reichsfuehrer SS* Heinrich Himmler. Grothmann's replies suggested that Himmler had become fumbling and ineffective during the final days of the Nazi regime, and the *Reichsfuehrer* reacted with consternation to Hitler's absolute refusal to leave Berlin.[34] Trevor-Roper also questioned Dr Rudolf Brandt, Himmler's personal adjutant, about his master's final relations with Hitler, but Brandt added nothing to Grothmann's answers. Trevor-Roper later admitted that 'I believe that Brandt and Grothmann know (or knew) a lot more than has ever been extracted from them; but I doubt if they are worth much now [March 1946]. Brandt especially seems a very shady character.'[35]

After questioning Grothmann and Brandt, later on during 26 September Trevor-Roper travelled south to Nienburg, where he interviewed Hermann Karnau, one of the detectives responsible for Hitler's personal safety. Douglas writes that 'there is no evidence that Trevor-Roper ever spoke to Karnau personally' yet admits 'It is ... possible Trevor-Roper visited Karnau in Nienburg.' Indeed, Trevor-Roper interrogated him twice.[36] Karnau had been arrested by Canadian Field Security on 25 May 1945 and interrogated at Bad Salzuflen on 19 June by Captain K.W.E. Leslie.[37] Afterwards, Leslie had concluded that there was reason for further examination of the detective, whom Trevor-Roper questioned 'on the subject of the burning of Hitler's body, in continuation of previous interrogation reports on the same subject'. Among the points that emerged during the interrogation were: 'The fact that Karnau saw the bodies burning was purely accidental. Hitler was lying on his back with his knees drawn up. Eva Braun was face downwards. There was no pyre or fuel under the bodies.'[38]

Not quite satisfied, four days later Trevor-Roper questioned Karnau again and this time Karnau 'finally yielded the facts', according to his interrogator, about the events he witnessed on 1 May: 'After rounding a concrete tower which served as a guard post he came suddenly upon the bodies of Hitler and his wife lying close to the door to the air raid shelter. He was no more than three metres away from the bodies when they suddenly burst into flames ... The setting alight could not have been through enemy action as Karnau was close enough to the bodies to be wounded if any missile were employed. Karnau can NOT explain the actual method of the burning; it is possible that someone threw a match from the doorway.'[39] Trevor-Roper's questions prompted Karnau to give a more revealing account of what he witnessed on Hitler's last day. The value of this evidence would become clear later in the enquiry.

Between his interrogations of Karnau Trevor-Roper had travelled to Berlin, where on 28 September 1945 he called on Dr Rudolf Birkner, a radiologist at the Robert Koch Institute in Moabit. Two other doctors from the Institute were also present, and Trevor-Roper questioned all three about Hitler's physicians. The institute staff told him about Professor Carl von Eicken, ear, nose and throat specialist at Berlin's Charité Hospital. They also mentioned Professor Gohrbandt, Medical Director of their institute and patron of Hitler's surgeon, Dr Ludwig

Stumpfegger.[40] Trevor-Roper sought out Gohrbandt and Eicken, who were both still working in Berlin.

On 29 September Trevor-Roper questioned Professor Gohrbandt about Dr Stumpfegger. Gohrbandt told Trevor-Roper that, 'Stumpfegger's position as a favourite of Hitler was assured less by his medical proficiency than by his general subservience; he thought Hitler was divinely inspired, and said so.'[41] On 30 September Trevor-Roper interrogated Professor von Eicken, who in 1935 had operated to remove a polyp from Hitler's vocal chords. Von Eicken also treated Hitler in the aftermath of the assassination attempt of 20 July 1944.[42]

After questioning von Eicken in Berlin, Trevor-Roper returned to the British Zone, first to re-interrogate Karnau and then to interview an unusual and informative witness, Baroness Irmengard von Varo. The Baroness had been under the protection of an SS officer, who brought her to the Reich Chancellery about ten days before the fall of Berlin. There she remained, working as a waitress. She met Hitler shortly before his death. Leslie Randall of the British *Evening Standard* had interviewed the Baroness for a story in his paper, but did not publish her name. In September 1945 von Varo was living near Berlin at Glienicke in the Russian Zone. She told Randall that her one desire was to return to her parents, who lived near Bad Oeynhausen in the British Zone.[43]

Baroness von Varo did succeed in returning to her parents, though without getting permission from the British. Trevor-Roper first tried unsuccessfully to find her in Berlin. When he came to question her on 1 October in the British Zone, she had every reason to co-operate. Otherwise, she could be deported back to the Russians. Trevor-Roper interviewed Varo at her mother's house in Bueckeburg. He reported that that 'she had a purely accidental connexion with the Fuehrerbunker, where she ate her meals in the general dining-corridor. Her personal knowledge of events in the Bunker is therefore limited to the relatively few occasions when she was in it.' Von Varo told Trevor-Roper about reactions of Hitler's entourage to the key events of his final days: 'Hitler's marriage. Von Varo says that this took place one or two days before Hitler's death. The fact was announced at the time, and left everyone dumbfounded. No one could think of a satisfactory explanation for what was regarded as very eccentric behaviour. Hitler's marriage was openly discussed by everyone, unlike his death which was officially kept secret so that the soldiers should not know of it.'[44]

Although Baroness von Varo was not a witness to the circumstances of Hitler's death, she gave interesting testimony about a prelude during the night of 29–30 April 1945: 'one of the SS Begleitkommando [escort battalion] came into the dining passage of the Fuehrerbunker, and said that Hitler wished to say goodbye to the ladies ... he walked round the room alone, and spoke a few words to most of the women with whom he shook hands ... After the ceremony was over and Hitler had withdrawn, everyone asked each other what the meaning of it could be, and they concluded that it must be the preliminary to suicide.'[45]

After interrogating von Varo, Trevor-Roper began the hunt for Hitler's personal pilots, Hans Baur and Georg Beetz, so he could disprove rumours that Hitler had escaped from Berlin by aeroplane. On 6 October 1945 he called on Frau Beetz, who had heard nothing from her husband since the end of April.[46] Next Trevor-Roper tried to locate Baur. He reported that, 'On the 7th October [a Sunday] I called at Frau Baur's house at Pilsensee, near Munich. Frau Baur was out at her devotions, but her mother told me that they had just received a letter from Baur dated 10th September ... and in it Baur stated that he was in hospital where he had had a leg amputated ... He said that he expected to be cured in a month to six weeks, and would then go to Russia ... I requested C.I.C. Tegernsee to keep in contact with Frau Beetz and through her with Frau Baur.'[47]

Trevor-Roper also hoped to get more information on Baur and Beetz from Erich Kempka, Hitler's chauffeur, who like the two pilots had tried to escape from the Chancellery on 1 May and was hit by an explosion in Friedrichstrasse that had also struck Beetz. Afterwards Kempka had made his way to Berchtesgaden, where he was arrested by the CIC.[48] On the afternoon of 7 October, as Trevor-Roper reported, he 'interrogated Erich Kempka, officer in charge of Hitler's transport, at No.6 Internment Camp, Moosburg. Asked about Beetz and Baur he stated that when he (Kempka) had recovered consciousness after the explosion in the Friedrichstrasse ... he found Beetz with a bad head wound ... Beetz told him that Baur had gone on ahead with the first group of the escape party. It is thus clear ... Beetz and Baur did not escape or attempt to escape by plane from Berlin.'[49] Subsequently Beetz was killed while trying to cross the Weidendammer Bridge over the river Spree.

Kempka was an important witness for the investigation, though Douglas asserts in a footnote that 'he [Kempka] was not interrogated by Trevor-Roper'.[50] Yet not only did Trevor-Roper interrogate Kempka on 7 October 1945, he succeeded in obtaining remarkably vivid testimony. Kempka told Trevor-Roper that during the early afternoon of 30 April 1945 he received a phone call from *SS Sturmbannfuehrer* Otto Guensche, Hitler's personal adjutant, who wanted a large amount of petrol. Kempka obtained this, and then went to the Fuehrerbunker, where he met Guensche, who told him that 'Hitler had shot himself through the mouth. Eva Braun was also dead ... Then the door of room 19 was opened, and Kempka saw Stubaf [*Sturmbannfuehrer*] Linge [Hitler's valet] and another man ... who came out carrying a body wrapped in a blanket. Only the legs of the body, up to the knees, were visible. They were clothed in black trousers, black socks, and black shoes. Guensche helped the two bearers to carry the body upstairs, and then returned. Next, Bormann came out of room 19, alone, carrying the body of Eva Braun, which was not wrapped in a blanket. She was clothed in a dark dress. Kempka took the body of Eva Braun from Bormann, and carried it to the foot of the stairs. There he gave it to Guensche, who had returned from carrying the other body upstairs. Guensche then carried the body of Eva Braun upstairs into the garden and laid it next to the other body ... Kempka waited in the Bunker until both bodies had been carried upstairs. He then fell in behind Bormann and Goebbels and followed them upstairs ... some of the party ... poured a part of the petrol over the two bodies. The bodies were lying on sandy ground, and the petrol sank quickly into the sand. They then withdrew under the shelter of the emergency exit, as Russian artillery firing was in progress. There Guensche struck a match, and lit a rag which he had previously dipped in the petrol. When he had lit the rag, he threw it out on to the petrol-soaked bodies, and they burst into flames. The party then stood to attention, gave the Hitler salute, and withdrew downstairs into the Bunker.' Trevor-Roper noted that 'this account explains part of the independent account given by Karnau. Karnau, coming round the corner-tower, saw the bodies, and then saw them burst into flames. He could not explain why or how they burst into flames. Kempka's story, if accurate, provides the explanation; the light was thrown out from the Emergency Exit by persons who would themselves be invisible from the place where Karnau stood.' Trevor-Roper commented later that, 'The truth of the incident is attested by the rational discrepancy of the evidence.'[51] The American prisoner Kempka and the British prisoner

Karnau confirmed each other's stories. Given quite independently, very specific detail in their narratives dovetailed perfectly: this was powerful evidence for Hitler's fate. Overy writes that Trevor-Roper's 'conclusion was heavily derived from the interrogation of Kempka in June [by Leslie] ... and the American interrogation of Kempka'.[52] But Trevor-Roper also interrogated both these witnesses himself and elicited testimony of vital importance to his investigation.

By late September 1945 Trevor-Roper was already interested in locating Gerda Christian, one of Hitler's secretaries. On 27 September he telephoned British Army of the Rhine HQ asking for Christian's characteristic features. These were obtained from Else Krueger.[53] Frau Christian had told Krueger she was going to visit her mother-in-law. Trevor-Roper interviewed this lady, Frau Krau, on two occasions, namely 6 October and 7 November, at Ebernburg near Kreuznach in the French Zone, but to no avail.[54] Indeed, Gerda Christian proved most elusive. Although on 9 November 1945 Trevor-Roper asked the British Security Officer for Hannover to locate her, only four months later, on 8 March 1946, could the BAOR inform Trevor-Roper via the War Room that the Americans had arrested Frau Christian. Trevor-Roper compiled a questionnaire for her the same day.[55]

Meanwhile, Trevor-Roper had interrogated Frau Christian's husband, General Eghard Christian, Chief of Luftwaffe Command Staff, at the Combined Services Detailed Interrogation Centre [CSDIC] in Latimer House, Buckinghamshire, on 15 October 1945. He noted that Christian had been present at the military conference on 22 April when Hitler learned that an attack by *SS Obergruppenfuehrer* Felix Steiner to relieve Berlin had not materialised. According to Christian, Hitler announced that 'he would stay in Berlin. Anyone else could go.' Trevor-Roper commented that he 'did not get the impression that Christian was altogether objective in his account. He was reluctant to give any personal account of characters which were mentioned to him, and in general seemed anxious to excuse (by omission or implication) the court [of Hitler] from which he could not pretend to be distinct.'[56]

On 3 November 1945 Trevor-Roper interrogated *SS Hauptsturmfuehrer* Hermann Bornholdt at Neumuenster in Schleswig-Holstein. Bornholdt had been on duty with the SS escort battalion until he left Berlin on 24 April, and was able to identify some of the battalion's officers who remained in the capital.[57] The most bizarre of Trevor-Roper's interviews during this autumn sequence was with Hitler's butler, Artur Kannenberg, who offered to work for his interrogator.[58]

Of the witnesses in Russian hands, Trevor-Roper was particularly interested in *SS Gruppenfuehrer* Johann Rattenhuber, commander of the Reich Security Service, which provided detectives such as Karnau to watch over Hitler's personal safety. In mid-October Trevor-Roper wrote to Brigadier E.R. 'Ronnie' Haylor, head of the British Intelligence Bureau in Germany, stressing the importance of interrogating Rattenhuber and asking to be involved: 'I should welcome the opportunity of either carrying out the interrogation or of briefing the interrogators.' Trevor-Roper also tried to inspect adjutants' diaries that Marshal Zhukov, the Soviet Commander-in-Chief in Germany, had cited publicly. The Russians noted Trevor-Roper's requests concerning Rattenhuber and the diaries but never replied to them.[59]

The witnesses Trevor-Roper did interrogate provided evidence between them that Hitler had intended to kill himself, that he had committed suicide with Eva Braun, and that their bodies had been burned in the garden of the Reich Chancellery. Nevertheless, Trevor-Roper had to consider whether his witnesses were perpetrating a deception by telling him a cover story in which they had all been carefully briefed. He rejected this possibility on the grounds that such a story would break down once the witnesses were pressed by their interrogator on new details concerning which there had been no opportunity to concert their accounts.[60]

Trevor-Roper's enquiry was by no means based on interrogations alone. He also drew on extensive documentation, including telegrams from Bormann and Goebbels to Hitler's successor, Grand Admiral Doenitz, informing him of the Fuehrer's death. Trevor-Roper also saw other records of the Doenitz Government. He studied the diaries of Hitler's Finance Minister, Lutz Graf Schwerin von Krosigk, and those of the Luftwaffe Chief of Staff, General Karl Koller. From the War Room he had a copy of an autobiography compiled during June 1945 by Schellenberg.[61] He also consulted a diary kept by Hitler's valet and a tear-off engagement pad covering the dates 15 to 21 April 1945, which listed Hitler's more formal meetings with Nazi ministers.

In his report for the meeting of the Quadripartite Intelligence Committee of the Allies on 10 November Trevor-Roper described the evidence for Hitler's death as 'positive, circumstantial, consistent and independent'. An appendix to the report asked whether any of the powers held eight further witnesses from the Bunker and asked the Russians to make a statement on the body recognized as Hitler's by the teeth. But no information was forthcoming from the taciturn Russians.[62]

Trevor-Roper's Enquiry into Hitler's Wills

Within weeks of his enquiry's conclusion, Trevor-Roper was faced with a new problem concerning Hitler's wills. He solved this rapidly in perhaps his most remarkable achievement as an intelligence officer. Douglas describes this work as 'exceptional', but says little about it, even though it is a particularly revealing example of Trevor-Roper's methods as an investigator and interrogator.[63] The new challenge for Trevor-Roper came about when a prisoner under arrest in the British Zone was told to move on by a sergeant of the guard. The sergeant grabbed the prisoner by the shoulder, and pushed him in the right direction. In doing so he felt paper in a shoulder pad. This paper consisted of Hitler's personal and political testaments plus an appendix to the latter by Goebbels.[64]

The prisoner's real name was Heinz Lorenz. He had been a senior editor at the German News Service and during late April 1945 personally took its bulletins to Hitler's bunker. He was interrogated at CSDIC in Germany on 30 November. According to its report, Lorenz was summoned by Bormann in the late morning of 29 April 1945. Bormann gave him copies with original signatures of Hitler's two testaments, personal and political, which he was to take to Doenitz. Next Lorenz was given a supplementary statement by Goebbels. According to Lorenz, Wilhelm Zander, an official of the Nazi Party Chancellery, was given copies of the personal and political testaments and also the Hitler–Braun marriage certificate. Furthermore, Major Wilhelm Johannmeier, Hitler's army adjutant, was given the political testament for delivery to Field Marshal Schoerner, Commander of Army Group Centre in Bohemia. In his will Hitler appointed Schoerner Commander in Chief of the Army.[65]

Lorenz, Johannmeier and Zander met shortly after midday on 29 April and left the Bunker, Johannmeier accompanied by a corporal from his staff. They made their way to Pichelsdorf in west Berlin, from where they travelled south by boat, and then on foot west to the Elbe in the general flood of refugees. According to Lorenz, by 10 May, as they neared Hanover, 'they had all realized that it was futile to attempt to deliver the wills to any German authority and they were now only interested in their personal fates'.[66]

British intelligence turned to Trevor-Roper for an opinion on whether the wills found on Lorenz were authentic. On December 1 1945 Trevor-Roper replied by telegram: 'Consider Hitler's will certainly genuine on internal evidence. Telegrams sent by Bormann and Goebbels refer to will of 29 April of which copies being sent to Doenitz and Schoerner. Known that copy sent to Doenitz failed to arrive. Telegrams quote and thus confirm second part of political testament. Other evidence confirming authenticity is given in written comments following by bag.'[67] In his written comments Trevor-Roper confirmed his view of the newly found documents: 'The evidence supplied by them is consistent in all particulars with the evidence derived from other sources concerning the last days in the Bunker.' William Skardon, a hand-writing expert from MI5, the British Security Service, had already examined Hitler's personal will, his political testament, and the appendix by Goebbels to Hitler's political testament. He was in no doubt that the signatures on the documents were genuine.[68]

Trevor-Roper later recalled that, 'My investigation was, officially, complete. However, at the end of November 1945 a document purporting to be Hitler's will was discovered ... and I was asked to return to Germany and investigate this matter too.'[69] On 14 December 1945 Trevor-Roper went back to Germany, and stayed for three weeks. Lorenz and his documents were in British hands. Lorenz had identified Major Wilhelm Johannmeier as a document bearer and the latter had been arrested on 11 December near Iserlohn in the British Zone. But although Johannmeier was in custody, there was no sign of the documents he was supposed to have. Trevor-Roper's purpose was to interrogate Johannmeier, find the third bearer Zander, and locate their documents.

When Trevor-Roper confronted Johannmeier, the latter claimed that he was merely escorting the other two messengers and had no documents himself. Yet when Trevor-Roper subsequently interrogated Lorenz on 18 December, the latter protested that he had seen Hitler's political testament in Johannmeier's hand. Who was telling the truth? Before returning to the obdurate Johannmeier, Trevor-Roper decided not only to find Zander, but first to carry out a secondary mission he had planned for some time, namely, to investigate a reported sighting of Bormann in Austria.[70]

On 5 December 1945 Trevor-Roper had interviewed Emil Otto Hoppe, a leading London photographer. Hoppe had been born in Munich but was now a British citizen. He owned a farm in Upper Austria [not Schleswig-Holstein, as Douglas asserts.][71] According to Trevor-Roper's report, 'Mr Hoppe referred to a recent newspaper report that Martin Bormann's chauffeur had been seen driving a car out of Linz.' Hoppe's farm was at Molln in the Steyr valley: 'Mr Hoppe suggested that it might be worth searching this area for missing war criminals. In his own farm, when he left, there remained his bailiff, Balthasar Schoettel … anti-Nazi and reliable.'[72]

Trevor-Roper felt that, 'All the available positive evidence is that Martin Bormann himself was killed in the Friedrichstrasse in Berlin on the night of 1/2 May; but this evidence is not conclusive … It seems certainly worthwhile to make an examination of this district.'[73] On 21 December Trevor-Roper travelled to Linz in Austria and the following day from there to St Florian, Molln and Salzburg. As he reported to Hoppe, 'I paid a visit to Austria and made some local investigations. I did not find any evidence that this particular area [the Steyr valley] was sheltering such people [as war criminals]; and I still believe … that Bormann was killed in the Friedrichstrasse … I made enquiries of your bailiff, Balthasar Schoettel; but his answers did not support the view that anyone was now in hiding in the neighbourhood.'[74]

Having drawn a blank in Austria, Trevor-Roper resumed the search for Zander. He needed Zander's evidence to break the deadlock between the testimonies of Lorenz and Johannmeier, and he also wanted to locate the missing copies of Hitler's wills in Zander's possession. The focus of his search was in the American Zone, and Trevor-Roper had the advantage of orders from American Intelligence enabling him to request help from CIC units. He later wrote that, 'This assistance was invaluable. Without the assistance of the CIC units at Munich, Deggendorf, and Tegernsee, the mission could not have been successfully completed.'[75]

On 1 January 1946, within days of its completion, Trevor-Roper wrote a revealing account of his search for Zander: 'On 24th December, 1945, I [Trevor-Roper] called at Frau Zander's flat in Munich … I spoke to Frau Buckwitz, who had taken over the flat. She merely repeated … that Zander was missing, having never returned from … Berlin. At this point, however, some further evidence came accidentally to hand from Mr. Rosener, [an American interrogator] … who had come across

Frau Zander personally while in Munich. From an unguarded observation by Frau Zander, Mr. Rosener had deduced that she knew her husband to be alive; and following up this evidence he had discovered (i) that more about Zander's history was known to two families, the Oesterreichers and the Greithers ... (ii) that Zander had arrived, under an assumed name, in the Seeheim hospital at Tegernsee (owned by the brothers Greither) in May or June and had been treated there for broken feet, having walked from Hanover. No action had been taken on this evidence, since no special significance had hitherto been attached to Zander.[76]

'On 26th December, 1945, I [Trevor-Roper] therefore interrogated the brothers, Hans and Otto Greither, at their home, 10 Schoenstrasse, Munich, and from them learnt the address of Frau Oesterreicher. Under persistent cross-examination at CIC Munich, Frau Oesterreicher admitted that Zander had been at the Oesterreichers' house in Tegernsee in June, and had been treated by Dr. Thelen, who treated many SS men and is now in prison for having removed identification marks of members of the SS ... the course of interrogation obliged Frau Oesterreicher to admit, inter alia, the name [Paustin] under which Zander had been admitted to the hospital at Tegernsee.' Trevor-Roper was much impressed by the American interrogation of Frau Oesterreicher, which he described as 'lengthy and clever'.[77]

On 27 December Trevor-Roper travelled on to the CIC office in Tegernsee, which identified Paustin's local address as Bahnhofstrasse 87: 'On the morning of 27th December, accompanied by an officer of CIC Tegernsee, I [Trevor-Roper] therefore entered the house Bahnhofstrasse 87 to arrest Paustin, but learnt that he was away for the period from Christmas to New Year, staying at Aidenbach, near Passau, with a friend Ilse Unterholzner (known to have been one of the secretaries of Martin Bormann). A search of Paustin's room and possessions in the house yielded nothing of interest.[78]

'On the afternoon of 27th December, accompanied by an officer of Munich CIC, I [Trevor-Roper] went to Deggendorf (being the CIC office nearest to Aidenbach), and thence, with representatives of CIC Deggendorf, to Aidenbach, arriving there at about 12.30 am on 28 December. After some local enquiries, the house in which Ilse Unterholzer was staying was identified, and at about 0230 on 28 December it was entered. Paustin, who was in bed, was arrested, and easily identified by his photographs [as Zander] ... Fraeulein Unterholzer, who refused to answer questions, was also arrested. The two prisoners were removed to Deggendorf, and, next morning, to CIC Munich.'[79]

'On the afternoon of 28th December, with the assistance of CIC Munich, I [Trevor-Roper] interrogated the prisoner [Zander] ... Throughout his interrogation, he made no false and no reluctant statements; and it was very soon clear that he was only inhibited from telling the whole truth by his determination to involve no other living person in his narrative ... He alone, he insisted, was to blame for everything. Thus, whenever Zander omitted anything from his account, it was apparent whom he was seeking to protect; and it was only necessary for his interrogator to show that that person was known, and could not be affected by Zander's revelation, for the even tide of his narrative to flow smoothly on again.'[80]

Zander admitted that he had been given copies of both Hitler's wills and two other documents, namely the Hitlers' marriage certificate and a note from Bormann to Doenitz. He told Trevor-Roper that he had concealed his documents in a trunk in Tegernsee, under the care of Ilse Unterholzer's sister-in-law. He promised to lead his interrogators to the documents, but this was not necessary. To avoid trouble the sister-in-law had voluntarily surrendered Zander's trunk to CIC Tegernsee. Inside were the expected documents including the marriage certificate.[81]

Sarah Douglas writes that 'Searle also obtained Hitler's marriage certificate, which, albeit a minor piece of the puzzle, verified that Hitler and Braun had indeed been married in the bunker less than two days before they committed suicide.' But Searle did not obtain Hitler's marriage certificate. Trevor-Roper had given decisive impetus to the surrender of this document, but the Americans naturally kept the original, even though Trevor-Roper asked them for it 'as a trophy of the chase'. Searle only got some copies through the post.[82]

Zander confirmed that Johannmeier had also been given a copy of Hitler's political testament. Meanwhile, Johannmeier had been interrogated on 27 December at Camp 032 by Sergeant S.J.B. Botes of 1 Corps, British Army of the Rhine. Johannmeier told Botes a story that neatly blended fact and fiction. After distinguished service on the Russian front, for which he had been decorated with the Oak Leaves to the Knight's Cross of the Iron Cross, in November 1944 Johannmeier had reported for duty with General Burgdorf, Hitler's Chief Wehrmacht Adjutant. Johannmeier claimed that 'as a non-political character, he [himself] was viewed with some reserve at the Chancellery'. On the morning of 29 April 1945 Burgdorf informed Johannmeier 'that he was to be entrusted with a special mission; namely to take out of Berlin two individuals, Lorenz and Zander. These two had documents of great importance.'[83]

Sergeant Botes noted that 'Johannmeier denies emphatically that he was given any documents to bring out of Berlin; he states further that he was not aware of the nature of the documents carried by his two companions; they did not refer to them in their conversation and Johannmeier did not ask. He observes also that, if he had been ordered to take the documents to any authority, he would certainly have done so. This observation is in keeping with his character.' Botes concluded that, 'Johannmeier is probably telling the truth. He has been shown photostats of the documents carried by Lorenz and therefore, if he is lying, it is difficult to see what his motive can be. It is doubted whether this subject was the type of person who would have been entrusted with documents of a political nature ... his gallantry alone gained him access to a political holy of holies where he was not held in much esteem.'[84] Johannmeier had fooled Botes, but Trevor-Roper was to prove more sceptical.

After his return to the British Zone, Trevor-Roper re-interrogated Johannmeier on 1 January 1946. Johannmeier had been ordered that on no account was he to let his documents fall into enemy hands, and those orders he intended to follow. According to a report on their encounter that Trevor-Roper finished two days later, once Johannmeier had decided upon his narrative 'he was too fearless to be deterred, and too proud to be cajoled, away from it. The appeal was therefore made to reason. Johannmeier was given all the evidence against him and persuaded that, on that evidence, it was quite impossible for us to accept his story.' For two hours the Wehrmacht veteran held firm. Then Trevor-Roper took a break from his interrogation. He explained years later that 'in interrogation pressure must [usually] be uninterrupted, but persuasion needs pauses, for only during a pause can a man reason with himself and catch up with the argument'. During the interval Johannmeier realized the futility of his silence. When the interrogation resumed, Johannmeier first sought assurance that he would not be punished and then finally confessed the truth: he had indeed been given documents. He led Trevor-Roper to a corner of his garden in Iserlohn and dug up a bottle containing, as his interrogator expected, Hitler's political testament and a covering note from General Burgdorf to Schoerner.[85]

The tracking down of Hitler's wills was a remarkable personal achievement by Trevor-Roper, during which he had interrogated Lorenz, Freytag von Loringhoven, Zander, the Greither brothers, and Johannmeier twice. In his subsidiary investigation concerning Bormann he had questioned Emil Hoppe and Balthasar Schoettl. Brigadier Haylor wrote that 'I would like to congratulate you … immediately on the successful conclusion of your Hitler enquiry. I do think that it was an excellent piece of work, for which nearly all the credit is due to you, but for which we are claiming all the undeserved credit that we can.'[86] Peter Ramsbotham wrote that 'everyone … is full of admiration for the speed and efficiency with which your investigations were concluded'. Ramsbotham sized up Trevor-Roper very well. In early 1947 he wrote from the Hamburg Intelligence Office to Trevor-Roper praising 'your dogged pertinacity, "debrouillard" [demystifying] instinct, and astonishing knack of accomplishing what you want'.[87]

There had been much discussion in Whitehall whether the wills found on Lorenz should be made public. Although the CIC had promised to wait before publishing Zander's documents, Lieutenant General L.K. Truscott Jr., Commander of the American Third Army in Bavaria, ordered their immediate publication. This caused a rumpus that threatened to involve Trevor-Roper. Haylor's superior, Major-General John Lethbridge, wrote on 7 January 1946 that, 'I should like to get the full story of the American disclosure regarding Hitler's Will as we shall be asked by J.I.C. (London) [the British Joint Intelligence Committee] to give it to them.'[88]

The Joint Intelligence Committee had a general supervisory role in matters relating to British Intelligence. As expected, a message promptly arrived at the Intelligence Bureau in the British Zone to the effect that the 'J.I.C. is not satisfied about two points in connection with discovery Hitler Will. First was British representative [Trevor-Roper] who assisted in discovery of copy in US Zone fully briefed on security aspect of release of them and if so why was he unable to prevent premature release of them by Third US Army. Second. Why was J.I.C. London not informed earlier (a) that one copy had been found in British Zone (b) that clues were being followed up in US Zone relative to another copy. Request early reply.' Lethbridge replied the following day with an effective defence of Trevor-Roper: 'First. British rep [Trevor-Roper] when at Third American Army arranged with them and USFET that matter should be and remain top secret. USFET issued instructions this sense. Story broke when

British rep had returned to USFET who were unable to explain why their instructions to Third U.S. Army had been disregarded. Second. JIC London was informed ... as soon as authenticity of first copy was reasonably established. Third. Suspected existence of second and third copies was reported in same letter ... Subsequent investigations were routine procedure.'[89]

Trevor-Roper and Interrogations by Colleagues

It was unfortunate that the Third Army publication had passed over the British role in the discovery of Zander's documents. Nevertheless, Trevor-Roper later wrote that 'I do not feel, and never did feel, any chagrin at not being personally mentioned or given any credit for the discovery. I was a serving officer at the time, and serving officers are normally anonymous. They do not expect anything else.'[90] In the aftermath of this Anglo–American misunderstanding for a time Trevor-Roper was *persona non grata* in the American Zone, so he was unable to interrogate directly some significant prisoners. Although Colonel Sands of American Counter-Intelligence in Frankfurt promised to put Trevor-Roper's questions to prisoners, Trevor-Roper recalled that this 'was not very satisfactory, as the interrogators did not have the necessary background to pursue such topics as might emerge during interrogation, or to detect possible errors or lies at the time'.[91] The advantage of carrying out interrogations personally was that he could observe the demeanour, facial expression and other physical reactions of the witness. Trevor-Roper's forced absence was a handicap in respect of various prisoners, in particular Artur Axmann, formerly Reich Youth Leader, captured by the Americans in December 1945.

On 14 January 1946 Lieutenant Leo Barton of the American Army interrogated Axmann according to a special brief from Trevor-Roper.[92] In his statement Axmann stressed Hitler's sense of abandonment by those he had trusted most of all, particularly Himmler. He told Barton that he was in the Fuehrer Bunker on 30 April and 'entered Hitler's room. Axmann states that he saw both bodies [of Hitler and Eva Braun] ... Both were carried to the garden exit of the Bunker. Axmann did not go upstairs. He only heard that the bodies were burnt in gasoline ... but he did not hear what happened to the ashes.'[93]

Trevor-Roper was not wholly convinced by Axmann's testimony about Hitler's remains. He wrote that 'Axmann said that he knew nothing about the fate of the ashes. On the other hand, I have second hand information [from Gertraud Junge, one of Hitler's secretaries] that the remains were put in a box which was delivered to Axmann … Either Axmann is telling the truth or he is lying. If he is telling the truth, no further information is of value. If he is lying, he will presumably lie again, and the truth will only be got from him, not by direct and open questioning, but indirectly as a result of skilful interrogation. I think this might be done in the following general way: Firstly, he should be asked to define exactly where his headquarters were before he left Berlin … no hint should be given to him as to the purpose for which the information is required. When the position of his command post has been established with sufficient certainty so that no subsequent evasion can conceal it, Axmann should be asked what he did with the box which was delivered to him on the evening of 30th April … His reactions to this question should be very carefully watched. In the course of interrogation on this subject, it should appear that in fact we know definitely rather more than we do.'[94] Trevor-Roper's thinking was that 'if Hitler's remains were to be preserved as a relic, the most natural trustees of such a relic would be the Hitler Youth … It is very unlikely that Axmann, or anyone else, could have escaped from Berlin carrying a (presumably) cumbrous box of relics, and the most natural thing for him to do would be to deposit it in some secret place in or near his command-post, which we know that he visited between the death of Hitler and the mass-escape [of bunker inmates].'[95] But it seems that Axmann was not pinned down in the way Trevor-Roper proposed.

Although Trevor-Roper suggested very specific questions for interrogators, he had recurrent problems with interviews carried out by others. Some interrogators simply lacked the concentration to work steadily through the questionnaires he provided; others jumped to the wrong conclusions. Even though Barton had elicited much evidence from Axmann, he had not carried out Trevor-Roper's brief fully. Even more problematic was the interrogation of Colonel Nicholas von Below, Luftwaffe adjutant with Hitler since 1937, who was arrested at Bad Godesberg on 7 January 1946. Trevor-Roper was asked for a questionnaire to put to Below and duly sent Peter Ramsbotham a brief.[96]

Below was interrogated by a sergeant at Camp 032 on 23 January. Although the resulting transcript filled nearly seventeen pages,[97] some of Trevor-Roper's questions were not answered. He found the extensive material from Below disappointing, and its interpretation by his interrogator little short of absurd. In his annoyance Trevor-Roper contacted Brigadier Haylor: 'Von Below was interrogated at Camp 032 on a brief sent by me. The 032 interrogators, quite naturally, do not know all the background; and in consequence committed themselves to some statements, and to an evaluation of the man's accuracy, which they were not really able to judge. Thus, in particular, they start straight off by saying that von Below is "up to the present the last living man to have left the Fuehrerbunker at Berlin, and to have seen Hitler alive"; whence they infer, and state, that he is the most reliable and accurate source at our disposal. This is nonsense. We, or the Americans, have four men (Karnau, Kempka, Lorenz and Mansfeld)[98] and two women (Krueger and von Varo), all of whom saw Hitler after von Below had left Berlin, and all of whom, together with others in our hands, left the Bunker later than Below. Further, on the internal evidence of Below's interrogation report, he is not very accurate; much less accurate, for instance, than either Krueger, Lorenz, or Zander. He is particularly inaccurate on dates ... Unfortunately, before the report on my brief could reach me, it, or a version of it including Camp 032's confident assertion of his accuracy, was issued to the Press. The Press quickly detected some inconsistencies of times and dates between this officially sponsored version and the previous official statement; and have tried to revive the whole mystery, on the grounds that obviously we don't know anything for certain.'

Trevor-Roper continued that 'I think you would agree that this is unfortunate, as in fact there is no difficulty in seeing where Below is wrong. In these circumstances may I ask that if (as seems likely) Frau Christian is brought in, no hand-out based on local interrogation is issued until it has been fully checked? If it is possible for me, and convenient for you, I should like to interrogate her myself.' Haylor replied that 'I agree that in view of the Press anxiety to revive the Hitler story it was unfortunate that this mistake [concerning a date] was made. If further information is obtained, we shall certainly be more careful in our checking, and if possible shall consult you. We should, of course, be very glad if Frau Christian is arrested, if you could come over and interrogate her.'[99]

Trevor-Roper found the testimony from Below incomplete and inadequate. So too were the answers he received from prisoners in US custody. On 3 July 1946 Trevor-Roper sent Dick White a questionnaire for the Americans to put to Gertraud Junge. Junge was an informative witness, and had much to say on the subject of Himmler's treachery.[100] But there were still loose ends after the interrogation, particularly the mistaken claim by Junge that the ashes of Adolf and Eva Hitler were collected in a box that was given to Axmann. In October 1946 Trevor-Roper wrote to Dick White that 'unfortunately, as you know, it takes three months to get a question answered by any prisoner in U.S. hands. At least that has been my experience in the cases of Frau Christian, Frau Junge, and [Guenther] Schwaegermann. And since Frau Junge is in Third Army and Axmann was at Frankfurt, there is probably no prospect of systematic interrogation.' For example, it would not be possible to confront Junge with Axmann. Trevor-Roper found that interrogations carried out by others were often unsatisfactory, whether the questioners were British or American. Although he had to draw on such interrogations, such reliance was by no means his method of choice.[101]

Trevor-Roper's enthusiasm for questioning witnesses himself was so great that when the Soviet Union freed its last German captives in 1955 and 1956, he travelled to Germany twice to question Baur, Rattenhuber and Harry Mengershausen. Mengershausen was a member of the Reich Security Service who had helped to bury Hitler. Trevor-Roper left Oxford for two days during term so he could question this last witness fifteen days after his release. He was jubilant about the results: 'I was entirely successful, getting from him everything that I wanted.'[102] By then *The Last Days of Hitler* had long been an international bestseller.

The Evidence for Trevor-Roper's Book

Even before his missions, Trevor-Roper had been planning a book on Hitler's regime, and he was encouraged to do so by Dick White.[103] Trevor-Roper began writing the book by hand at great speed well before he finished accumulating evidence. The initial text, which Trevor-Roper described as about 70,000 words long, was finished by 22 May 1946.[104] Douglas writes that 'Searle's timeline ... must have proved of immense help to Trevor-Roper as he drafted *Last Days*.'[105] But Trevor-Roper's writing was well under way by the time he received Searle's useful timetable, which was merely a drop in the ocean of evidence at his disposal.

What material did Trevor-Roper use for his book? How far, if at all, was *The Last Days* the result of a 'collective effort' by post-war interrogators as Douglas argues? Trevor-Roper certainly drew on his own interrogations during autumn 1945, in particular those with von Eicken, Grothmann, Bornholdt, Krueger, Karnau, and Kempka. During the period of writing Trevor-Roper continued to interrogate witnesses.

To clarify the dates of Himmler's attendance on Hitler in April 1945, Trevor-Roper had been advised by Speer to question Dr Hans Gebhardt, head of Hitler's medical staff.[106] Trevor-Roper finally interrogated Gebhardt on 27 March 1946. But he came too late. When Trevor-Roper asked him about dates, Gebhardt explained that, 'I can no longer remember precisely the exact date, it is too long ago and the days were full of developments, I can no longer remember these details, my overriding concern was to care for the wounded.' Gebhardt tried to put a benevolent gloss on his own activities, relating how Goebbels would not allow the evacuation of his six small children from Berlin, preferring to murder them instead. Gebhardt's concern for saving children contrasted sharply with his previous record of horrific experimentation on Polish female prisoners, subsequent to which he was appointed President of the German Red Cross.[107]

For his book Trevor-Roper did rely heavily on another interrogator's questioning of Speer. In *The Last Days* Trevor-Roper highlighted 'the indispensable Speer' amongst 'many other sources of evidence,' and frequently quoted him.[108] Most of this material came from interviews with Speer during June and July 1945 carried out by Otto Hoeffding, who worked for the Economic and Financial Branch of the American Field Information Agency. Hoeffding gathered Speer's material in reports that covered such subjects as 'Politicians and Politics in Nazi Germany' and 'Nazi Foreign Policy and Military Leadership'. Trevor-Roper deployed five quotations from 'Politicians and Politics in Nazi Germany' in *The Last Days*. These include Speer's characterisation of the struggle within the Nazi elite as a 'War of the Diadochi' and his assessment of Goebbels' propaganda as 'Latin'.[109] Trevor-Roper marked on his own copy of Speer's 'Nazi Foreign Policy and Military Leadership' the section dealing with the Nazi Foreign Minister, Joachim von Ribbentrop, and cited in his book Hitler's ludicrous characterization of Ribbentrop as 'a second Bismarck'.[110]

Speer also wrote a fourteen-page account of Adolf Hitler. Again Trevor-Roper marked his own copy of this document and drew on it for his book, for example in describing Hitler's habit of making appointments by intuition. Trevor-Roper also quoted on ten occasions from Speer's Hitler document in *The Last Days,* including such memorable phrases as 'A few critical words from Hitler, and all Bormann's enemies would have jumped at his throat', 'For all writers of history, Eva Braun is going to be a disappointment', and that 'I [Speer] noticed during my activities as architect that being in his presence for any length of time made me tired, exhausted and void. Capacity for independent work was paralysed.'[111]

The prominence of Speer's testimony owed something to artifice. For security reasons Trevor-Roper attributed to Speer conclusions he had originally drawn from secret material. Trevor-Roper wrote in the introduction to the second edition: 'I have relied primarily on the great mass of evidence which became increasingly available to us during the war, and only secondarily on Speer.' Yet it seemed imprudent 'to quote unverifiable secret reports and numerous obscure sources when the same conclusion was lucidly and cogently expressed by Speer'.[112]

The majority of evidence in *The Last Days of Hitler* did not come from interrogations, whether by Trevor-Roper or his British and American colleagues. During his six years in British Intelligence Trevor-Roper had worked through many thousands of secret documents on Nazi Germany. For his book he redeployed some material that he had written during his work as an intelligence officer. During the second half of 1945 he had composed a paper on 'The German Intelligence Service and the War', pointing to the lack of centralisation in German intelligence as 'one aspect of a phenomenon which was of much wider relevance in Nazi Germany. For although in theory the structure of the administration was "pyramidal" and centralised, in fact the apex of the pyramid, or the centre of the circle, was not a unitary structure at all but a vortex of competing personal ambitions.' This text and the following sentence appeared in a vigorous paraphrase on page two of *The Last Days of Hitler.*[113]

Trevor-Roper also incorporated eavesdropping material into *The Last Days*. According to Soenke Neitzel, the British had perfected this surreptitious art. British Intelligence systematically recorded the conversations between captured German generals, who chattered away even though they had been warned about the possibility of eavesdropping.[114] Trevor-Roper was particularly interested in the overheard talk of *SS Obergruppenfuehrer* Gottlob Berger, former chief of the SS Head Office. Berger's conversation circulated by CSDIC on 5 June 1945 had included verbatim accounts of dramatic interviews with Himmler and Hitler six weeks earlier.[115] Trevor-Roper needed to question Berger himself to assess the value of this material.

Nearly ten months after the CSDIC report, on 26 March 1946 Trevor-Roper finally interrogated Berger at Nuremberg for ninety minutes.[116] Afterwards Trevor-Roper was still unsure about the value of the SS General's testimony, and inserted in *The Last Days* a caveat that Berger's 'accounts of his conversations with Himmler and Hitler, which rest on his testimony alone, are given with some reservations'. Trevor-Roper included in the book some of Berger's material, in particular Hitler's bitter reproaches, but omitted the SS General's improbable reproof to Himmler: 'What sort of a *Reichsfuehrer* are you?'[117]

In preparing his manuscript Trevor-Roper drew on another CSDIC report of conversation by Otto Ohlendorf, former head of department three of the Reich Security Head Office, who bore responsibility for the murder of 90,000 Jews while commander of Task Force D in Russia.[118] During his monitored talk, Ohlendorf had described *SS Gruppenfuehrer* Hermann Fegelein, Himmler's liaison officer with Hitler, as 'a thoroughly disreputable fellow … By his marriage to Eva Braun's sister he won himself a position entirely independent of Himmler. It made him a member of the family circle.'[119]

In his book Trevor-Roper used the phrase 'family circle' in describing Fegelein's position and also drew on Ohlendorf for his graphic writing about Himmler in Flensburg. Trevor-Roper sought to follow up the CSDIC report for himself. In early April 1946 he submitted questions for Ohlendorf that explored whether there had been an SS plot to murder Hitler.[120] Once again Trevor-Roper's submission was so extensive and specific that it did not require much input on the part of the interrogator, but it seems the questions were never put to Ohlendorf. Although the manuscript shows some later improvements to the expression of the passages based on Ohlendorf's testimony, there are no changes of substance.[121]

For his book Trevor-Roper also made extensive use of German manuscripts, particularly the diary by Hitler's valet he had used in the initial enquiry.[122] Trevor-Roper also cited Schwerin von Krosigk's diary on numerous occasions, and drew on it heavily for the final ten pages of his chapter on 'The Court in Defeat'. Furthermore, Trevor-Roper made considerable use of what he called the 'long, complacent, insensitive account ... of his endless manoeuvres' by Schellenberg. Himmler's spy-master had spent June 1945 in Stockholm and there composed his 'autobiography', a document of just over thirty-four substantial pages that he described as 'chronological jottings from memory'. Schellenberg's account mostly focused on the final stages of the Third Reich. A comparison of the marking on Trevor-Roper's own copy of the autobiography with his book shows that he could not resist improving the wording of his quotations from Schellenberg. For example, 'it was a fight, in which I fought like a Devil fighting for a soul' became 'I struggled with him [Himmler], like a devil struggling for a soul'.[123] Trevor-Roper regarded Schellenberg and Krosigk with contempt, writing that 'the two form a perfect pair, the Tweedledum and Tweedledee of pretentious German silliness'.[124]

By contrast, Trevor-Roper saw the Luftwaffe Chief of Staff, General Karl Koller, as a sober and realistic figure who had kept a particularly informative chronicle. Trevor-Roper later wrote that 'Koller's diary, covering the period 16th April to 9th May 1945, is a detailed record of great value.'[125] General Koller had formed the habit of writing down in shorthand all telephone conversations, other discussions and verbal orders. He found this useful when Hitler later disputed a verbal order that he had simply forgotten or if he claimed it meant something different to his obvious original intention.[126] When Koller was in British custody during 1945, he read out his shorthand notes to be typed in full and translated.[127]

In his book Trevor-Roper made extensive use of Koller's diary, which provided significant evidence for Chapter Five, 'The Siege of the Bunker'. General Koller's pedestrian character made him the perfect foil in the narrative for the hectic fanaticism of Hanna Reitsch, the Luftwaffe test pilot who accompanied Ritter von Greim, Goering's successor as commander-in-chief of the Luftwaffe. Yet Trevor-Roper did not quote the strangest passage in Koller's account, namely a complaint by Reitsch and Greim that they had not been allowed to commit suicide: Trevor-Roper marked the relevant text but merely alluded to it in his book.[128]

In addition to diaries, Trevor-Roper cited extensively single documents of particular importance, such as a letter from Speer to Hitler on 18 March 1945 used as evidence at Nuremberg, and a vivid account of Goebbels by one of his secretaries.[129] The most significant individual documents at Trevor-Roper's disposal were Hitler's political and personal wills and Goebbels' testament. Trevor-Roper filled the best part of five pages with extensive quotations from Hitler's wills and reproduced Goebbels' document in full.[130]

Trevor-Roper also made substantial use of published sources for his book. He quoted Sir Neville Henderson, Britain's ambassador to Germany before the war, and much more extensively from Hermann Rauschning's controversial book *Hitler Speaks*.[131] Trevor-Roper repeatedly cited *Mein Kampf* and contrasted Hitler's actions during the war with the positions he took up in *Mein Kampf*. Trevor-Roper also drew on *The Fall of the Curtain*, an account by the Swedish Count Folke Bernadotte of his negotiations with Himmler in 1945 to liberate Scandinavian prisoners from concentration camps.[132] In describing Hanna Reitsch's intrepid flight to Berlin in late April Trevor-Roper drew 'with caution' on her account published by the *News Chronicle* in three instalments on 28, 29 and 31 December 1945.[133]

So in writing *The Last Days*, Trevor-Roper drew not only on the transcripts of interrogations carried out by himself and others, important though these were, but also, and more extensively, on a considerable array of pre-war books, wartime intelligence documents, eavesdropping material, diaries, memoirs, post-war publications, and documents originating from Hitler or the Doenitz government. Under these circumstances the description of his book as due to a 'collective effort' by himself and other interrogators is unconvincing. Such a characterisation also underestimates Trevor-Roper's intellectual and literary contribution as a professional historian. *The Last Days of Hitler* was far more than the sum of its evidence. Trevor-Roper brought to his book a unique combination of writing skill and historical understanding. Has the conundrum of Hitler's end ever been more tellingly evoked than in the following lines?: 'Besieged in the shattered capital, cooped up fifty feet below the ground, cut off from ordinary communication, a physical and mental wreck, without power to enforce, or reason to persuade, or machinery to execute, Hitler still remained, in the universal chaos he had caused, the sole master whose orders were implicitly obeyed.'[134]

Changes to Trevor-Roper's Text in Later Editions

Just as Sarah Douglas' characterisation of *The Last Days of Hitler* as the result of a 'collective effort' fails to convince, so too her view of its publishing history is open to question. Douglas asserts that 'the actual text of the book remains the same through every edition.'[135] But the text did not remain the same, as the following alterations, by no means a complete list, demonstrate. Trevor-Roper even made some changes to the American first edition, which was published in the same year as the British.[136] For the American edition he amended the characterisation of Wilhelm Canaris, Chief of the Abwehr. In the British edition Trevor-Roper wrote of the Abwehr that 'Under the incompetent rule of Admiral Canaris, a shady political intriguer who had filled its highly-paid offices with his inefficient naval friends, for the first two years of the war it had been borne along, a happy parasite.' For the American edition Trevor-Roper wrote that 'under the negligent rule of Admiral Canaris, an enigmatical figure, more interested in anti-nazi intrigue than in his official duties, for the first two years' etc.[137] For the American edition Trevor-Roper also revised his account of Canaris' death.[138] Trevor-Roper included his revised characterisation of Canaris in the British second edition.[139]

Trevor-Roper had to make various changes for the British second edition to avert legal proceedings from Hanna Reitsch. Her stridency had drawn Trevor-Roper's particular fire. He replaced four scathing paragraphs assessing Reitsch with a single more restrained paragraph which can also be found in subsequent editions.[140] Furthermore, for the second edition Trevor-Roper had to abandon a parallel he had drawn between Goebbels and the Jesuits, in which he described Goebbels as 'the prize pupil of a Jesuit seminary'.[141]

Trevor-Roper's Acknowledgments

Trevor-Roper had written to White on 12 March 1946 asking him to read the draft book. On 18 March White replied enthusiastically 'please send me the m.s. [manuscript] as soon as possible. I am all eagerness.' White also pressed on with obtaining official approval for publication, which was successfully achieved.[142] If Trevor-Roper was so busy claiming for his own credit due to others such as Ramsbotham and White, why did they praise him so highly and seek to help him whenever they could? During the Cold War, British former and serving intelligence officers did not usually identify themselves publicly nor were their secret roles mentioned by friends. Acknowledgement in Trevor-Roper's book would have done no favours to the later diplomat Peter Ramsbotham. Indeed, a blatant link with military intelligence might have drawn unwelcome scrutiny during his overseas postings. During the war Ramsbotham had served in MI5, the Intelligence Corps, and as a counter-intelligence officer in France before his work in Germany. For many decades he deliberately kept his intelligence connections secret. Indeed, the Foreign Office List described his service with no mention of the word intelligence, though this left a puzzling gap: 'Served in H.M. Forces from 1940 to 1945. Temporarily employed in the Control Office for Germany and Austria from 1947.' Nor did Ramsbotham's *Who's Who* entry for 1973 mention intelligence, a prudent omission as that year he became Ambassador to America for a period of service during which intelligence became a dirty word in Washington. By the end of his life Ramsbotham conceded that he had served in the Intelligence Corps.[143]

Professor Parker writes that Trevor-Roper mentioned Dick White by name in the preface to the first edition, but that 'even that acknowledgement disappeared in subsequent editions'.[144] No, Dick White was also mentioned in the preface to the second edition of 1950; but by the publication of third edition in 1956 he was head of a British secret department and would scarcely have wanted a mention at the front of Trevor-Roper's best-seller. So Trevor-Roper excised Dick White from the third edition of *The Last Days*. Instead he inserted detailed acknowledgments to a long list of academics and other intellectual figures who had helped in the preparation of the new edition.[145] As these people were not intelligence officers, Trevor-Roper could make generous acknowledgement. After Dick White's death in 1993, Trevor-Roper could finally restore him to the preface of the seventh edition: 'Sir Dick White persuaded me to write this book, which was first published in March 1947. I then dedicated it to him. I now dedicate it to his memory, as its only begetter, and my constant friend.'[146]

In 1945 Dick White entrusted a specific mission to one person, Trevor-Roper, who had to carry it out, write the report, and take responsibility for the findings. For the colleagues who helped, the enquiry into Hitler's fate was usually one task among many. But it was Trevor-Roper's primary and overriding concern. Had the investigation misfired, Trevor-Roper would have taken the blame. So the prestige he won was thoroughly deserved. It tells us much that two of Trevor-Roper's closest colleagues, Dick White and Peter Ramsbotham, realized the unique quality of his achievement and never begrudged his success.

* I am very grateful to Professor Blair Worden, Literary Executor of Hugh Trevor-Roper, Baron Dacre of Glanton, for his kind permission to quote from the Dacre Papers in Christ Church Oxford and much other generous assistance. Judith Curthoys, archivist of Christ Church, was also exceptionally helpful. I would also like to thank the late Eilis de Burca, the late Jeremy Catto, Richard Davenport-Hines, Miriam Gross, S.J.V. Malloch, the late A.J. Nicholls, P.G.J. Pulzer, Adam Sisman and Gina Thomas.

Bibliography

Unpublished Sources

Abteiarchiv Muensterschwarzach (AaM):
A 910 & 950
IX D4, 5, 11, 12 & 15

Bayerisches Hauptstaatsarchiv (BHSA):
Reichsstatthalter 619, 620, 626 & 647

Berlin Document Centre (BDC):
Hauptarchiv B-323
Party File Dr Otto Helmuth
Party and SS Files Dr Oskar Dengel
Party and SS Files Raimund Rueth
SA File Helldorf
SA-P Helldorf
SS File Fritz Glitz

British Library (BL):
Macmillan Archive Letter Book 490/420, 491/95 & 415, 492/273,
493/119, 494/339, 497/606, 526/501

Bundesarchiv Koblenz (BAK):
NS 6/336, 19/282, 1227 & 26/1350
059/000150
R22/3355
R43 II/1271a
Sammlung Schumacher 243 II/2

Bundesarchiv Potsdam (BAP):
RKM 23318

Christ Church Oxford:
SOC.Dacre 6/34; 9/13; 10/2, 4, 5, 7, 9, 12, 13, 16, 14, 17, 18, 20, 22, 28, 29, 30 & 31; 13/29, 58

Institut fuer Zeitgeschichte, Archiv (AdIfZ):
Fa 156, 172, 292
ED 82
MA 261 & 1560
ZS 539

Landesarchiv Berlin (LAB):
20/7249 & 58/20

Landesarchiv Speyer:
Gestapo Neustadt B2303

The National Archives (TNA), Kew, United Kingdom:
CAB 118/56
DEFE 1/134
FO 371/46748 & 46778; 938/196; 1005/1706; 1093/8, 10 & 11
HO 144/22492
HS 6/623 & 624
INF 1/292 & 857
KV 4/100, 217 & 354
PREM 3/219/5 & 7
WO 199/3288A, 208/3779, 3787, 3790, 4475 & 4701

NSDAP Hauptarchiv [Microfilm] Reel 16A Folder 1634

Staatsarchiv Wuerzburg (SAW):
NSDAP Gau Mainfranken 16
Gestapo Wuerzburg 299, 3693, 5556, 5761, 6677, 6739, 6753, 7995, 12136, 12421, 12877, 15770, 16273 & 16309
Wiener Library London, (WLL):
PIIIa & PIIIf

BIBLIOGRAPHY

Published Sources

Abshagen, Karl Heinz, *Canaris* (London: Hutchinson & Co. 1956). Translated by Alan Houghton Brodrick.

Adam, Uwe Dietrich, 'Wie spontan war der Pogrom?' in Pehle, Walter H., *Der Judenpogrom 1938. Von der 'Reichskristallnacht' zum Voelkermord* (Frankfurt am Main: Fischer, 1988).

Adolph, Walter, *Geheime Aufzeichnungen aus dem nationalsozialistischen Kirchenkampf* (Mainz: Mathias Gruenewald, 1987).

Akten zur Deutschen Auswaertigen Politik 1918–1945 Serie E: 1941–1945 8 vols (Goettingen: Vandenhoeck & Ruprecht, 1969–79).

Baranowski, Shelley, *The Sanctity of Rural Life. Nobility, Protestantism and Nazism in Weimar Prussia* (Oxford University Press, 1995).

Baynes, Norman H., *A Short List of Books on National Socialism* Historical Association Pamphlet 125 (London, 1943).

Benz, Wolfgang and Walter H. Pehle, *Lexikon des deutschen Widerstandes* (Frankfurt am Main: SF, 1994).

Bernadotte, Count Folke, *The Fall of the Curtain. Last Days of the Third Reich* (London: Cassell, 1945).

Beevor, Antony, *Berlin. The Downfall* (London: Penguin, 2003).

Bethge, Eberhard, *Dietrich Bonhoeffer. Theologian, Christian, Contemporary* (London: Fount, 1977).

Boberach, Heinz (ed), *Berichte des SD und der Gestapo ueber Kirchen und Kirchenvolk in Deutschland, 1934–1944* (Mainz: Mathias Gruenewald, 1971).

Boeselager, Philipp von with Florence and Jerome Fehrenbach, *Valkyrie. The Plot to Kill Hitler* (London: Phoenix, 2009).

Boldt, Gerhard, *In the Shelter with Hitler* edited by Ernst A. Hepp (London: The Citadel Press, 1948).

Borovik, Genrikh, *The Philby Files. The Secret Life of the Master Spy – KGB Archives Revealed* (London: Little Brown, 1994).

Botz, Gerhard, *Wien vom 'Anschluss' zum Krieg. Nationalsozialistische Machtuebernahme und politisch-soziale Umgestaltung am Beispiel der Stadt Wien, 1938/39* (Vienna: Jugend und Volk, 1980).

Bower, Tom, *The Perfect English Spy. Sir Dick White and the Secret War 1935–90* (London: Heinemann, 1995).

171

Bracher, Karl Dietrich, *Die Aufloesung der Weimarer Republic. Eine Studie zum Problem des Machtverfalls in der Demokratie* (Koenigstein: ADT, 1978).

Bracher, Karl Dietrich et al., *Deutschland Zwischen Krieg und Frieden. Beitraege zur Politik und Kultur im 20. Jahrhundert. Festchrift fuer Hans-Adolf Jacobsen* (Duesseldorf: Droste, 1991).

Brodrick S.J., J., 'Jesuits and Nazis', *The Tablet*, 21 June 1947.

Broszat, Martin, *Nationalsozialistische Polenpolitik, 1939–1945* (Stuttgart: Deutsche Verlags-Anstalt, 1961).

Broszat, Martin, *Der Staat Hitlers* (Munich: Deutscher Taschenbuch Verlag, 1969).

Broszat, Martin, *Hitler and the Collapse of the Weimar Republic* (Leamington Spa: Berg, 1987).

Bruening, Heinrich, *Memoiren 1918–34* (Stuttgart: Deutsche Verlags-Anstalt, 1970).

Hans Buchheim, 'The SS – Instrument of Domination', in Helmut Krausnick, Hans Buchheim, Martin Broszat and Hans-Adolf Jacobsen, *The Anatomy of the SS State* (London: Collins, 1968).

Bullock, Alan, *Hitler. A Study in Tyranny* (London: Odhams, 1952).

Butler, J.R.M. (ed), *Grand Strategy* (6 vols, London: HMSO, 1956–76).

Butler, Rohan and J.P.T. Bury (eds) Documents on British Foreign Policy 1919–1939 first series [*DBFPFS*] vol. xi (London: HMSO, 1961).

Canaris, Wilhelm, 'Politik und Wehrmacht' in Richard Donnevert (ed), *Wehrmacht und Partei* (Leipzig: Johann Ambrosius Barth, 1938).

Charisius, Albrecht and Julius Mader, *Nicht laenger geheim. Entwicklung, System und Arbeitsweise des imperialistischen deutschen Geheimdienstes* (Berlin: Militaerverlag, 1978).

Colville, John, *The Fringes of Power. Downing Street Diaries 1939–1955* (London: Hodder and Stoughton, 1985).

Conway, J.S., *The Nazi Persecution of the Churches* (London: Weidenfeld and Nicolson, 1968).

Curthoys, Judith, *The Cardinal's College: Christ Church, Chapter and Verse* (London: Profile Books, 2012).

Davies, Norman, *Uprising '44. 'The Battle for Warsaw'* (London: Macmillan, 2003).

De Gaulle, Charles, *The Complete War Memoirs of Charles de Gaulle* (New York: Simon & Schuster, 1972).

Deakin, F.W., *The Brutal Friendship. Mussolini, Hitler and the Fall of Italian Fascism* (London: Weidenfeld and Nicolson, 1962).

BIBLIOGRAPHY

Dear, I.C.B. (ed), *The Oxford Companion to the Second World War* (Oxford University Press, 1995).

Degener, Herrmann A.L. (ed), *Degeners Wer ist's* (Berlin: Herrmann Degener, 1935).

Delmer, Sefton, *Trail Sinister. An Autobiography* vol. 1 (London: Secker & Warburg, 1961).

Deutsch, Harold C., *The Conspiracy against Hitler in the Twilight War* (Minneapolis: The University of Minnesota Press, 1968).

Devrient, Ernst, *Das Geschlecht von Helldorff* vol. 1 *Familiengeschichte* (Berlin: Herrmann Degener, 1931).

Dilks, David (ed), *The Diaries of Sir Alexander Cadogan 1939–1945* (London: Cassell, 1971).

Dodd Jr., William E. and Martha Dodd, *Ambassador Dodd's Diary* (London: Victor Gollancz, 1941).

Douglas-Hamilton, James, *Motive For A Mission. The Story Behind Hess's Flight to Britain* (London: Macmillan, 1971).

Duering, Jonathan (Pater Jonathan OSB), *'Unsere Heimat kann man uns nicht rauben'. Die Antwort der Moenche von Muensterschwarzach auf die Verfolgungsmasshnahmen und die Aufhebung ihrer Abtei durch die Nationalsozialisten im Jahre 1941* Diploma diss., Institut fuer fraenkische Kirchengeschichte, Julius-Maximilians Universitaet (Wuerzburg 1986)

Eberle, Henrik and Mathias Uhl (eds), *The Hitler Book. The Secret Dossier Prepared for Stalin* (London: John Murray, 2005).

Eden, Anthony, *The Eden Memoirs. The Reckoning* (London: Cassell, 1965).

Evans, Richard J., *The Third Reich at War 1939–1945* (London: Allen Lane, 2008).

Fest, Joachim, *Inside Hitler's Bunker. The Last Days of the Third Reich* (London: Pan, 2005).

The Foreign Office List and Diplomatic and Consular Year Book 1951 (London: Harrison and Sons).

Francois-Poncet, André, *Souvenirs d'une Ambassade à Berlin* (Paris: Flammarion, 1946).

Franz-Willing, Georg, *Putsch und Verbotszeit der Hitlerbewegung November 1923-Februar 1925* (Preussisch Oldendorf: K.W. Schuetz, 1977).

Freytag von Loringhoven, Bernd with Francois d'Alancon, *In the Bunker with Hitler 23 July 1944 – 29 April 1945* (London: Weidenfeld & Nicolson, 2006).

Frieser, Karl-Heinz, *Blitzkrieglegende. Der Westfeldzug 1940* (Munich: R. Oldenbourg 1996)

Froehlich, Elke (ed), *Die Tagebuecher von Joseph Goebbels. Saemtliche Fragmente* Part 1 *Aufzeichnungen 1924–1941* vol. 4 (Munich: K.G. Saur, 1987).

Garnett, David, *The Secret History of PWE. The Political Warfare Executive 1939–1945* with an introduction and notes by Andrew Roberts (London: St Ermin's Press, 2002).

Gauger, Hildegard, *Die Psychologie des Schweigens in England* (Heidelberg: Carl Winters Universitaetsbuchhandlung, 1937).

Gellately, Robert, *The Gestapo and German Society. Enforcing Racial Policy, 1933–1945* (Oxford: Clarendon Press, 1990).

Gerwarth, Robert, *Hitler's Hangman. The Life of Heydrich* (New Haven, Yale University Press, 2012).

Geyer, Michael, 'National Socialist Germany: The Politics of Information' in May, Ernest R. (ed), *Knowing One's Enemies. Intelligence Assessment before the two World Wars* (Princeton University Press, 1986).

Gilbert, Martin, *Winston S. Churchill* vol. VII *Road to Victory, 1941–1945* (London: Heinemann, 1986).

Gisevius, Hans-Bernd, *To the Bitter End* (London: Jonathan Cape, 1948).

Goerlitz, Walter (ed), *Generalfeldmarschall Keitel. Verbrecher oder Offizier? Erinnerungen, Briefe, Dokkumente des Chefs OKW* (Goettingen, 1961).

Goldhammer, *Katholische Jugend Frankens im Dritten Reich* (Frankfurt am Main, 1986).

Gordon, Harold J., *Hitler and the Beer Hall Putsch* (Princeton University Press, 1972).

Gorodetsky, Gabriel, *Stafford Cripps' Mission to Moscow 1940–42* (Cambridge University Press, 1984).

Gorodetsky, Gabriel, 'The Hess Affair and Anglo-Soviet Relations on the eve of "Barbarossa"', *The English Historical Review* vol. ci no. 399 (April 1986).

Graml, Hermann and Klaus-Dietmar Henke (eds), *Nach Hitler. Der schwierige Umgang mit unserer Geschichte. Beitraege von Martin Broszat* (Munich: Oldenbourg 1987)

Granier, Gerhard, *Magnus von Levetzow. Seeoffizier, Monarchist und Wegbereiter Hitlers. Lebensweg und ausgewaehlte Dokumente* (Boppard am Rhein: Harald Boldt, 1982).

BIBLIOGRAPHY

Groner, Franz (ed), *Kirchliches Handbuch. Amtliches statistisches Jahrbuch der katholischen Kirche Deutschlands* vol. xxiii *1944–51* (Cologne: J.P. Bachem, 1951).

Groscurth, Helmuth, *Tagebücher eines Abwehroffiziers 1938–1940 Mit weiteren Dokumenten zur Militäropposition gegen Hitler* edited by Helmut Krausnick and Harold C. Deutsch with Hildegard von Kotze (Stuttgart: Deutsche Verlags-Anstalt, 1970).

Gruchmann, Lothar, *Justiz im Dritten Reich 1933–1940. Anpassung und Unterwerfung in der Aera Guertner* (Munich: Oldenbourg, 1988).

Gruchmann, Lothar, 'Korruption im Dritten Reich. Zur "Lebensmittelversorgung" der NS-Fuehrerschaft', *Vierteljahrshefte fuer Zeitgeschichte* 42 (1994).

Grunberger, Richard, *A Social History of the Third Reich* (London: Penguin, 1991).

Haenel, Wolfgang, *Hermann Rauschnings 'Gespraeche mit Hitler' - Eine Geschichtsfaelschung* (Veroeffentlichung der zeitgeschichtlichen Forschungsstelle Ingolstadt vol. 7, 1984).

Harris, J.P. and F.H. Toase (eds), *Armoured Warfare* (London: BT Batsford, 1990).

Harrison, Edward, *The Young Kim Philby. Soviet Spy and British Intelligence Officer* (Exeter University Press, 2012).

Harrison, Edward, *Secret Service* (Barnsley: Pen & Sword, 2022).

Harrison, E.D.R., 'The Nazi Dissolution of the Monasteries: A Case-Study', *The English Historical Review* vol. cix no. 431 (April 1994).

Harrison E.D.R., '"Alte Kaempfer" im Widerstand. Graf Helldorff, die NS-Bewegung und die Opposition gegen Hitler', *Vierteljahrshefte fuer Zeitgeschichte* 45/3 (July 1997).

Harrison, E.D.R., 'Something Beautiful for 'C': Malcolm Muggeridge in Lourenco Marques' in K.G. Robertson, *War, Resistance and Intelligence. Essays in Honour of M.R.D. Foot* (Barnsley: Pen & Sword, 1999).

Harrison, E.D.R., 'British Subversion in French East Africa, 1941–42: SOE's Todd Mission', *English Historical Review* vol. cxiv no. 456 (April 1999).

Harrison, E.D.R., '"wir wurden schon viel zu oft hereingelegt" Mai 1941: Rudolf Hess in englischer Sicht' in Kurt Paetzold and Manfred Weissbecker, *Rudolf Hess. Der Mann an Hitlers Seite* (Leipzig: Militzke Verlag, 1999).

Harrison, E.D.R., 'Kim Philby: The End of a Myth' in Alistair Horne (ed), *Telling Lives. From W.B. Yeats to Bruce Chatwin* (London: Macmillan, 2000).

Harrison, E.D.R., 'The British special operations executive and Poland', *The Historical Journal* 43/4 (Dec. 2000).

Harrison, E.D.R., '*The Last Days of Hitler* revisited', *The Spectator* 303/9318 (17 March 2007).

Harrison, E.D.R., 'On Secret Service for the Duce: Umberto Campini in Portuguese East Africa', *English Historical Review* vol. cxxii no. 499 (Dec. 2007).

Harrison, E.D.R., 'Hugh Trevor-Roper und *Hitlers letzte Tage*', *Vierteljahrshefte fuer Zeitgeschichte* 57/1 (Jan. 2009).

Harrison, E.D.R., 'British Radio Security and Intelligence 1939–43', *English Historical Review* vol. cxxiv no. 506 (Feb. 2009).

Harrison, E.D.R., 'J.C. Masterman and the Security Service, 1940–72', *Intelligence and National Security* 24/6 (Dec. 2009).

Harrison, E.D.R., 'Carton de Wiart's Second Military Mission to Poland and the German Invasion of 1939', *European History Quarterly* 41/4 (Oct. 2011).

Harrison, E.D.R., '"An Absolute Non-Ducker": Carton de Wiart in the Great War', *Journal of the Society for Army Historical Research* vol. 91 no. 366 (Summer 2013)

Harrison, E.D.R., 'Spurensuche: Hugh Trevor-Ropers Sondermissionen 1945/46 und seine Quellen fuer "Hitlers Letzte Tage"', *Vierteljahrshefte fuer Zeitgeschichte* 65/4 (Oct. 2017).

Hassell, Ulrich von, *Vom Andern Deutschland* (Atlantis Verlag, Zuerich, 1946).

Hassell, Ulrich von, *Die Hassell-Tagebuecher 1938–1944 Aufzeichnungen vom anderen Deutschland. Nach der Handschrift revidierte und erweiterte Ausgabe* edited by Friedrich Freiherr Hiller von Gaertringen (Berlin: Siedler Verlag, 1988).

Hastings, Max, *The Secret War. Spies, Codes and Guerillas* (London: William Collins 2017).

Hauner, Milan, *India in Axis Strategy. Germany, Japan and Indian Nationalists in the Second World War* (Stuttgart: Klett Cotta, 1981).

Hehl, Ulrich von, *Katholische Kirche und Nationalsozialismus im Erzbistum Koeln, 1933–1945* (Mainz: Mathias Gruenewald, 1977).

Heiden, Konrad, *Der Fuehrer. Hitler's Rise to Power* (New York, 1944).

Heinemann, Ulrich, *Ein Konservativer Rebell. Fritz-Dietlof von der Schulenburg und der 20. Juli* (Berlin, 1990).

BIBLIOGRAPHY

Heinemann, Ulrich, '"Kein Platz fuer Juden und Polen." Der Widerstandskaempfer Fritz-Dietlof Graf von der Schulenburg und die Politik der Verwaltung in Schlesien 1939/40' in Christoph Klessmann (ed), *September 1939. Krieg,Besatzung,Widerstand in Polen. Acht Beitraege* (Goettingen: Vandenhoeck & Ruprecht, 1989).

Heinemann, Winfried, 'Der militaerische Widerstand und der Krieg' in Militaergeschichtliches Forschungsamt, *Das Deutsche Reich und der Zweite Weltkrieg* vol. 9 part 1 (Munich: Deutsche Verlags-Anstalt, 2004).

Hess, Father Sales OSB, *KZ-Dachau. Eine Welt ohne Gott* (Muensterschwarzach: Turm, 1985).

Hitler, Adolf, *Mein Kampf* (Munich: Franz Eher Nachfolger, 1933).

Hitler's Table Talk 1941–1944 (London: Weidenfeld and Nicolson, 1953).

Hoehne, Heinz, *Canaris. Patriot im Zwielicht* (Munich: C. Bertelsmann, 1976).

Hoehne, Heinz & Hermann Zolling, *Network. The Truth about General Gehlen and his Spy Ring*. Translated from the German by Richard Barry. Introduction by H.R. Trevor-Roper (London: Secker & Warburg, 1972).

Hoellen, Martin, *Heinrich Wienken: Der 'unpolitische' Kirchenpolitiker. Eine Biographie aus drei Epochen des deutschen Katholizismus* (Mainz: Mathias Gruenewald, 1981).

Hoettl, Wilhelm, *The Secret Front. The Inside Story of Nazi Political Espionage* With an Introduction by Ian Colvin (London: Phoenix Press, 2000).

Howard, Michael, *Grand Strategy* Vol. IV *August 1942–September 1943* (London: HMSO, 1972).

Howard, Michael, *British Intelligence in the Second World War* vol. v *Strategic Deception* (London: HMSO, 1990).

Huerten, Heinz (ed), *Deutsche Briefe 1934–1938. Ein Blatt der katholischen Emigration* vol. 1 *1934–1935* (Mainz: Mathias Gruenewald, 1969).

Irving, David, *Hess. The Missing Years 1941–1945* (London: Macmillan, 1987).

Jacobsen, Hans-Adolf (ed), *'Spiegelbild einer Verschwoerung'. Die Opposition gegen Hitler und der Staatsstreich vom 20. Juli 1944 in der SD-Berichterstattung. Geheime Dokumente aus dem ehemaligen Reichssicherheitshauptamt* (Stuttgart: Seewald, 1984).

Janssen, Karl-Heinz and Fritz Tobias, *Der Sturz der Generaele. Hitler und die Blomberg-Fritsch Krise 1938* (Munich: Beck, 1994).

Jeffery, Keith, *MI6. The History of the Secret Intelligence Service, 1909–1949* (London: Bloomsbury, 2010).

Joachimsthaler, Anton, *The Last Days of Hitler. The Legends, the Evidence, the Truth* (London: Brockhampton, 1999).

John, Otto, *Zweimal kam ich heim. Vom Verschwoerer zum Schuetzer der Verfassung* (Duesseldorf: Econ Verlag, 1969).

Kahn, David, *Hitler's Spies. German Military Intelligence in World War II* (New York: Da Capo Press 2000).

Keegan, John, *The Second World War* (London: Hutchinson, 1989).

Kengel, Rainer, *Die Aufhebung der Abtei Muensterschwarzach* (St Ottilien, 1948).

Kershaw, Ian, *The 'Hitler Myth'. Image and Reality in the Third Reich* (Oxford University Press, 1987).

Kershaw, Ian, *The Nazi Dictatorship. Problems and Perspectives of Interpretation* 4th edition (London: Arnold, 2000).

Kershaw, Ian, '"Working Towards the Fuehrer": Reflections on the Nature of the Hitler Dictatorship' in idem, *Hitler, the Germans, and the Final Solution* (Yad Vashem International Institute for Holocaust Research and Yale University Press, 2008).

Kershaw, Ian, *The End. Hitler's Germany, 1944–45* (London: Allen Lane, 2011).

Kimball, Warren F., *Churchill and Roosevelt. The Complete Correspondence* vol. 1 *Alliance Emerging* (Princeton University Press, 1984).

Kirkpatrick, Ivone *The Inner Circle. Memoirs* (London: Macmillan, 1959).

Klee, Ernst, *'Euthanasie' im NS Staat. Die 'Vernichtung lebensunwerten Lebens'* (Frankfurt am Main: Fischer, 1986).

Klee, Ernst, *Dokumente zur 'Euthanasie'* (Frankfurt am Main: Fischer, 1986).

Kleine, Georg H., 'Adelsgenossenschaft und Nationalsozialismus', *Vierteljahrshefte fuer Zeitgeschichte* 26 (1978).

Klemperer, Klemens von, 'Widerstand-Résistance: The Place of the German Resistance in the European Resistance against National Socialism' in Hedley Bull (ed), *The Challenge of the Third Reich. The Adam von Trott Memorial Lectures* (Oxford: Clarendon Press, 1986).

Klemperer, Klemens von, 'Sie gingen ihren Weg ... Ein Beitrag zur Frage des Entschlusses und der Motivation zum Widerstand' in

BIBLIOGRAPHY

Juergen Schmaedeke and Peter Steinbach, *Der Widerstand gegen den Nationalsozialismus. Die deutsche Gesellschaft und der Widerstand gegen Hitler* (Munich: Piper, 1986).

Koller, Karl, *Der letzte Monat. Die Tagebuchaufzeichnungen des ehemaligen Chefs des Generalstabes der deutschen Luftwaffe vom 14. April bis zum 27. Mai 1945* (Mannheim: Wohlgemuth, 1949).

Krebs, Alfred, *Fritz-Dietlof Graf von der Schulenburg. Zwischen Staatsraison und Hochverrat* (Hamburg, 1964).

Kroener, Bernhard R., *'Der Starke Mann im Heimatskriegsgebiet'. Generaloberst Friedrich Fromm. Eine Biographie* (Paderborn: Ferdinand Schoeningh, 2005).

Kuropka, Joachim (ed), *Zur Sache – Das Kreuz! Untersuchungen zur Geschichte des Konflikts um Kreuz und Lutherbild in den Schulen Oldenburgs, zur Wirkungsgeschichte eines Massenprotests und zum Problem nationalsozialistischer Herrschaft in einer agrarisch-katholischen Region* (Vechta: Vechtaer Druckerei und Verlag, 1987).

Lange, Annemarie, *Berlin in der Weimarer Republik* (Berlin, 1987).

Leon, R.W., *The Making of an Intelligence Officer* (London: Date Luce, 1994).

Leugers, Antonia, 'Adolf Kardinal Bertram als Vorsitzender der Bischofskonferenz waehrend der Kriegsjahre, 1939–1945' *Archiv fuer schlesische Kirchengeschichte* xlvii–viii (1990).

Leverkuehn, Paul, *German Military Intelligence* (London: Weidenfeld and Nicolson, 1954).

Lewy, Guenter, *The Catholic Church and Nazi Germany* (London: Weidenfeld and Nicolson, 1964).

Lochner, Louis P. (ed), *The Goebbels Diaries* (London: Hamish Hamilton, 1948).

Loeffler, Peter (ed), *Bischof Clemens August Graf von Galen. Akten, Briefe und Predigten* vol. ii *1939–1946* (Mainz: Mathias Gruenewald, 1988).

Longerich, Peter, *Die braunen Bataillone. Geschichte der SA* (Munich: C.H. Beck, 1989).

Luza, Radomir, *Austro-German Relations in the Anschluss Era* (Princeton University Press, 1975).

McDonogh, Giles, *A Good German. Adam von Trott zu Solz* (London, 1989).

McLaine, Ian, *Ministry of Morale. Home Front Morale and the Ministry of Information in World War II* (London: Routledge, 1979).

Maier, Klaus A. et al., *Germany in the Second World War* vol. 2 (Oxford University Press, 2000).

Manstein, Erich von, *Aus Einem Soldatenleben* (Bonn: Athenaeum, 1958).

Mehringer, Hartmut, *Waldemar von Knoeringen. Eine politische Biographie. Der Weg vom revolutionaeren Sozialismus zur sozialen Demokratie* Schriftenreihe der Georg-von-Vollmar Akademie vol. 2 (Munich: K.G. Saur, 1989).

Meissner, Otto, *Magda Goebbels. A Biography* (London: Sidgwick and Jackson, 1980).

Mendelsohn, John, *Covert Warfare. Intelligence, Counterintelligence and Military Deception During the World War II Era* vol. 14 *A Man Called A.H.* (London: Garland Publishing, 1989).

Michaelis, Herbert and Ernst Schraepler (eds), *Ursachen und Folgen. Vom deutschen Zusammenbruch 1918 und 1945 bis zur staatlichen Neuordnung Deutschlands in der Gegenwart* (Berlin: Dokumenten Verlag Wendler no year).

Mommsen, Hans, 'The Indian Summer and the Collapse of the Third Reich: The Last Act' in idem, *The Third Reich Between Vision and Reality. New Perspectives on German History 1918–1945* (Oxford: Berg, 2001).

Mueller, Rolf-Dieter and Hans-Erich Volkmann (eds), *Die Wehrmacht. Mythos und Realitaet* (Munich: R. Oldenbourg, 1999).

Muggeridge, Malcolm (ed), *Ciano's Diary 1939–43* (London: William Heinemann, 1947).

Neuhaeusler, Johann, *Kreuz und Hakenkreuz* (Munich, 1946).

Neitzel, Soenke, *Abgehoert. Deutsche Generaele in britischer Kriegsgefangenschaft 1942–1945* (Berlin: List Taschenbuch, 2009).

Neumann, Franz, *Behemoth. The Structure and Practice of National Socialism* (London: Victor Gollancz, 1943).

Nicolson, Nigel (ed), *Harold Nicolson. Diaries and Letters 1939–1945* (London: Collins, 1967).

Jeremy Noakes, 'The Oldenburg Crucifix Struggle of November 1936: A Case Study of Opposition in the Third Reich' in Peter D. Stachua (ed), *The Shaping of the Nazi State* (London: Croom Helm, 1978).

Novak, Kurt, *'Euthanasie' und Sterilisierung im 'Dritten Reich'. Die Konfrontation der evangelischen und der katholischen Kirche mit dem 'Gesetz zur Verhuetung erbkranken Nachwuchses' und der 'Euthanasie'-Aktion* (Goettingen: Vandhoeck & Ruprecht, 1980).

Oven, Wilfred von, *Finale Furioso. Mit Goebbels bis zum Ende* (Tuebingen: Grabert, 1974).

Overy, Richard, *Interrogations. The Nazi Elite in Allied Hands, 1945* (London: Allen Lane, 2001).

Overy, Richard, '"The Chap with the Closest Tabs": Trevor-Roper and the Hunt for Hitler' in Worden (ed), *Hugh Trevor-Roper.*

Paehler, Katrin, *The Third Reich's Intelligence Services. The Career of Walter Schellenberg* (Cambridge University Press, 2019).

Papen, Franz von, *Memoirs* (London: Andre Deutsch, 1952).

Parker, Geoffrey and Sarah K. Douglas, 'The Search for Hitler: Hugh Trevor-Roper, Humphrey Searle, and the Last Days of Hitler', *The Journal of Military History* 78 (Jan. 2014).

The Persecution of the Catholic Church in German-Occupied Poland (London: Burns Oates, 1941).

Picker, Henry (ed), *Hitlers Tischgespraeche im Fuehrerhauptquartier* (Stuttgart: Seewald, 1977).

Portmann, Heinrich, *Cardinal von Galen* (London: Jarrolds, 1957).

Preussisches Staatsministerium (ed), *Handbuch ueber den Preussischen Staat fuer das Jahr 1938, 140 Jahrgang* (Berlin).

Rauschning, Hermann, *Germany's Revolution of Destruction* (London: William Heinemann, 1939).

Rauschning, Hermann, *Hitler Speaks* (London: Thornton Butterworth, 1939).

'Die Religionsgliederung im Deutschen Reich, in den Laendern, Verwaltungsbezirken und Gemeinden mit 10,000 und mehr Einwohnern nach der Volkszaehlung vom 16. Juni 1933', supplement to *Wirtschaft und Statistik* vol. xiv (1934).

Reuth, Ralf Georg (ed), *Goebbels Tagebuecher* 4 vols (Munich: R. Piper, 1992).

Reuth, Ralf Georg, *Goebbels* (London: Constable, 1993).

Ribbentrop, Joachim von, *The Ribbentrop Memoirs* with an introduction by Alan Bullock (London: Weidenfeld and Nicholson, 1954).

Ritter, Gerhard (ed), *Hitlers Tischgespraeche im Fuehrerhauptquartier 1941–42* (Bonn: Athenaeum, 1951).

Roberts, Frank, *Dealing with Dictators. The Destruction and Revival of Europe 1930-70* (London: Weidenfeld & Nicholson, 1991).

Roehm, Ernst, *Die Geschichte eines Hochverraeters* 2nd edn, (Munich: Franz Eher Nachfolger, 1930).

Rose, P. Ambrosius O.S.B., *Kloster Gruessau* (Stuttgart: Konrad Theiss, 1974).

Schacht, Hjalmar, *My first Seventy-Six Years* (London: Allan Wingate, 1955).

Schellenberg, Walter, *The Schellenberg Memoirs* edited and translated by Louis Hagen introduction by Alan Bullock (London: Andre Deutsch, 1956).

Schenk, Dieter, *Hitlers Mann in Danzig* (Bonn: J.H.W. Dietz Nachf., 2000).

Schmidt, Matthias, *Albert Speer: Das Ende eines Mythos. Speers wahre Rolle im Dritten Reich* (Bern: Scherz, 1982).

Schmidt, Rainer F., *Rudolf Hess 'Botengang eines Toren'? Der Flug nach Grossbritannien vom 10. Mai 1941* (Duesseldorf: Econ, 1997).

Schmidt, Ulf, *Karl Brandt: The Nazi Doctor. Medecine and Power in the Third Reich* (London: Continuum, 2007).

Schmuhl, Hans-Walter, *Rassenhygiene, Nationalsozialismus, Euthanasie. Von der Verhuetung zur Vernichtung 'lebensunwerten' Lebens, 1890–1945* (Goettingen: Vandhoeck & Ruprecht, 1987).

Schneider, Burkhart (ed), *Die Briefe Pius XII an die deutschen Bischoefe, 1939–1944* (Mainz: Mathias Gruenewald, 1966).

Schwendemann, Heinrich, 'Drastic Measures to Defend the Reich at the Oder and the Rhine': A Forgotten Memorandum of Albert Speer of 18 March 1945', *Journal of Contemporary History* 38/4 (Oct. 2003).

Schwerin, Detlef Graf von, '*Dann sind's die besten Koepfe, die man henkt.' Die junge Generation im deutschen Widerstand* (Munich: Piper, 1994).

Shirer, William L., *End of a Berlin Diary* (London: Hamish Hamilton, 1947).

Sisman, Adam, *Hugh Trevor-Roper. The Biography* (London: Weidenfeld & Nicholson, 2010).

Smelser, Ronald and Enrico Syring (eds), *Die Militaerelite des Dritten Reiches. 27 biographischen Skizzen* (Frankfurt am Main: Ullstein, 1997).

Speer, Albert, *Erinnerungen* (Frankfurt am Main: Propylaen, 1969).

Speer, Albert, *Spandauer Tagebuecher* (Frankfurt am Main: Ullstein, 1975)

Straesser, Susanne, 'Hans Bernd Gisevius – Ein Oppositioneller auf "Aussenposten"' in Klemens von Klemperer, Enrico Syring and

BIBLIOGRAPHY

Rainer Zitelmann (eds), *'Fuer Deutschland.' Die Maenner des 20. Juli* (Frankfurt am Main, 1994).

Szarota, Tomasz, *Warschau unter dem Hakenkreuz* (Paderborn: Ferdinand Schoeningh, 1985).

Taylor, A.J.P., 'The Bunker Revisited' *New Statesman and Nation*, 8 July 1950.

Taylor, A.J.P., 'Funeral in Berlin' *The Observer*, 29 September 1968.

Tedder, Lord, *With Prejudice. The War Memoirs of Marshal of the Royal Air Force Lord Tedder* (London: Cassell, 1966).

Thamer, Hans-Ulrich, *Verfuehrung und Gewalt. Deutschland 1933–1945* (Berlin: Siedler, 1986).

Thomas, Gina, 'Himmler's Masseur' in Worden (ed) *Hugh Trevor-Roper.*

Thomson, David, review of *The Last Days of Hitler*, *Cambridge Review*, May 1947.

Tobias, Fritz, *The Reichstag Fire. Legend and Truth* (London: Secker & Warburg, 1963).

Trevor-Roper, H.R., *The Last Days of Hitler* 1st edition (London: Macmillan, 1947), (New York: Macmillan, 1947), 2nd edition (London: Macmillan, 1950), 3rd edition (Macmillan, 1956) 7th edition (Macmillan, 1995).

Trevor-Roper, H.R., *Hitlers letzte Tage* (Zuerich: Amstutz Herdeg, 1948).

Trevor-Roper, H.R., 'Portraet des wirklichen Nazi-verbrechers' (1949) in Adalbert Reif (ed), *Albert Speer. Kontroversen um ein deutsches Phaenomen* (Munich, 1978).

Trevor-Roper, H.R., 'The Mind of Adolf Hitler' in *Hitler's Table-Talk* (London: Weidenfeld and Nicolson, 1953).

Trevor-Roper, H.R., 'Kersten, Hitler and Count Bernadotte', *The Atlantic Monthly* 151/2 (Feb. 1953).

Trevor-Roper, H.R., 'Hitlers Kriegsziele', *Vierteljahrshefte fuer Zeitgeschichte* 8/2 (April 1960).

Trevor-Roper, H.R. (ed), *Hitler's War Directives 1939–1945* (London: Sidgwick and Jackson, 1964).

Trevor-Roper, Hugh, 'Recherchen der ersten Stunde. Hugh Trevor-Roper ueber 'Hitlers letzte Tage' in Henning Ritter (ed), *Werksbesichtigung Geisteswissenschaften. Fuenfundzwanzig Buecher von ihren Autoren gelesen* (Frankfurt am Main, 1990).

Trevor-Roper, Hugh, 'Hess: The Incorrigible Intruder' in Stafford, David (ed), *Flight From Reality. Rudolf Hess and his Mission to Scotland, 1941* (London: Pimlico, 2002).

Trevor-Roper, Hugh, 'Secrets that survived the Bunker', *The Times*, 23 April 1983.

Trevor-Roper, Hugh, 'Hitler: a catalogue of errors', *The Times*, 14 May 1983.

Trevor-Roper, Hugh, *The Wartime Journals* edited by Richard Davenport-Hines (London: I.B. Tauris, 2012).

Trevor-Roper, Hugh, *The Secret World. Behind the Curtain of British Intelligence in World War II and the Cold War* edited by Edward Harrison with an introduction by Sir Michael Howard (London: Bloomsbury Academic, 2020).

Trial of the Major War Criminals before the International Military Tribunal vols xxv, xxxii & xxxiii (Nuremberg 1947–49).

Vassiltchikov, Marie, *The Berlin Diaries 1940–1945 of Marie 'Missie' Vassiltchikov* (London: Chatto and Windus, 1985).

Vinogradov, V.K., J.F. Pogonyi and N.V. Teprzov, *Hitler's Death. Russia's Last Great Secret from the Files of the KGB* Foreword by Andrew Roberts (London: Chaucer Press, 2005).

Vogelsang, Thilo, *Reichswehr, Staat und NSDAP* (Stuttgart: Deutsche Verlags-Anstalt, 1962).

Volk, Ludwig (ed), *Akten deutscher Bischoefe ueber die Lage der Kirche, 1933–1945* vol. v: *1940–1942* (Mainz: Mathias Gruenewald, 1983).

Volk, Ludwig (ed), *Akten Kardinal Michael Faulhabers 1917–45* 2 vols (Mainz: Mathias Gruenewald, 1975 & 1978).

Volk, Ludwig, 'Episkopat und Kirchenkampf im Zweiten Weltkrieg. Pt. I: Lebensvernichtung und Klostersturm, 1939–1942' in Dieter Albrecht (ed), *Katholische Kirche und Nationalsozialismus.Ausgewaehlte Aufsaetze von Ludwig Volk* (Mainz: Mathias Gruenewald, 1987).

Wegner, Bernd, 'The War against the Soviet Union, 1942–1943' in Militaergeschichtliches Forschungsamt (ed), *Germany and the Second World War* vol. vi *The Global War* (Oxford: Clarendon Press, 2001).

Wehrenalp, Erwin Barth von, *Auf den Spuren des Secret Service* (Berlin: Nibelungen, 1940).

Weiss, Hermann and Paul Hoser (eds), *Die Deutschnationalen und die Zerstoerung der Weimarer Republik. Aus dem Tagebuch von Reinhold Quaatz 1928–1933* (Munich: Oldenbourg, 1989).

Who's Who 1973 & 2009.

Wiedemann, Fritz, *Der Mann, der Feldherr werden wollte* (Velbert & Kettwig, 1964).

Wildt, Michael, *Generation des Unbedingten. Das Führungskorps des Reichssicherheitshauptamtes* (Hamburger Edition, 2003).

Wittstadt, Klaus (ed), *Die kirchliche Lage in Bayern nach den Regierungspraesidentenberichten, 1933–1943* vol. vi: *Regierungsbezirk Unterfranken, 1933–1944* (Mainz: Mathias-Gruenewald-Verlag, 1981).

Woodward, F.L., and Rohan Butler (eds), *Documents on British Foreign Policy 1919–1939* Second Series vol. iv 1932–33 (London: HMSO, 1950).

Woodward, Llewellyn, *British Foreign Policy in the Second World War* vol. 1 (London: HMSO, 1970).

Worden, Blair, 'Hugh Redwald Trevor-Roper 1914–2003', *Proceedings of the British Academy* 150, 247–284, *Biographical Memoirs of Fellows*, VI.

Worden, Blair (ed), *Hugh Trevor-Roper. The Historian* (London: Bloomsbury Academic, 2020).

Wright, J.R.C., *'Above Parties': The Political Attitudes of the German Protestant Church Leadership, 1918–1933* (Oxford University Press, 1974).

Wrigley, Chris, *A.J.P. Taylor. A Complete Annotated Bibliography and Guide to His Historical and Other Writings* (Brighton: Harvester, 1980).

Young, Kenneth (ed), *The Diaries of Sir Robert Bruce Lockhart 1939–1965* (London: Macmillan, 1980).

Zahn, Gordon, *German Catholics and Hitler's Wars* (London: Sheed and Ward, 1963).

Zeller, Eberhard, *Geist der Freiheit. Der Zwanzigste Juli* 5th edition (Munich: Gotthold Mueller, 1965).

Zimmer, Detlev, 'Soziale Lebenslaeufe und individuelle politische Biographie. Das Beispiel der Familie von Helldorf (Haus St Ulrich)', *Zeitschrift fuer Geschichtswissenschaft* 40 (1992).

Zitelmann, Rainer, *Hitler. Selbstverstaendnis eines Revolutionaers* (Stuttgart: Herbig, 1991).

Endnotes

Chapter 1: Rudolf Hess: The Uninvited Guest

1. H.R. Trevor-Roper, *The Last Days of Hitler* (London, 1947), pp. 29–30; Erwin Barth von Wehrenalp, *Auf den Spuren des Secret Service* (Berlin, 1940), pp. 88–91.
2. Malcolm Muggeridge, *Chronicles of Wasted Time* vol. 2 *The Infernal Grove* (London, 1973), p. 120; H.R. Trevor-Roper, *The Philby Affair* (London, 1968), p. 73; F.H. Hinsley and C.A.G. Simkins, *British Intelligence in the Second World War* vol. 4 *Security and Counter-Intelligence* (London, 1990).
3. Rainer F. Schmidt, *Rudolf Hess 'Botengang eines Toren'? Der Flug nach Grossbritannien vom 10. Mai 1941* (Duesseldorf, 1997), pp. 144–9.
4. T[he] N[ational] A[rchives] CAB 118/56, ALBRECHT HAUSHOFER. Note by the Security Service; DEFE 1/134, Mr. Herbert to the Director-General [Ministry of Information] 26 May 1941; James Douglas-Hamilton, *Motive For A Mission. The Story Behind Hess's Flight to Britain* (London, 1971), pp. 146–7.
5. TNA CAB 118/56, ALBRECHT HAUSHOFER. Note by the Security Service; Douglas-Hamilton, *Motive for a Mission,* pp. 148–9 & 175.
6. TNA CAB 118/56, S [the Earl of Swinton] to Director-General [of MI5] 20 May 1941; Hinsley and Simkins, *Security and Counter-Intelligence,* pp. 52 & 69.
7. TNA WO 199/3288A, Report by O.C. 3rd Battalion Renfrewshire Home Guard of the incidents of the nights 10th, 11th May 1941; FO 1093/11 C/6756 to H.L. d'A. Hopkinson Esq., 11 June 1941 and Gen. 5/12/B.R. 11, The Interrogation of Rudolph Hess by Roman Battaglia, 30 May 1941.

8. TNA WO 199/3288A, 'German P.O.W. Captured Night 10/11 May 1941 – Report by Night Duty Officer [Captain Anthony C. White] 15 May 1941, 1020/A; Major James Barrie to Officer Commanding, 3rd Battalion Home Guard Renfrewshire, 11 May 1941; Lieutenant Whitby to Officer Commanding, 11th Battalion The Cameronians (Scottish Rifles), 11 May 1941.

9. Douglas-Hamilton, *Motive for a Mission*, pp. 157–9.

10. Ibid., pp. 161–4; Anthony Eden, *The Eden Memoirs. The Reckoning* (London, 1965), p. 255; Ivone Kirkpatrick, *The Inner Circle. Memoirs* (London, 1959), p. 176; David Dilks (ed), *The Diaries of Sir Alexander Cadogan* (London, 1971), p. 377.

11. Kirkpatrick, *The Inner Circle*, pp. 177–8; John Colville, *The Fringes of Power. Downing Street Diaries 1939–1955* (London, 1985), p. 387.

12. Foreign Office, Weekly Political Intelligence Summary no. 84, 14 May 1941; TNA PREM 3/219/7, Report by Officer in charge Medical Division, Military Hospital, Drymen, 13 May 1941; Kirkpatrick, *Inner Circle*, pp. 177–80; John Colville, *The Fringes of Power. Downing Street Diaries 1939–1955* (London, 1986), p. 387.

13. TNA PREM 3/219/7, REPORT ON THE CUSTODY AND MOVEMENTS OF RUDOLPH HESS, Director of Prisoners of War, 22 May 1941; FO 1093/8, Graham to Lieutenant Colonel A.M. Scott, Scots Guards, 21 May 1941; EXTRACT FROM A LETTER FROM CAMP COMMANDANT 'Z' CAMP TO D.D.P.W., 22 May 1941; P/39/D.P.W. Hunter to Sir Alexander Cadogan, 22 May 1941; Hunter to Foreign Office, 16 June 1941; David Irving, *Hess. The Missing Years 1941–1945* (London, 1987), p. 103.

14. TNA FO 1093/11, Memorandum on Jonathan (No. 3) dated 29th May, 1941; Llewellyn Woodward, *British Foreign Policy in the Second World War* vol. 1 (London, 1970), p. 614.

15. TNA FO 1093/11, John [Simon] to Anthony [Eden], 27 May 1941; PREM 3/219/7, Cadogan minute of 6 June 1941, Desmond Morton minute to Churchill of 6 June 1941; Kirkpatrick, *Inner Circle*, pp. 182–4.

16. Kirkpatrick, *ibid*; TNA PREM 3/219/5 No. 28, 9 June 1941 and Prime Minister's personal minute no. 645/1, 14 June 1941, 3/219/7, Rudolf Hess preliminary report, 10 June 1941.

17. TNA FO 1093/10, Colonel J.R. Rees to D.D.P.W., 19 June 1941.
18. Ian McLaine, *Ministry of Morale. Home Front Morale and the Ministry of Information in World War II* (London, 1979), pp. 219–20.
19. Ben Pimlott, *Hugh Dalton* (London, 1985), pp. 320–6.
20. TNA FO 1093/11, Third Nazi Communiqué and Preliminary Propaganda about Hess for immediate use on all British and foreign broadcasts; Douglas-Hamilton, *Motive for a Mission*, p. 173.
21. Dilks (ed), *Diaries of Sir Alexander Cadogan*, p. 379; Eden, *The Reckoning*, p. 256.
22. McLaine, *Ministry of Morale*, pp. 220 & 235; Nigel Nicolson (ed), *Harold Nicolson. Diaries and Letters 1939–1945* (London, 1967), pp. 166-7.
23. TNA INF 1/857, Ministry of Information to the Minister, 21 May 1941 and enclosed paper by Walter Monckton and Cyril Radcliffe.
24. TNA INF 1/857, Walter Monckton to Alfred Duff Cooper, 27 May 1941.
25. Warren F. Kimball (ed), *Churchill and Roosevelt. The Complete Correspondence* vol. 1 *Alliance Emerging* (Princeton University Press, 1984), pp. 186–8; Eden, *The Reckoning*, p. 259.
26. Douglas-Hamilton, *Motive for a Mission* p. 178.
27. TNA FO 1093/11, Deputy Fuehrer Hess's Flight: its Exploitation in Propaganda to Germany.
28. TNA FO 1093/11, O. Sargent to Strang, 16 May, A.C. note of 20 May and Strang note of 29 May 1941; FO 1093/6, Henry L. d'A Hopkinson to Brigadier R.A.D. Brooks, 23 May 1941.
29. TNA HO 144/22492, 'The Hess Danger', *Daily Mail*, 21 June 1941; Kenneth Young (ed), *The Diaries of Sir Robert Bruce Lockhart 1939–1965* (London, 1980), p. 99.
30. Elke Froehlich (ed), *Die Tagebuecher von Joseph Goebbels. Saemtliche Fragmente* Teil 1 *Aufzeichnungen 1924–1941* Band 4 (Munich, 1987), pp. 638–45.
31. Louis P. Lochner (ed), *The Goebbels Diaries* (London, 1948), p. 386; TNA FO 1093/10, minute of R.M. Makins, 11 July 1941.
32. TNA INF 1/292, Ministry of Information, Weekly Reports by Home Intelligence nos. 32 & 33.
33. Mclaine, *Ministry of Morale* p. 221; TNA DEFE 1/134, POSTAL CENSORSHIP REPORTS 23 & 27 May 1941; INF 1/292, Ministry of Information, Weekly report by Home Intelligence no. 32.

34. Ibid; TNA HO 144/22492, M. Hiley to Mr Morrison, 13 May 1941, Anonymous [to Home Secretary] no date, Miss A. Leigh Pemberton [to Home Secretary] 14 May 1941, B. Winsbury [to Home Secretary], 19 May 1941.

35. TNA INF 1/292, Ministry of Information Home Intelligence Weekly Report No. 34; DEFE 1/134, POSTAL CENSORSHIP REPORTS 23 & 27 May 1941; HO 144/22492, W.J. Harbord to the Minister of Home Security, 16 May 1941.

36. TNA INF 1/292, Ministry of Information Home Intelligence Weekly Report No. 33; DEFE 1/134, POSTAL CENSORSHIP REPORTS 23 & 27 May 1941.

37. TNA FO 1093/11, Prime Minister's personal minutes M.540/1 & 550/1, 13 May & 16 May 1941.

38. Gabriel Gorodetsky, *Stafford Cripps' Mission to Moscow 1940–42* (Cambridge University Press, 1984), pp. 126–7; idem, 'The Hess affair and Anglo-Soviet relations on the eve of "Barbarossa"', *The English Historical Review* vol. CI no. 399 (April 1986), pp. 409–12.

39. TNA FO 1093/11, RAB 16 May 1941.

40. Genrikh Borovik, *The Philby Files. The Secret Life of the Master Spy – KGB Archives Revealed* (London, 1994), pp. 183–5; F.W. Deakin and G.R. Storry, *The Case of Richard Sorge* (London, 1966), p. 229.

41. Gorodetsky, 'The Hess Affair', pp. 419–20.

42. TNA HS 6/623 & 624, X/PLANS to AD/X, 18 Dec. 1944 and 8 Jan. 1945.

43. Malcolm Muggeridge (ed), *Ciano's Diary 1939–43* (London, 1947), p. 342; Hildegard Gauger, *Die Psychologie des Schweigens in England* (Heidelberg, 1937).

Chapter 2: Nazi Against Hitler: Count Wolf-Heinrich von Helldorf

1. Konrad Heiden, *Der Fuehrer. Hitler's Rise to Power* (London, 1944), Book 1 p. 294; André Francois-Poncet, *Souvenirs d'une Ambassade à Berlin* (Paris, 1946), p. 97; Giles McDonogh, *A Good German. Adam von Trott zu Solz* (London, 1989), p. 2; Hans-Bernd Gisevius, *To the Bitter End* (London, 1948).

2. Detlef Zimmer, 'Soziale Lebenslaeufe und individuelle politische Biographie. Das Beispiel der Familie von Helldorf (Haus St Ulrich)', *Zeitschrift fuer Geschichtswissenschaft* 40 (1992), p. 850; Wolfgang Benz and Walter H. Pehle, *Lexikon des deutschen Widerstandes* (Frankfurt am Main, 1994).

3. Klemens von Klemperer, '*Widerstand-Résistance*: The Place of the German Resistance in the European Resistance against National Socialism' in Hedley Bull (ed), *The Challenge of the Third Reich. The Adam von Trott Memorial Lectures* (Oxford, 1986), p. 43 and idem, 'Sie gingen ihren Weg ... Ein Beitrag zur Frage des Entschlusses und der Motivation zum Widerstand' in Juergen Schmaedeke and Peter Steinbach (eds), *Der Widerstand gegen den Nationalsozialismus. Die deutsche Gesellschaft und der Widerstand gegen Hitler* (Munich, 1986), p. 1103.

4. Ernst Devrient, *Das Geschlecht von Helldorff* vol. 1 *Familiengeschichte* (Berlin, 1931), pp. 6–7 and passim.

5. Berlin Document Center (BDC), SA File Helldorf; Archiv des Instituts fuer Zeitgeschichte (AdIfZ) ZS 539; Herrmann A.L. Degener (ed), *Degeners Wer ist's* (Berlin 1935) entry for Helldorf.

6. BDC SA File Helldorf; Shelley Baranowski, *The Sanctity of Rural Life. Nobililty, Protestantism and Nazism in Weimar Prussia* (Oxford, 1995), p. 31; Devrient, *Das Geschlecht von Helldorff*, p. 310; AdIfZ ZS 539.

7. Detlev Zimmer, 'Soziale Lebenslaeufe', p. 848; Harold J. Gordon, *Hitler and the Beer Hall Putsch* (Princeton, 1972), pp. 250–1; Georg Franz-Willing, *Putsch und Verbotszeit der Hitlerbewegung November 1923–Februar 1925* (Preussisch Oldendorf, 1977) pp. 77–8; Ernst Roehm, *Die Geschichte eines Hochverraeters* (2nd ed. Munich, 1930), p. 292; AdIfZ ZS 539.

8. NSDAP Hauptarchiv Reel 16A Folder 1634.

9. Ibid; Peter Longerich, *Die braunen Bataillone. Geschichte der SA* (Munich, 1989), pp. 46–7.

10. Roehm, *Geschichte eines Hochverraeters*, p. 295; AdIfZ ZS 539.

11. Roehm, *Geschichte eines Hochverraeters*, pp. 308 & 315; BDC File Count Helldorf; AdIfZ ZS 539.

12. Bundesarchiv Koblenz (BAK) NS 26/1350; BDC SA-P Count Helldorf.

13. BDC SA File Helldorf; BAK NS 26/1350; Elke Froehlich (ed), *Die Tagebuecher von Joseph Goebbels. Saemtliche Fragmente* Part 1 *Aufzeichnungen 1924–1941* vol. 2 (Munich, 1987), pp. 92, 98, 471 & 729.

14. Froehlich (ed), *Tagebuecher von Joseph Goebbels* vol. 2, pp. 92 & 98; BDC SA File Helldorf; BAK NS 26/1350.

15. BDC Hauptarchiv B-323; AdIfZ Fa 172; Landesarchiv Berlin (LAB) 58/20 vol. 3.

16. LAB 58/20 vols 1 & 3; BDC Hauptarchiv B-323; Heinrich Bruening, *Memoiren 1918–1934* (Stuttgart, 1970), p. 411.

17. BDC Hauptarchiv B-323; LAB 58/20 vol. 3; Thilo Vogelsang, *Reichswehr, Staat und NSDAP* (Stuttgart, 1962), p. 395; Annemarie Lange, *Berlin in der Weimarer Republik* (Berlin, 1987), pp. 1015–17; Froehlich (ed), *Tagebuecher von Joseph Goebbels* vol. 2, p. 114; Ralf Georg Reuth, *Goebbels* (London, 1993), p. 138; *Degeners Wer ist's* (1935) entry for Helldorf.

18. Sefton Delmer, *Trail Sinister. An Autobiography* vol. 1 (London, 1961), p. 129.

19. Martin Broszat, *Hitler and the Collapse of the Weimar Republic* (Leamington Spa, 1987), pp. 112 & 119; Hermann Weiss and Paul Hoser (eds), *Die Deutschnationalen und die Zerstoerung der Weimarer Republik. Aus dem Tagebuch von Reinhold Quaatz 1928–1933* (Munich, 1989), p. 187; Vogelsang, *Reichswehr, Staat und NSDAP*, pp. 189 & 263.

20. Ralf Georg Reuth (ed), *Goebbels Tagebuecher* vol. 2: 1930–1934 (Munich, 1992), p. 680; Rainer Zitelmann, *Hitler. Selbstverstaendnis eines Revolutionaers* (Stuttgart, 1991), p. 87.

21. Franz von Papen, *Memoirs* (London, 1952), p. 195; Froehlich (ed), *Tagebuecher von Joseph Goebbels* vol. 2, p. 202; Delmer, *Trail Sinister*, pp. 166–7.

22. Longerich, *Die braunen Bataillone* p. 145; Fritz Wiedemann, *Der Mann, der Feldherr werden wollte* (Velbert & Kettwig, 1964), p. 145; Alan Bullock (intro), *The Ribbentrop Memoirs* (London, 1954), p. xii.

23. BDC SA File Helldorf; Zimmer, 'Soziale Lebenslaeufe', p. 848.

24. BDC SA File Helldorf and SA-P Helldorf.

25. Gerhard Ritter (ed), *Hitlers Tischgespraeche im Fuehrerhauptquartier 1941–42* (Bonn, 1951), p. 430; Karl Dietrich Bracher, *Die Aufloesung*

der Weimarer Republic Eine Studie zum Problem des Machtverfalls in der Demokratie (Koenigstein, 1978), p. 630.

26. Hans-Ulrich Thamer, *Verfuehrung und Gewalt. Deutschland 1933–1945* (Berlin, 1986), p. 241; F.L. Woodward and Rohan Butler (eds), *Documents on British Foreign Policy 1919–1939* Second Series vol. iv *1932–33* (London, 1950), pp. 425–6.

27. BDC SA File Helldorf; Heinz Huerten (ed), *Deutsche Briefe 1934–1938. Ein Blatt der katholischen Emigration* vol. 1 *1934–1935* (Mainz, 1969), p. 82.

28. Georg H. Kleine, 'Adelsgenossenschaft und Nationalsozialismus', *Vierteljahrshefte fuer Zeitgeschichte* 26 (1978), pp. 115–18 & 125–6.

29. Fritz Tobias, *The Reichstag Fire. Legend and Truth* (London, 1963), p. 118.

30. Ibid., pp. 150–1; Delmer, *Trail Sinister*, pp. 185–90.

31. BDC SA File Helldorf; Erich von Manstein, *Aus Einem Soldatenleben* (Bonn, 1958), p. 187; Lothar Gruchmann, *Justiz im Dritten Reich 1933–1940. Anpassung und Unterwerfung in der Aera Guertner* (Munich, 1988), pp. 443–5.

32. William E. Dodd Jr. and Martha Dodd, *Ambassador Dodd's Diary* (London, 1941), pp. 141–2.

33. BAK NS 19/1227; BDC SA-P Count Helldorf.

34. Ibid.

35. BDC SA-P Helldorf and SA File Helldorf.

36. BAK NS 19/1227.

37. Gerhard Granier, *Magnus von Levetzow. Seeoffizier, Monarchist und Wegbereiter Hitlers. Lebensweg und ausgewaehlte Dokumente* (Boppard am Rhein, 1982), pp. 177 & 192–4; Reuth (ed), *Goebbels Tagebuecher* vol. 2 *1930–1934*, pp. 849–51; vol. 3 *1935–1939*, pp. 864 & 869–70; Huerten (ed), *Deutsche Briefe*, p. 477.

38. Granier, *Magnus von Levetzow*, p. 194; Huerten (ed), *Deutsche Briefe*, p. 588.

39. Susanne Straesser, 'Hans Bernd Gisevius – Ein Oppositioneller auf "Aussenposten"' in Klemens von Klemperer, Enrico Syring and Rainer Zitelmann (eds), *'Fuer Deutschland'. Die Maenner des 20. Juli* (Frankfurt am Main, 1994), pp. 57–9 & 66; AdIfZ ED 82: the documents in the file were collected by Gisevius.

40. Wiener Library London, (WLL) PIIIf no. 109; BDC SA File Count Helldorf.

41. BDC SA File Count Helldorf.

42. Ibid.

43. Reuth (ed), *Goebbels Tagebuecher* vol. 3 *1935–1939*, pp. 1082–3 & 1139; Froehlich, *Tagebuecher von Joseph Goebbels* vol. 3, pp. 150 & 251.

44. Karl-Heinz Janssen & Fritz Tobias, *Der Sturz der Generaele. Hitler und die Blomberg-Fritsch Krise 1938* (Munich, 1994), pp. 38 & 45–6.

45. Ibid; AdIfZ ED 82; Froehlich (ed), *Tagebuecher von Joseph Goebbels* vol. 3, pp. 415 & 427.

46. Janssen & Tobias, *Sturz der Generaele*, pp. 48–50; Heinz Hoehne, *Canaris. Patriot im Zwielicht* (Munich, 1976), pp. 245–7; Walter Goerlitz (ed), *Generalfeldmarschall Keitel. Verbrecher oder Offizier? Erinnerungen, Briefe, Dokumente des Chefs OKW* (Goettingen, 1961), pp. 103–4.

47. Reuth (ed), *Goebbels Tagebuecher* vol. 3 *1935–1939*, pp. 1218–1229; Landesarchiv Berlin 20/7249; Froehlich (ed), *Tagebuecher von Joseph Goebbels* vol. 3, pp. 470 & 492; AdIfZ MA 261.

48. BDC SA File Helldorf.

49. Preussisches Staatsministerium (ed), *Handbuch ueber den Preussischen Staat fuer das Jahr 1938 140. Jahrgang* (Berlin), p. 245; Richard Grunberger, *A Social History of the Third Reich* (London, 1991), p. 138; WLL PIIIf no. 547 & PIIIa no. 502; Otto Meissner, *Magda Goebbels. A Biography* (London, 1980), p. 280.

50. Froehlich (ed), *Tagebuecher von Joseph Goebbels* vol. 3, pp. 476 & 479.

51. Reuth (ed), *Goebbels Tagebuecher* vol. 3 *1935–1939*, pp. 1279–81.

52. Uwe Dietrich Adam, 'Wie spontan war der Pogrom?' in Walter H. Pehle (ed), *Der Judenpogrom 1938. Von der 'Reichskristallnacht' zum Voelkermord* (Frankfurt am Main, 1988), p. 91; Gisevius, *Bitter End*, p. 335.

53. Hans-Adolf Jacobsen (ed), *'Spiegelbild einer Versschwoerung'. Die Opposition gegen Hitler und der Staatsstreich vom 20. Juli 1944 in der SD-Berichterstattung. Geheime Dokumente aus dem ehemaligen Reichssicherheitshauptamt* vol. 1 (Stuttgart, 1984), p. 436; Huerten (ed), *Deutsche Briefe* vol. 2 *1936–1938*, pp. 266–7.

54. Albert Speer, *Erinnerungen* (Frankfurt am Main, 1969), p. 123; Lothar Gruchmann, 'Korruption im Dritten Reich. Zur 'Lebensmittelversorgung' der NS-Fuehrerschaft,' *Vierteljahrshefte fuer Zeitgeschichte* 42 (1994), pp. 572–5; Jacobsen (ed), '*Spiegelbild einer Verschwoerung*' vol. 1, p. 417; BAK NS 19/1227.

55. AdIfZ Fa 156 & ZS 539; BDC SA File Helldorf; Jacobsen, '*Spiegelbild einer Verschwoerung*', p. 479.

56. Ibid., pp. 103–4 & 448.

57. Ian Kershaw, *The 'Hitler Myth'. Image and Reality in the Third Reich* (Oxford, 1987) p. 75; Froehlich (ed), *Tagebuecher von Joseph Goebbels* vol. 2, p. 569, & vol. 3, pp. 51, 147 & 255.

58. Ulrich Heinemann, *Ein Konservativer Rebell. Fritz-Dietlof von der Schulenburg und der 20. Juli* (Berlin, 1990), pp. 46–7 & 271; idem, '"Kein Platz fuer Juden und Polen." Der Widerstandskaempfer Fritz-Dietlof Graf von der Schulenburg und die Politik der Verwaltung in Schlesien 1939/40' in Christoph Klessmann (ed), *September 1939. Krieg, Besatzung, Widerstand in Polen. Acht Beitraege* (Goettingen, 1989), pp. 39–40 & 51; Alfred Krebs, *Friz-Dietlof Graf von der Schulenburg. Zwischen Staatsraison und Hochverrat* (Hamburg, 1964), pp. 154–7; Eberhard Zeller, *Geist der Freiheit. Der Zwanzigste Juli* (5th edition, Munich, 1965), p. 165.

59. Hjalmar Schacht, *My first Seventy-Six Years* (London, 1955), p. 386; Detlef Graf von Schwerin, '*Dann sind's die besten Koepfe, die man henkt.' Die junge Generation im deutschen Widerstand* (Munich, 1994), pp. 140–41.

60. Reuth (ed), *Goebbels Tagebuecher* vol. 3 *1935–1939*, p. 1265; Klaus-Juergen Mueller, *General Ludwig Beck. Studien und Dokumente zur politisch-militaerischen Vorstellungswelt und Taetigkeit des Generalstabschefs des deutschen Heeres 1933–1938* (Boppard am Rhein, 1980), p. 560; Gisevius, *Bitter End*, p. 319; Wiedemann, *Der Mann Der Feldherr Werden Wollte*, p. 114; AdIfZ A1560.

61. Helmuth Groscurth, *Tagebuecher eines Abwehroffiziers 1938–1940. Mit weiteren Dokumenten zur Militaeropposition gegen Hitler* (Stuttgart, 1970), pp. 183–6 & 197.

62. Eberhard Bethge, *Dietrich Bonhoeffer. Theologian, Christian, Contemporary.* (London, 1977), pp. 529 & 576; F. Hiller von Gaertringen (ed), *Die Hassell-Tagebuecher 1938–1944.*

Aufzeichnungen vom Andern Deutschland. Nach der Handschrift revidierte und erweiterte Ausgabe (Berlin, 1988), pp. 137–9.

63. Groscurth, *Tagebuecher*, pp. 466–8.

64. Froehlich (ed), *Tagebuecher von Joseph Goebbels* vol. 4, p. 148; Reuth (ed), *Goebbels Tagebuecher* vol. 4 *1940–1942*, p. 1449; Jacobsen (ed), '*Spiegelbild einer Verschwoerung*' vol. 1, p. 419.

65. Froehlich (ed), *Tagebuecher von Joseph Goebbels* vol. 4, pp. 542 & 566.

66. AdIfZ Fa 292; Schwerin, *Die junge Generation*, pp. 281–3; BDC SA File Helldorf; Bernhard R. Kroener, '*Der starke Mann im Heimatskriegsgebiet*', *Generaloberst Friedrich Fromm. Eine Biographie* (Paderborn, 2005), p. 727.

67. *The Berlin Diaries 1940–1945 of Marie 'Missie' Vassiltchikov* (London, 1985), pp. 83, 91–2 & 162; Jacobsen (ed), '*Spiegelbild einer Verschwoerung*' vol. 1, p. 99.

68. Zeller, *Geist der Freiheit*, pp. 362 & 487; AdIfZ MA 1560; BDC SA File Helldorf.

69. Jacobsen (ed), '*Spiegelbild einer Verschwoerung*' vol. 2, p. 769, & vol. 1, p. 341; Gisevius, *Bitter End*, pp. 509 & 517; *Berlin Diaries of 'Missie Vassiltchikov*, p. 205.

70. Gisevius, *Bitter End*, pp. 490–2.

71. Ibid., pp. 529–31.

72. AdIfZ Fa 292; Gisevius, *Bitter End*, pp. 529–35; Schwerin, *die junge Generation*, p. 399.

73. Gisevius, *Bitter End*, pp. 536, 546 & 558–9; AdIfZ MA Fa 292 & MA 1560; Wilfred von Oven, *Finale Furioso. Mit Goebbels bis zum Ende* (Tuebingen, 1974), pp. 415–17.

74. Jacobsen (ed), '*Spiegelbild einer Verschwoerung*' vol. 1, pp. 47–8, & vol. 2, p. 773; Zeller, *Geist der Freiheit*, p. 384; Gisevius, *Bitter End*, pp. 573–5; *Berlin Diaries of 'Missie' Vassiltchikov*, pp. 197–8 & 219.

75. *Berlin Diaries of 'Missie' Vassiltchikov*, p. 205; John Mendelsohn, *Covert Warfare. Intelligence, Counterintelligence and Military Deception During the World War II Era* vol. 14 *A Man Called A.H.* (London, 1989), pp. 153–4.

76. Oven, *Finale Furioso*, pp. 447–8.

77. Herbert Michaelis and Ernst Schraepler (eds), *Ursachen und Folgen. Vom deutschen Zusammenbruch 1918 und 1945 bis zur*

staatlichen Neuordnung Deutschlands in der Gegenwart (Berlin, no year) no. 3525; BDC SA File Helldorf.

78. BDC Hauptarchiv B-323; AdIfZ MA 1560; *Berlin Diaries of 'Missie' Vassiltchikov*, p. 224.

79. BAK NS 19/227.

Chapter 4: The Nazi Dissolution of the Monasteries: a Bavarian Case Study

1. For the Nazi monastery dissolutions see Guenter Lewy, *The Catholic Church and Nazi Germany* (London, 1964), J.S. Conway, *The Nazi Persecution of the Churches* (London, 1968), Johann Neuhaeusler, *Kreuz und Hakenkreuz* (Munich, 1946) and Ludwig Volk, 'Espiskopat und Kirchenkampf im Zweiten Weltkrieg. Pt. I: Lebensvernichtung und Klostersturm, 1939–1941' in Dieter Albrecht (ed), *Katholische Kirche und Nationalsozialismus. Ausgewaehlte Aufsaetze von Ludwig Volk* (Mainz, 1987) pp. 83–97. Neuhaeusler altered some of the documents in his book to spare church leaders embarrassment: Gordon Zahn, *German Catholics and Hitler's Wars* (London, 1963) p. 76.

2. Frierich Freiherr Hiller von Gaertringen (ed), *Die Hassell-Tagebuecher, 1938–1944. Ulrich von Hassell, Aufzeichnungen vom andern Deutschland* (rev. edition Berlin, 1988), p. 282.

3. Zahn, *German Catholics*, p. 103; Antonia Leugers, 'Adolf Kardinal Bertram als Vorsitzender der Bischofskonferenz waehrend der Kriegsjahre, 1939–1945', *Archiv fuer schlesische Kirchengeschichte*, xlvii–viii (1990), pp. 15 & 18.

4. Leugers, 'Adolf Kardinal Bertram' p. 27.

5. Bayerisches Hauptstaatsarchiv [BHSA], Reichsstatthalter 619 & 620.

6. BHSA Reichsstatthalter 619.

7. Bundesarchiv Koblenz [hereafter BAK] NS 6/336; Lewy, *Catholic Church*, p. 253.

8. J.R.C. Wright, *'Above Parties': The Political Attitudes of the German Protestant Church Leadership, 1918–1933* (London, 1974), pp. 154–5.

9. Volk, 'Episkopat und Kirchenkampf', p. 92.

10. Franz Groner (ed), *Kirchliches Handbuch. Amtliches statistisches Jahrbuch der katholischen Kirche Deutschlands* vol. xxiii: *1944–51* (Cologne, 1951), p. 264.

11. BAK NS 19/282.

12. P. Ambrosius Rose OSB, *Kloster Gruessau* (Stuttgart, 1974), pp. 191–2.

13. Ludwig Volk (ed), *Akten deutscher Bischoefe ueber die Lage der Kirche, 1933–1945* vol. v: *1940–1942* (Mainz, 1983), pp. 253–6; BAK NS 19/282.

14. *Trial of the Major War Criminals before the International Military Tribunal* [hereafter IMT] vol. xxxiii (Nuremberg, 1949), 3927-PS, p. 537.

15. BAK R43 II/1271a.

16. Radomir Luza, *Austro-German Relations in the Anschluss Era* (Princeton, 1975), pp. 189–91; Adolf Hitler, *Mein Kampf* (Munich, 1933), pp. 3–4.

17. Luza, *Austro-German Relations* ibid; Gerhard Botz, *Wien vom 'Anschluss' zum Krieg. Nationalsozialistische Machtuebernahme und politisch-soziale Umgestaltung am Beispiel der Stadt Wien, 1938/39* (Vienna, 1980), pp. 394–5; *IMT* vol. xxxiii, 3927-PS, pp. 538–40.

18. Ibid., pp. 727–8.

19. Volk (ed), *Akten deutscher Bischoefe* vol. v, pp. 345–8.

20. Abteiarchiv Muensterschwarzach [hereafter AaM] IX D11, Deutsche Arbeitsfront [hereafter DAF] Kitzingen 1 July 1941; A 950, Abbot Burkard Utz 12 March 1942 and IX D12, Abbot Utz 12 May 1941.

21. Staatsarchiv Wuerzburg [hereafter SAW], G[estapo] W[uerzburg] 16309.

22. Johannes Duering [Pater Jonathan OSB], *'Unsere Heimat kann man uns nicht rauben.' Die Antwort der Moenche von Muensterschwarzach auf die Verfolgungsmassnahmen und die Aufhebung ihrer Abtei durch die Nationalsozialisten im Jahre 1941* [Diploma diss., Institut fuer fraenkische Kirchengeschichte, Julius-Maximilians Universitaet Wuerzburg 1986], p. 17.

23. SAW GW 5761 & 16309; Heinz Boberach (ed), *Berichte des SD und der Gestapo ueber Kirchen und Kirchenvolk in Deutschland, 1934–1944* (Mainz, 1971), p. 313; Volk (ed), *Akten deutscher Bischoefe* vol. v, p. xlix.

24. Klaus Wittstadt (ed), *Die kirchliche Lage in Bayern nach den Regierungspraesidentenberichten, 1933–1943* vol.vi: *Regierungsbezirk Unterfranken, 1933–1944* (Mainz, 1981), p. xlix; Groner (ed), *Kirchliches Handbuch* vol.xxiii, pp. 374 & 386.

25. 'Die Religionsgliederung im Deutschen Reich, in den Laendern, Verwaltungsbezirken und Gemeinden mit 10,000 und mehr Einwohnern nach der Volkszaehlung vom 16. Juni 1933', supplement to *Wirtschaft und Statistik* vol. xiv (1934), p. 11.

26. SAW, GW 15770 & NSDAP Gau Mainfranken 16.

27. B[erlin] D[ocument] C[enter], SA file Willy Heer; Alan Bullock, *Hitler. A Study in Tyranny* (revised edition (London, 1964), p. 73.

28. SAW NSDAP Gau Mainfranken 16.

29. BAK Sammlung Schumacher 243 II/2.

30. AaM IX D4; Voelkl was the deputy of Criminal Commissioner Gramowski, head of the Wuerzburg Gestapo. At the end of the war Voelkl poisoned himself together with his wife and youngest daughter. Keil was a devout Catholic who had been transferred to the Gestapo against his will, according to Frau Roellich, a former Gestapo secretary, in a deposition to Father Rainer Kengel OSB on 15 Nov. 1946, ibid. Kengel interviewed as many witnesses as he could find to the abbey's history during the war years. These interviews were preserved as 'Protocols' in the abbey archive. Kengel used them to write a short survey of his abbey's dissolution: *Die Aufhebung der Abtei Muensterschwarzach, 1941–1945* (St Ottilien, 1948).

31. AaM, IX D4 & A 950.

32. AaM IX D4, Protocol of the discussion between the former Gestapo official Karl Immel and Father Rainer Kengel in the library of Muensterschwarzach Abbey, 19 May 1948.

33. AaM IX D4, Abbot Burkard Protocol 20 Nov. 1945; SAW GW 5761.

34. SAW GW 5761; AaM IX D4, Frau Roellich Protocol 15 Nov. 1946 & Abbot Burkard Protocol, 20 Nov. 1945.

35. AaM IX D4, Father August Falkenstein Protocol 20 Nov. 1945.

36. BDC SS File Fritz Glitz; AaM IX D4, Karl Immel Protocol 19 May 1948.

37. AaM IX D4, Abbot Burkard Protocol 20 Nov. 1945.

38. BDC Party File Dr Otto Helmuth.

39. AaM IX D4, statement made by Dr Oskar Dengel in Dachau, 5 Dec. 1946.

40. BDC Party and SS files Dr Oskar Dengel; Tomasz Szarota, *Warschau unter dem Hakenkreuz* (Paderborn, 1985), p. 232.

41. AaM IX D4, statement made by Dr Oskar Dengel in Dachau, 5 Dec. 1946.

42. AaM IX D4, Abbot Burkard Protocol 20 Nov. 1945. For Gramowski's career, see Robert Gellately, *The Gestapo and German Society. Enforcing Racial Policy, 1933–1945* (Oxford, 1990).

43. SAW GW 299.

44. SAW GW 3693.

45. SAW GW 6739.

46. Kengel, *Aufhebung der Abtei Muensterschwarzach*, pp. 20–1; Karl-Werner Goldhammer, *Katholische Jugend Frankens im Dritten Reich* (Frankfurt am Main, 1986), p. 365.

47. Kengel, *Die Aufhebung*, p. 21.

48. Father Sales Hess OSB, *KZ-Dachau. Eine Welt ohne Gott* (Muensterschwarzach, 1985), pp. 19–20.

49. Ibid., pp. 20–3.

50. Ibid., pp. 20–4, 31, 42, 47, 52.

51. Landesarchiv Speyer, Gestapo Neustadt B2303.

52. AaM IX D11; SAW GW 6677; BHSA Reichsstatthalter 626 & 647.

53. Volk (ed), *Akten deutscher Bischoefe* vol.v, p. 356; Bundesarchiv Potsdam [hereafter BAP], RKM 23318.

54. SAW GW 5556; BAK R22/3355.

55. Ian Kershaw, *The 'Hitler Myth'. Image and Reality in the Third Reich* (Oxford, 1987), p. 116.

56. SAW GW 12877, 5556, 16273, 12421; Boberach (ed), *Berichte des SD und Gestapo*, p. 665.

57. See Chapter 3 for the popular protests against the removal of crucifixes from schools in Oldenburg.

58. SAW GW 5761, 12136 & 6753.

59. SAW GW 7995.

60. AaM IX D11 & 15; IMT vol. xxv (Nuremberg, 1947), 076-PS pp. 139–40.

61. AaM, IX D11 & A910.

62. AaM IX D11.

63. BAK NS6/336; AaM A910.
64. AaM A910 & 950, IX D11.
65. AaM A910, IX D4, IX D11.
66. AaM, A910 & 950, IX D11.
67. BAK 059/000150.
68. AaM A910; Kengel, *Die Aufhebung*, pp. 49–50.
69. AaM A910.
70. Kengel, *Die Aufhebung*, p. 40; BDC, Party and SA Files Raimund Rueth.
71. AaM IX D4, Abbot Burkard and Brother Dunstan [Karl Rueger] OSB Protocols, 20 Nov. 1945.
72. AaM IX D4, note of a conversation between Abbot Burkard and Father Rainer Kengel, 14 March 1947.
73. AaM IX D11.
74. Ibid.
75. AaM, A910 & IX D11; Kengel, *Die Aufhebung*, p. 43.
76. Walter Adolph, *Geheime Aufzeichnungen aus dem nationalsozialistischen Kirchenkampf*(Mainz, 1987), p. 277; Martin Hoellen, *Heinrich Wienken: Der 'unpolitische' Kirchenpolitiker. Eine Biographie aus drei Epochen des deutschen Katholizismus* (Mainz, 1981), p. 78.
77. AaM A950.
78. AaM IX D4 & 5.
79. Volk (ed), *Akten deutscher Bischoefe* vol. v, pp. 354–6; BAK R43 II/1271a.
80. Volk (ed), *Akten deutscher Bischoefe* vol. v, pp. 464–5.
81. Ibid., pp. 469–73; Conway, *Nazi Persecution*, pp. 393–7.
82. Ulrich von Hehl, *Katholische Kirche und Nationalsozialismus im Erzbistum Koeln, 1933–1945* (Mainz, 1977), p. 220.
83. Groner (ed), *Kirchliches Handbuch* vol. xxiii, pp. 390–3.
84. Peter Loeffler (ed), *Bischof Clemens August Graf von Galen. Akten, Briefe und Predigten* vol. ii *1939–1946* (Mainz, 1988), pp. 844–7; Conway, *Nazi Persecution*, pp. 277–8.
85. Loeffler (ed), *Graf von Galen*, vol. ii pp. 852, 857 & 864–6.
86. Ibid., pp. 874–83; Volk, 'Episkopat und Kirchenkampf', p. 94; Conway, *Nazi Persecution*, pp. 278–84.
87. Ernst Klee, *Dokumente zur 'Euthanasie'* (Frankfurt am Main, 1986), pp. 194–8; Hans-Walter Schmuhl, *Rassenhygiene,*

Nationalsozialismus, Euthanasie (Goettingen, 1987), p. 350; Kurt Nowak, *'Euthanasie' und Sterilisierung im 'Dritten Reich'. Die Konfrontation der evangelischen und der katholischen Kirche mit dem 'Gesetz zur Verhuetung erbkranken Nachwuchses' und der 'Euthanasie'-Aktion* (Goettingen, 1980), p. 162.

88. Schmuhl, *Rassenhygiene, Nationalsozialismus, Euthanasie*, p. 354.
89. Volk (ed), *Akten Faulhabers* vol. ii, pp. 801, 853 & 915; Burkhart Schneider (ed), *Die Briefe Pius XII an die deutschen Bischoefe, 1939–1944* (Mainz, 1966), p. 155.
90. BAK R43 II/1271a; BHSA Reichsstatthalter 619; Lewy, *Catholic Church* pp. 253–4.
91. BAK R43 II/1271a.
92. Volk (ed), *Akten deutscher Bischoefe* vol. v, p. 1032.
93. BAP RKM 23318.
94. Schneider, *Briefe Pius XII*, p. 155.
95. BAK R43 II/1271a; Volk (ed), *Akten Faulhabers* vol. ii, p. 997.
96. Ibid., pp. 802–3 & 997.
97. Henry Picker (ed), *Hitlers Tischgespraeche im Fuehrerhauptquartier* (Stuttgart, 1977), p. 203.
98. Heinrich Portmann, *Cardinal von Galen* (London, 1957), pp. 101 & 106.
99. Ernst Klee, *'Euthanasie' im NS Staat. Die 'Vernichtung lebensunwerten Lebens'* (Frankfurt am Main, 1986), p. 335.
100. Volk (ed), *Akten Faulhabers* vol. ii, pp. 851 & 937; Portmann, *Cardinal von Galen*, pp. 11–12.
101. Martin Broszat, *Nationalsozialistische Polenpolitik, 1939–1945* (Stuttgart, 1961), pp. 158, 160 & 173; *IMT* vol. xxxii (Nuremberg, 1948), 3264-PS, pp. 96–97; *The Persecution of the Catholic Church in German-Occupied Poland* (London, 1941), p. 122.

Chapter 5: Hugh Trevor-Roper and The Last Days of Hitler

1. H.R. Trevor-Roper, *The Last Days of Hitler* (London, 1947); Christ Church Oxford SOC.Dacre 10/29, L.B. Namier to H.R. Trevor-Roper, 28 April 1947; Joachim Fest, *Inside Hitler's Bunker. The Last Days of the Third Reich* (London, 2005), p. 177; A.J.P. Taylor, 'The Bunker Revisited', *New Statesman and Nation,* 8 July 1950.

Taylor described the French translation of *The Last Days* as a book that developed its story with all the brilliance of a symphony conducted by a great master: Chris Wrigley, *A.J.P. Taylor. A Complete Annotated Bibliography and Guide to His Historical and Other Writings* (Brighton, 1980), p. 308.

2. SOC.Dacre 6/34. In 1979 Hugh Trevor-Roper was raised to the peerage as Baron Dacre of Glanton. All SOC.Dacre references are to the Dacre Papers in the archive at Christ Church Oxford.

3. Hugh Trevor-Roper, 'Recherchen der ersten Stunde. Hugh Trevor-Roper ueber 'Hitlers Letzte Tage' in Henning Ritter (ed), *Werksbesichtigung Geisteswissenschaften. Fuenfundzwanzig Buecher von ihren Autoren gelesen* (Frankfurt am Main, 1990), p. 45; idem, 'Hitlers Kriegsziele', *Vierteljahrshefte fuer Zeitgeschichte* 8/2 (April 1960), p. 124.

4. SOC.Dacre 13/29, pp. 167–75.

5. SOC.Dacre 10/20, Dick White to Lord Dacre, June 1985.

6. Henrik Eberle and Mathias Uhl (eds), *The Hitler Book. The Secret Dossier Prepared for Stalin* (London, 2005); V.K. Vinogradov, J.F. Pogonyi and N.V. Teprzov, *Hitler's Death. Russia's Last Great Secret from the Files of the KGB* (London, 2005). Vinogradov's book is based on documents provided by the Russian Federal Security Service and includes interrogations from bunker inmates captured by the Soviets. Often these are very informative and appear authentic, though Hans Rattenhuber's comment [purportedly in May 1945] that the defences of Hitler's HQ 'were the equal of the fortifications of the Berlin Wall' does not inspire confidence: ibid., p. 186.

7. Antony Beevor, *Berlin. The Downfall* (London, 2003), p. 399; H.R. Trevor-Roper, *The Last Days of Hitler* (2002), Introduction to the Third Edition [hereafter Introduction] xx; SOC.Dacre 10/20, 12 A.G. Interrogation Report of Friedrich Olmes of 19 May 1945; SOC.Dacre 20/29, Excerpt from the *Evening Standard* of Saturday, 9 June 1945 and 'Public Statements by the Russians on Hitler's death; T[he]N[ational] A[rchives] WO 208/3787, CX CF/IV/73 17 Sept. 1945.

8. TNA KV 4/217, A.D.B.1. [White] to D.B. [Liddell] 14 March 1943; SOC.Dacre 13/29, pp. 338–39.

9. TNA KV 4/100, Major General K.W.D. Strong to Sir David Petrie, 10 Nov. 1944, ROLE OF THE SPECIAL AGENCIES IN

COMBATTING UNDERGROUND ACTIVITIES IN GERMANY, Note of a meeting held in the Director-General's Room at 5 p.m. on 23rd November, 1944, to consider the SHAEF Proposals for the Creation of a German War Room in London, for the Servicing of the C.I. Staffs in Germany.

10. TNA WO 208/2701, *History of the Counter Intelligence War Room.*

11. Ibid.

12. TNA WO 208/3787, C.I.B. [Dick White] to Lt. Col. T.A. Robertson, 10 Sept. 1945, 10 Sept. 1945, Counter Intelligence War Room [T.A. Robertson] to Brigadier D.G. White, 14 and 19 Sept. 1945; WO 208/4701, *History of the Counter Intelligence War Room.*

13. SOC.Dacre 13/29, pp. 338–9; Introduction, pp. xxvii & xxxvi.

14. TNA WO 208/3787, GSI (b), HQ, BAOR [Peter Ramsbotham] to GSI 1 Corps District etc., 18 Sept. 1945.

15. Introduction xxvi–xxvii; SOC.Dacre 10/20, Trevor-Roper to Randall, 6 Feb. 1946.

16. SOC.Dacre 10/28, *The Death of Hitler* and *The Death of Hitler* Revision note, 11 Feb. 1946; Trevor-Roper, 'Recherchen' p. 43.

17. SOC.Dacre 10/20, *The Enquiry into Hitler's end*; 10/7, R.W. Leon to Lord Dacre, 23 May 1995.

18. SOC.Dacre 10/7, *Willi Johannmeier HRT-R*, 17 Dec. 1945; Ronald Smelser and Enrico Syring (eds), *Die Militaerelite des Dritten Reiches. 27 biographischen Skizzen* (Frankfurt/M, 1997), p. 505.

19. SOC.Dacre 13/58, entries in Trevor-Roper's pocket diaries for December 1945 and January 1946; SOC.Dacre 10/7, *Willi Johannmeier HRT-R* 17 Dec. 1945.

20. SOC.Dacre 10/7, CSDIC (WEA) to IB, 21 Dec. 1945; *Wilhelm Zander* H.R. Trevor-Roper, Majór. Int. Corps, 1 Jan. 1946.

21. SOC.Dacre 10/7, *Wilhelm Zander* H.R. Trevor-Roper Major Int Corps, 1 Jan. 1946; SOC.Dacre 13/29 p. 358.

22. SOC.Dacre 10/20, *The Enquiry into Hitler's end*; SOC.Dacre 10/7, *Fortnightly Notes The Discovery of Hitler's Wills & Third Interrogation of Willi Johannmeier.*

23. SOC.Dacre 10/7, Maj. P.E. Ramsbotham to Maj. Trevor-Roper, 7 Jan. 1945; Trevor-Roper to Brian Melland, Cabinet Office, Historical Section, 8 April 1966; Vinogradov et al., *Hitler's Death*, p. 163.

24. SOC.Dacre 10/7, Trevor-Roper to Brian Melland, Cabinet Office, Historical Section, 8 April 1966.

25. SOC.Dacre 13/29, pp. 367–8; Trevor-Roper, 'Recherchen der ersten Stunde.'

26. Trevor-Roper, 'Recherchen der ersten Stunde', p. 44.

27. SOC.Dacre 10/31; SOC.Dacre 13/29: 368–69; SOC.Dacre 10/30, Trevor-Roper to Macmillan, 22 May 1946.

28. SOC.Dacre 10/30, White to Trevor-Roper, 18 March and 17 May 1946.

29. SOC.Dacre 10/30, *Extract from Minutes of the Meeting held on 14th June 1946*, White to Trevor-Roper, 19 June 1946. As an undergraduate at Christ Church 'Tim' Milne had lived on the same staircase as Trevor-Roper, and in later life was much amused that his contemporary had been elevated to the House of Lords.

30. SOC.Dacre 10/30, Trevor-Roper to White, 19 June 1946, Trevor-Roper to Solly Zuckerman, 19 June 1946, *Extract from JIC (46) 38th Meeting held on 29th June 1946 3. Publication of 'The Last Days of Hitler' by Mr Trevor Roper*, Zuckerman to Trevor-Roper, 4 July 1946; H.R. Trevor-Roper, *The Last Days of Hitler* (London, 1947), Foreword by Marshal of the RAF Lord Tedder … Deputy Supreme Commander Allied Expeditionary Force, 1943–45. Tedder's ponderous foreword is omitted from later English paperback editions and from the German paperback edition, *Hitlers letzte Tage* (Frankfurt/M, 1965).

31. SOC.Dacre 10/30, White to Trevor-Roper, 4 July 1946, Trevor-Roper to White, 6 July 1946, Caccia to White,17 July 1946, *Memorandum* [by Hugh Trevor-Roper].

32. SOC.Dacre 10/30, Trevor-Roper to Dick White, 10 May 1946, Trevor-Roper to Hamish Hamilton, 21 May 1946; B[ritish] L[ibrary] M[acmillan] A[rchive], letters from Dickson to Trevor-Roper, Letter Book 490/420 14 June, Letter Book 491/95 8 July 1946, Letter Book 491/415 8 Aug. 1946, Letter Book 492/273 17 Sept. 1946. The Oxford English Dictionary defines a mugwump as a great man or one who sits on the fence.

33. BLMA, letters from Dickson to Trevor-Roper, Letter Book 493/119 17 Oct. 1946 and 494/339 18 Dec. 1946; New Books and New Editions 23 Nov. 2/43 – Sept. 11/47.

34. SOC.Dacre 10/29, David Thomson, review of *The Last Days of Hitler*, *Cambridge Review*, May 1947.

35. *The Last Days of Hitler*, pp. 1–2 & 255.

36. Franz Neumann, *Behemoth. The Structure and Practice of National Socialism* (New York, 1944), pp. 396 & 469; Martin Broszat, *Der Staat Hitlers* (Munich, 1969).

37. Dieter Schenk, *Hitlers Mann in Danzig* (Bonn, 2000), p. 195; Wolfgang Haenel, *Hermann Rauschnings 'Gespraeche mit Hitler' – Eine Geschichtsfaelschung*-(Ingolstadt, 1984), pp. 4–6; Elke Froehlich (ed), *Die Tagebuecher von Joseph Goebbels. Saemtliche Fragmente Teil I Aufzeichnungen 1924–1941 Band 4* (Munich, 1987), pp. 41 & 73.

38. SOC.Dacre 10/29, L.B. Namier to H.R. Trevor-Roper, 28 April 1947.

39. Norman H. Baynes, *A Short List of Books on National Socialism* Historical Association Pamphlet 125 (London, 1943).

40. *The Last Days of Hitler* (1947), p. 4; *Hitler's Table-Talk 1941–1944* With an introductory essay on 'The Mind of Adolf Hitler' by H.R. Trevor-Roper (London, 1953) x; SOC.Dacre 10/29, Trevor-Roper to Namier, 30 April 1947; Alan Bullock, *Hitler. A Study in Tyranny* (London, 1952); Hermann Graml and Klaus-Dietmar Henke (eds), *Nach Hitler. Der schwierige Umgang mit unserer Geschichte. Beitraege von Martin Broszat* (Munich, 1987), p. 249.

41. Haenel, *Geschichtsfaelschung*, pp. 25–27 & 31–42; Hermann Rauschning, *Hitler Speaks* (London, 1939); Trevor-Roper, 'Recherchen' p. 49; Ian Kershaw, *The Nazi Dictatorship. Problems and Perspectives of Interpretation* (4th edition, London, 2000), p. 83.

42. Hermann Rauschning, *Germany's Revolution of Destruction* (London, 1939), pp. 16, 21, 34 & 196.

43. *The Last Days of Hitler* (1947), pp. 4–5; Fest, *Inside Hitler's Bunker*, p. 125. Trevor-Roper neatly summed up his emphasis on the centrality of Russia in Hitler's world view in 'Hitlers Kriegsziele': 'mit dem Russlandkrieg stand oder fiel der Nationalsozialismus,' *Vierteljahrshefte fuer Zeitgeschichte* 8/2, p. 129.

44. *The Last Days of Hitler* (1947), pp. 84 & 263. See also H.R. Trevor-Roper, 'Portraet des wirklichen Nazi-verbrechers' (1949) in Adelbert Reif (ed), *Albert Speer. Kontroversen um ein deutsches Phaenomen* (Munich, 1978).

45. SOC.Dacre 10/29, J.K. Galbraith to Trevor-Roper, 15 July 1947.

46. Matthias Schmidt, *Albert Speer: Das Ende eines Mythos. Speers wahre Rolle im Dritten Reich* (Bern, 1982). Trevor-Roper's

personal copy of Schmidt's book shows that he worked through it in his usual method, which was to mark significant passages and construct his own list of contents on the end-papers or inserts. He concluded: 'I cannot go as far as Matthias Schmidt' [in revising his view of Speer], 'Recherchen', p. 49.

47. Heinrich Schwendemann, 'Drastic Measures to Defend the Reich at the Oder and the Rhine': A Forgotten Memorandum of Albert Speer of 18 March 1945', *Journal of Contemporary History* 38 no. 4 (Oct. 2003), pp. 600–7.
48. Trevor-Roper, 'Recherchen der ersten Stunde', p. 49.
49. *The Last Days of Hitler* (1947), pp. 22–27 & 40–2; Hans Mommsen, 'The Indian Summer and the Collapse of the Third Reich: The Last Act' in idem, *The Third Reich Between Vision and Reality. New Perspectives on German History 1918–1945* (Oxford, 2001), pp. 109–110.
50. *The Last Days of Hitler* (1947), p. 8; SOC.Dacre 10/29, Dr Johann Neuhaeusler, Weihbischof to H.R. Trevor-Roper, 7 Jan. 1950; Trevor-Roper to Weihbischof Dr Johann Neuhaeusler, 18 Jan. 1950.
51. *The Last Days of Hitler* (1947), pp. 18–19.
52. J. Brodrick S.J., 'Jesuits and Nazis', *The Tablet*, 21 June 1947.
53. *The Last Days of Hitler* (1947), pp. 21–22; Brodrick, 'Jesuits and Nazis.'
54. SOC.Dacre 6/5, letter from Evelyn Waugh, 12 April 1947.
55. *The Last Days of Hitler* (2nd edition, London, 1950) lvi, pp. 18–19, & footnote to 22–3; SOC.Dacre 10/29, Bernard Bassett SJ to Trevor-Roper, 30 May 1947; F.W. Pick to H.R. Trevor-Roper, 26 May 1948; Trevor-Roper, *Hitlers letzte Tage*, pp. 52–3. It is unlikely Trevor-Roper had advance sight of the 1965 German edition, which reproduced the Swiss edition of 1948 published by Amstutz and Herdeg.
56. TNA FO 938/196, Francis Graham-Harrison to C.M. Anderson, 13 July 1947.
57. Ibid., Hugh Trevor-Roper to Robert Birley, 15 May 1947, Michael Balfour to D. Whyte, [PMD] Section, Foreign Office, 27 May 1947; BLMA Letter Book 497/606 Lovat Dickson to Trevor-Roper, 11 June 1947.
58. TNA FO 938/196, P.M.D. Section (Whyte) to R.F. Allen, Macmillan & Co., 29 Aug. 1947.

59. TNA FO 938/196, Michael Balfour, Control Commission for Germany (British Element) [CCG (BE)] to David Whyte, G.I. (PDM) Section, Foreign Office, 27 May 1947; Foreign Office PMD Section to M. Balfour CCG (BE) Berlin, 6 June 1947; H.R. Trevor-Roper, *Hitlers letzte Tage* (no place of publication, Spiegel Verlag, July 1947).

60. TNA FO 938/196, Foreign Office PMD Section to Verlag Amstutz, 6 Sept. 1947; Amstutz to D.H. Whyte, PMD Section, 17 Sept. 1947 & 5 Feb. 1948; D.H. Whyte to P.S. to Chancellor, 3 Dec. 1947; BLMA Letter Book 526/501, R.F. Allen to Dr Amstutz, 25 April 1952.

61. TNA FO 938/196, Information Centres Section Kiel to HQ Information Centres Section, March 1948; Land N. Rhine Westphalia *Reader's [sic] Reactions to the book 'The Last Days of Hitler';* PRISC Branch to Information Centres Control Branch, CCG (BE) ZEO, 4 March 1948.

62. TNA FO 938/196, D.H. Whyte to Mrs. Redlich, German and Austrian Service Desk, Norfolk House, 24 May 1948.

63. Anton Joachimstaler, *The Last Days of Hitler. The Legends, the Evidence, the Truth* (London, 1999); A.J.P. Taylor, 'Funeral in Berlin', *The Observer* 29 September 1968.

Chapter 6: Hugh Trevor-Roper's Special Missions in Germany

1. *The Last Days of Hitler* (London, 1947), henceforth LDOH (1947).

2. Hugh Trevor-Roper, 'Secrets that survived the Bunker', *The Times* 23 April 1983, and 'Hitler: a catalogue of errors', *The Times* 14 May 1983.

3. Adam Sisman, *Hugh Trevor-Roper. The Biography* (London, 2009). Trevor- Roper's posthumous books to date are: *Europe's Physician: The Various Life of Sir Theodore de Mayerne* (London, 2006), *Letters from Oxford: Hugh Trevor-Roper to Bernard Berenson* (London, 2006), *The Invention of Scotland: Myth and History* (London, 2008), *History and the Enlightenment* (London, 2010), *The Wartime Journals* (London, 2010), *The Secret World: Behind the Curtain of British Intelligence in World War II and the Cold War*

(London, 2014), *One Hundred Letters from Hugh Trevor-Roper* (London, 2014). Trevor-Roper's papers are held in the archive at Christ Church Oxford under the signature SOC.Dacre.

4. Edward D.R. Harrison, 'Hugh Trevor-Roper und "Hitlers letzteTage"' *Vierteljahrshefte fuer Zeitgeschichte* 57/1 (Jan. 2009) S. 33–60, republished as Chapter Five.

5. Geoffrey Parker and Sarah K. Douglas, 'The Search for Hitler: Hugh Trevor-Roper, Humphrey Searle, and the Last Days of Adolf Hitler', *The Journal of Military History* 78 (January 2014): pp. 159–210; Richard Overy, '"The Chap with the Closest Tabs": Trevor-Roper and the Hunt for Hitler' in Worden (ed), *Hugh Trevor-Roper*, pp. 192–206.

6. Parker and Douglas, 'The Search for Hitler', p. 161.

7. Parker and Douglas, 'The Search for Hitler', p. 162.

8. Parker and Douglas, 'The Search for Hitler', pp. 160 & 163.

9. Overy, 'The Chap with the Closest Tabs', p. 204.

10. Parker and Douglas, 'The Search for Hitler', p. 165 note 2 & p. 192.

11. T[he] N[ational] A[rchives] FO 371/46748, WSC 15.V.

12. Henrik Eberle and Mathias Uhl (eds.), *The Hitler Book. The Secret Dossier Prepared for Stalin* (London, 2005), pp. 280–1; Ian Kershaw, *The End. Hitler's Germany, 1944–45* (London, 2012), p. 372.

13. V.K. Vinogradov, J.F. Pogonyi and N.V. Teptzov, *Hitler's Death. Russia's Last Great Secret from the files of the KGB* Foreword by Andrew Roberts (London, 2005), pp. 99 & 108.

14. SOC.Dacre 10/20, Dick White to Lord Dacre, June 1985.

15. TNA WO 208/4475, folio 26, cx/12506, M.I.6 Political Report, Germany Description of Hitler's dentition 7 June 1945, folio 29, M.I.14(d)/1/OB/46/45 Major Norman Gash to D.D.L.M. (R.L.G.), 13 July 1945, folio 27, D.D.L.M. (R.L.G.) to D.D.M.L. (G), 14 July 1945; Anton Joachimsthaler, *The Last Days of Hitler. Legend, Evidence and Truth* (London, 2000), p. 297 note 102.

16. TNA FO 1005/1706, Headquarters Berlin Area, Intelligence Summary No. 3.

17. Hugh Trevor-Roper, *The Secret World. Behind the Curtain of British Intelligence in World War II and the Cold War* with a foreword by Sir Michael Howard and edited by Edward Harrison (London, 2014), pp. 6–8 & 19–20.

18. TNA WO 208/4701, *History of the Counter Intelligence War Room*, p. 18.

19. SOC.Dacre 10/30, Dick White to Winston M. Scott, Esq., Attach, American Embassy, 2 Aug. 1947.

20. SOC.Dacre 10/20, The Enquiry into Hitler's end.

21. Adam Sisman, *Hugh Trevor-Roper. The Biography* (London, 2010), p. 131.

22. 'At least' because it is not clear how many of Hitler's detective-guard, the Reich Security Service, were interviewed by Trevor-Roper, who wrote that 'about half of its members had been evacuated to Berchtesgaden on 22nd April, and captured there. I was able to interrogate them in their camps at Ludwigsburg and Garmisch-Partenkirchen': *The Last Days of Hitler* (London, 3rd edition 1956) henceforth (LDOH 1956) Introduction to third edition, p. xix.

23. SOC.Dacre 13/58, *The Badminton* [a pocket diary], 1945, p. 69, DEC. 18 TU entry of 'Bad Nenndorf'; Bernd Freytag von Loringhoven with Francois d'Alancon, *In the Bunker with Hitler 23 July 1944 – 29 April 1945* (London, 2006), p. 187.

24. Ulf Schmidt, *Karl Brandt: The Nazi Doctor. Medecine and Power in the Third Reich* (London, 2007), p. 337.

25. TNA FO 371/46778, minute by Victor Cavendish-Bentinck, 24 June 1945; Richard Overy, *Interrogations. The Nazi Elite in Allied Hands, 1945* (London, 2001), p. 136.

26. TNA KV 4/354, folio 6a, SPECIAL INTERROGATION OF ALBERT SPEER, 11/9/45. Although the special interrogations in KV 4/354 do not bear Trevor-Roper's signature, the dates and places tally with the sparse entries in his pocket diary. These entries, seemingly made soon before his travel, reveal many of his intended destinations. There is also separate documentation confirming that he had interrogated the person in question: see the endnotes below.

27. Parker and Douglas, 'The Search for Hitler', pp. 171 & 176, note 43.

28. Albert Speer, *Spandauer Tagebuecher* (Frankurt am Main, 1975), p. 109; SOC.Dacre 10/4, Albert Speer an den Herrn Lagerkommandanten, Kransberg, 12 Sept. 1945.

29. SOC.Dacre 10/4, Special Interrogation of SPEER From Major H. Trevor-Roper, C.I. Bureau c/o G.S.I. (b), H.Q., B.A.O.R.

to Major P.M. Wilson, Enemy Personnel Exploitation Section, F.I.A.T., 24 Sept. 1945. Trevor-Roper advised Macmillan to bid for Speer's memoirs after his release from Spandau Prison, commenting: 'I interrogated him myself in 1945 and was deeply struck by his personality': SOC.Dacre 10/4, ALBERT SPEER, ERINNERUNGEN.

30. TNA KV 4/354, folio 7a, SPECIAL INTERROGATION OF Dr. MORELL: this document is also to be found in SOC.Dacre 10/5, signed H.R. Trevor-Roper. Trevor-Roper gave a detailed account of Morell's activities as Hitler's doctor in LDOH (1947), pp. 65–69. He quoted with stylistic improvements a paragraph about Morell from the interrogation of Hitler's principal surgeon Karl Brandt on 24 June 1945 at Special Detention Center 'Ashcan', TNA FO 371/46778, C3728.

31. Parker and Douglas, 'The Search for Hitler', p. 173 note 31 and p. 170.

32. Military Intelligence in the British zone set up three interrogation camps with the numbers 030, 031 and 032. These camps held captured intelligence personnel from the Abwehr, Reich Security Head Office, German General Staff and similar organisations: R.W. Leon, *The Making of an Intelligence Officer* (London, 1994), p. 117.

33. SOC.Dacre 13/58, *The Badminton*, 1945, p. 55, SEPT. 24 MON entry of 'to Ploen' & 25 TU entry of 'Ploen'; TNA KV 4/354, folio 8a, Points emerging from special interrogation of Else KRUEGER, 25.9.45; WO 208/3790 folio 83, Major Trevor-Roper to Intelligence Bureau (attn. Captain Searle) Subject: Death of Hitler 21 Feb 46: 'Frl. Krueger stated that the arrest of Fegelein was carried out by *Staf.* Beetz ... Frl. Krueger said that she had heard these details from Beetz himself. The occasion on which she made these statements was when I interrogated her at Ploen on 25 Sept.' For Trevor-Roper's use of Krueger's testimony see LDOH (1947), p. 130. He later wrote that 'Frl. Else Krueger, Bormann's secretary, ... was detained at Ploen in Schleswig-Holstein and interrogated by me': LDOH (1956) Introduction to third edition, p. xx.

34. TNA KV 4/354, folio 9a, Special Interrogation of Werner GROTHMANN, 26.9.45. See LDOH (1947), p. 136 for use of Grothmann's testimony.

35. TNA KV 4/354, folio 9a, Special Interrogation of Werner GROTHMANN, 26.9.45; WO 208/3790 folio 48, Hugh Trevor-Roper to Captain H. Searle, 7 March 1946.

36. Parker and Douglas, 'The Search for Hitler', p. 175 note 40; SOC. Dacre 13/58, *The Badminton*, 1945, p. 55, SEPT. 26 W. entry of 'Nienburg (Karnau)' & p. 56, SEPT. 30 SUN entries include 'Karnau'. Trevor-Roper later wrote that Karnau 'was imprisoned at Nienburg and had been examined by Canadian and British authorities before he was cross-examined by me': LDOH (1956), Introduction to third edition, p. xx.

37. SOC.Dacre 10/13, Report on Interrogation of:- Revier Oberwachtmeister der Schutzpolizei Hermann Karnau, arrested 25 May 45 in Wilhelmshaven by 3 Cdn FS Sec; interrogated at Bad Salzuflen 1030 hrs 19 Jun 45 by Capt KWE Leslie, SSI (z) 21 Army Group.

38. TNA KV 4/354, folio 10a.

39. SOC.Dacre 10/13, REINTERROGATION OF KARNAU, Hermann I have expanded 'K.' in the original quotation to 'Karnau'.

40. TNA KV 4/354, folio 11a, HITLER'S DOCTORS.

41. TNA KV 4/354, folio 13a, PROFESSOR GOHRBANDT.

42. TNA KV 4/354, folio 14a, PROF. VON EICKEN. Carl von Eicken was director of the Ear, Nose and Throat Clinic at the Charité Hospital from 1926 until 1950. Trevor-Roper referred to this interrogation in a letter of 14 Feb. 1948, which Eicken later published: *Frankfurter Illustrierte Zeitung*, 28 Jan. 1951 in SOC. Dacre 10/29. Trevor-Roper made use of Eicken's testimony in LDOH (1947), pp. 64 & 70–72.

43. SOC. Dacre 10/22, Statement concerning interview with Baroness von Varo 20th September 1945 and supplementary note of 21 Sept. 1945, both by John Silver, Major [General Staff].

44. TNA KV 4/354, folio 15a, Interrogation of the Baroness von Varo; SOC. Dacre 13/58, *The Badminton*, 1945, p. 56, SEPT. 30 SUN entries include 'To Bad Oeyn[hausen] & OCT.1 MON entries include 'Bad Oeyn.' On 14 October 1945 Trevor-Roper noted that, 'I have interviewed both persons mentioned [in a report he was criticising], viz. Professor von Eicken ... and the Baroness von Varo', SOC. Dacre 10/22, B.1.B, 14.10.45. H R T-R [ink initials]. He later wrote that 'the Baroness von Varo ... was traced

and interrogated by me in her mother's home': LDOH (1956) Introduction to third edition, p. xxi.

45. TNA KV 4/354, folio 15a, Interrogation of the Baroness von Varo.

46. TNA KV 4/354, folio 16a, BAUR and BEETZ.

47. TNA KV 4/354, folio 16a, BAUR and BEETZ.

48. SOC.Dacre 10/29, George Allen [of Philadelphia] to Trevor-Roper, 19 July 1950.

49. TNA KV 4/354, folio 16a, BAUR and BEETZ; SOC.Dacre 13/58, *The Badminton*, 1945, p. 57, OCT. 7 SUN, entries include 'Moosburg.' Trevor-Roper later wrote that 'Erich Kempka ... was interrogated both by American officers and by myself at Moosburg': LDOH (1956) Introduction to third edition, p. xxi.

50. Parker and Douglas, 'The Search for Hitler', p. 175, note 41.

51. TNA KV 4/354, folio 17a, Special Interrogation of Erich Kempka: Trevor-Roper referred to 'my first "special interrogation of Erich Kempka"' in a letter to the historian Sir John Wheeler-Bennett of 26 Feb. 1949: SOC. Dacre 10/29; LDOH (1956) Introduction to third edition, p. xxiv.

52. Overy, 'The Chap with the Closest Tabs', p. 201.

53. SOC.Dacre 10/2, GSI(b), HQ BAOR 1 Oct 1945, to Control Commission, C.I. Bureau, 'For the attention of Major Trevor-Roper'.

54. SOC.Dacre 10/17, Frau CHRISTIAN.

55. SOC.Dacre 10/17, Frau CHRISTIAN.

56. TNA KV 4/354, folio 18a, Interrogation of Gen. (der Lw) Eghard Christian, Chef Luftwaffenfuehrungsstab (at Latimer, 15.10.45.) Trevor-Roper later recalled that, 'I don't think that I interrogated Frl Christian myself ... I conducted a long hunt for her, and interviewed her husband, General Christian, in Latimer prison-camp': Trevor-Roper to Brian Melland, Cabinet Office, Historical Section, 8 April 1966, SOC.Dacre 10/7. The C[ombined] S[ervices] D[etailed] I[nterrogation] C[entre] came under the jurisdiction of MI19 in the War Office. Besides interrogations, it also organized eavesdropping on prisoners, in particular the German generals housed at Trent Park in Cockfosters. CSDIC's interrogation centre in Britain was dissolved in November 1945 and its work taken over by CSDIC BAOR: Soenke Neitzel, *Abgehoert. Deutsche Generaele in britischer Kriegsgefangenschaft 1942–1945* (Berlin, 2009), pp. 12–15.

57. SOC.Dacre 13/58, *The Badminton*, 1945, p. 60, NOV. 3 SAT entries include 'Neumuenster' & 10/13, The S.S. FUEHRERBEGLEITKOMMANDO. Trevor-Roper wrote to Ramsbotham: 'Attached are five copies of the report on my interrogation of Bornholdt', ibid., To: G.S.I. (B), B.A.O.R. Major the Hon. P.E. Ramsbotham; From Major H.R. Trevor-Roper, 3rd December 1945. Trevor-Roper used Bornholdt's testimony for a footnote in his book: LDOH (1947) pp. 172-3 note 4. Trevor-Roper later wrote that 'Bornholdt ... had become an Allied prisoner and I was able to question him about his comrades': LDOH (1956) Introduction to third edition, p. xix.

58. Sisman, *Hugh Trevor-Roper*, p. 137; SOC.Dacre 13/58, *The Badminton*, 1945, p. 56, OCT. 6 SAT entry of 'Kannenberg'.

59. SOC.Dacre 10/28, Major Trevor-Roper to Brigadier E.R. Haylor, GSI/b, BAOR, 16 Oct. 1945; LDOH (1956) Introduction to third edition, p. xxi. Rattenhuber's name is given as 'Rattenhube' in T-R's memo to Haylor.

60. LDOH (1956) Introduction to third edition, pp. xxiii–iv.

61. SOC.Dacre 10/2, BRIGADEFUEHRER SCHELLENBERG, Amtschef VI, Autobiography, compiled during his stay in Stockholm, June 1945 [Copied in War Room, 14.8.45]. In the 'Note on Sources' for his eventual book Trevor-Roper wrote that 'While in Sweden between the end of hostilities and his surrender to SHAEF, Schellenberg compiled a careful diary [autobiography] of the events of the last month of the war, which is very important': LDOH (1947) NOTE ON SOURCES, p. 266. Trevor-Roper had questioned Schellenberg before he began his enquiry, as he wrote to Felix Kersten, Himler's masseur: 'I took a personal part in the examination of Walter Schellenberg', H.R. Trevor-Roper to Dr Felix Kersten, Linnegatan 8, Stockholm, 9 Dec. 1947, SOC.Dacre 10/29.

62. SOC.Dacre 10/28, THE DEATH OF HITLER and THE DEATH OF HITLER Revision note, 11 Feb. 1946.

63. Parker and Douglas, 'The Search for Hitler', pp. 170–71 note 22.

64. SOC.Dacre 10/7, R.W. Leon to Lord Dacre, 23 May 1995. Gertraud Junge, one of the two secretaries who remained with Hitler in Berlin until its capture, had typed the will and made three further copies.

65. SOC.Dacre 10/7, CSDIC (WEA) BAOR REPORT ON Heinz LORENZ 30 Nov. 1945. Lorenz brought Hitler news of Himmler's dealings with Count Folke Bernadotte on 28 April.
66. SOC.Dacre 10/7, CSDIC (WEA) BAOR REPORT ON Heinz LORENZ 30 Nov. 1945. I have substituted 'Lorenz' for prisoner in quoting this document.
67. SOC.Dacre10/7, War Room outgoing telegram GCCS 16799 from Major Trevor-Roper to G.S.I. (S), B.A.O.R., 1.12.45.
68. SOC.Dacre 10/7, Major H.R. Trevor-Roper to Lt. Colonel S.H. Noakes G.S.I.(b), B.A.O.R. HITLER's and GOEBBEL's Wills 1 December 1945; Statement by William James SKARDON, Capt Int Corps, MI 5 Liaison Section 1 Dec 45.
69. SOC.Dacre 10/20, The Enquiry into Hitler's end.
70. SOC.Dacre 10/7, Heinz LORENZ CSDIC (WEA) to IB, 21 Dec. 1945.
71. Parker and Douglas, 'The Search for Hitler', S. 180.
72. SOC.Dacre 10/22, Delitescent Nazis. H.R. Trevor-Roper, 7 Dec. 1945.
73. SOC.Dacre 10/22, Delitescent Nazis. H.R. Trevor-Roper, 7 Dec. 1945.
74. SOC.Dacre 13/58, *The Badminton*, 1945, p. 69, entries for DEC. 21 FRI & 22 SAT; 10/22, [H.R. Trevor-Roper] to E.O. Hoppe, 5 Jan. 1946.
75. SOC.Dacre 10/7/1, Major Trevor-Roper to Head, Intelligence Bureau, BAOR, 3 Jan. 1946.
76. SOC.Dacre 10/7, Wilhelm ZANDER H.R. Trevor-Roper, Major. Int. Corps to Intelligence Bureau c/o GSI Rhine Army, BAOR, 1 Jan. 1946.
77. SOC.Dacre 10/7, Wilhelm ZANDER H.R. Trevor-Roper, Major. Int. Corps to Intelligence Bureau c/o GSI Rhine Army, BAOR, 1 Jan. 1946 & FORTNIGHTLY NOTES The Discovery of Hitler's Wills.
78. SOC.Dacre 10/7, Wilhelm ZANDER H.R. Trevor-Roper, Major. Int. Corps to Intelligence Bureau c/o GSI Rhine Army, BAOR, 1 Jan. 1946.
79. SOC.Dacre 10/7, Wilhelm ZANDER H.R. Trevor-Roper, Major. Int. Corps to Intelligence Bureau c/o GSI Rhine Army, BAOR, 1 Jan. 1946.

80. SOC.Dacre 10/7, Wilhelm ZANDER H.R. Trevor-Roper, Major. Int. Corps to Intelligence Bureau c/o GSI Rhine Army, BAOR, 1 Jan. 1946.

81. SOC.Dacre 10/7, Wilhelm ZANDER H.R. Trevor-Roper, Major. Int. Corps to Intelligence Bureau c/o GSI Rhine Army, BAOR, 1 Jan. 1946.

82. Parker and Douglas, 'The Search for Hitler' p. 185; SOC.Dacre 10/14, [H.R. T-R] to Captain E. Burrows Smith, USFET, G-2, CIB, Frankfurt a/M, 11 Feb. 1946; WO 208/3790 folios 156 & 134, Capt. H. Searle for Brigadier, Head of Intelligence Bureau, to AC of S, G-2 (CI) HQ USFET (Attention Major Alfano), 29 Jan. 1946 & Feb. 1946: 'Reference your letter of 31 Jan 46 forwarding 3 copies of Hitler's marriage certificate and Bormann's covering letter to Doenitz for which we thank you.'

83. SOC.Dacre 10/7, 032 Case No 0258/JOHANNMEYER. I have substituted 'Johannmeier' for 'subject' in quoting this document.

84. SOC.Dacre 10/7, 032 Case No 0258/JOHANNMEYER.

85. SOC.Dacre 10/7, THIRD INTERROGATION OF WILLI JOHANNMEIER H. R. Trevor-Roper, Major, Int Corps, 3 Jan. 1946; LDOH (1956) Introduction to third edition, pp. xxviii–xxix.

86. SOC.Dacre 10/7, Brigadier E.R. Haylor to Major H.R. Trevor-Roper, 8 Jan. 1946.

87. SOC.Dacre 10/7, Maj. P.E. Ramsbotham to Maj. Trevor-Roper, 7 Jan. 1945; SOC.Dacre 1/2/1, Ramsbotham to Trevor-Roper, 8 Feb.1947.

88. TNA WO 208/3779 S.3, J.S. Lethbridge, M.G.I. [Major-General Intelligence] to Colonel Sanderson, G.S., 7 Jan. 1946. Major-General John Sydney 'Tubby' Lethbridge (1897–1961) headed the Intelligence Division in the British Element of the Control Commission for Germany.

89. TNA WO 208/3779 S. 44 & 43, War Office for Intelligence Bureau, BAOR, 7 Jan 1946, MGI to Troopers [War Office], 8 Jan. 1946.

90. SOC.Dacre 10/29, Hugh Trevor-Roper to S.S. Mahlab, 24 May 1955.

91. SOC.Dacre 10/7, Trevor-Roper to Brian Melland, Cabinet Office, Historical Section, 8 April 1966.

92. SOC.Dacre 10/7, Reference telephone conversation SANDS – RAMSBOTHAM.

93. SOC.Dacre 10/14, Interrogation of AXMANN on special brief by Major TREVOR-ROPER 14 Jan 1946. Trevor-Roper included testimony from Axmann that Hitler felt Speer was deserting him in LDOH (1947), p. 149.
94. SOC.Dacre 10/28, Trevor-Roper to Anthony Marreco, CCG(BE), 3 July 1947.
95. SOC.Dacre 10/28, Trevor-Roper to D.G. White, 2 Oct. 1946.
96. SOC.Dacre 10/7, Trevor-Roper to Major the Hon. P.E. Ramsbotham, Intelligence Bureau G.S.I. B.A.O.R. 10 Jan. 1946.
97. SOC.Dacre 10/9, 032 Case No. 0279/ VON BELOW, 23 Jan. 1946.
98. Erich Mansfeld was a Gestapo official who transferred to the Reich Security Service in June 1944. He was captured by the Americans on 14 July 1945: Joachimsthaler, *Last Days*, p. 293 note 74.
99. SOC.Dacre 10/7, H.R. Trevor-Roper to Brigadier E.R. Haylor, 30 Jan. 1946; Brigadier E.R. Haylor to Major H. Trevor-Roper, 6 Feb. 1946.
100. TNA KV 4/354/40c, Trevor-Roper to D.G. White, 26 July 1946; SOC.Dacre 10/17, Counter Intelligence Corps, Garmisch Sub-Region, 30 August 1946.
101. SOC. Dacre 10/28, Trevor-Roper to D.G. White, 2 Oct. 1946. *SS Hauptsturmfuehrer* Guenther Schwaegermann served as an adjutant to Goebbels. He escaped from the Chancellery on 1 May and was arrested by the Americans on 25 June 1945: Joachimsthaler, *Last Days*, p. 292 note 64.
102. SOC. Dacre 10/18, Trevor-Roper to Dr. P. Kluke, Institut fuer Zeitgeschichte, 1 Nov. 1955 & to Anthony Terry, Esq., c/o Foreign News Editor, Sunday Times, 30 Jan. 1956; Joachimsthaler, *Last Days*, p. 303 note 251.
103. SOC.Dacre 13/29, pp. 367–8.
104. Ibid.; SOC.Dacre 10/31, untitled manuscript of *The Last Days of Hitler*; SOC.Dacre 10/30, Trevor-Roper to Harold Macmillan, 22 May 1946.
105. Parker and Douglas, 'The Search for Hitler', p. 188. Overy also claims that Trevor-Roper 'was greatly helped by Searle': 'The Chap with the Closest Tabs', S. 203.
106. TNA KV 4/354, folio 6a, SPECIAL INTERROGATION OF ALBERT SPEER, 11/9/45.
107. SOC.Dacre 10/2, PROTOKOLL v. 27 Maerz 1946 Anwesend waren a) Vernehmer: Major H.R. Trevor-Roper British Officer

b) Internierter: Prof. Karl Gebhardt Nr.4 -5445. For Trevor-Roper's use of Gebhardt's testimony see LDOH (1947), pp. 75 & 137.

108. LDOH (1947), p. 58.

109. SOC.Dacre 10/4, U.S Group Control Council (Germany), Office of the Director of Intelligence, Field Information Agency, Technical, Intelligence Reports nos. EF/Min/1, no date, S. 4,7,9 [twice] 10 &15, and reproduced in LDOH (1947) at pp. 13, 15, 41 & 172, 23 & 18. The *Diadochi* were Alexander the Great's generals, who later fought over his empire.

110. SOC.Dacre 10/4, U.S Group Control Council (Germany), Office of the Director of Intelligence, Field Information Agency, Technical, Intelligence Reports nos. EF/Min/2, 28 Aug. 1945, p. 8, and LDOH (1947), p. 195.

111. SOC.Dacre 10/4, U.S Group Control Council (Germany), Office of the Director of Intelligence, Field Information Agency, Technical, Intelligence Reports nos EF/Min/3, 1 Oct. 1945. The quotations are to be found in the original document on pp. 3–4, 5, 7, 11[twice] 15, 19 [twice], 26 [twice] & 27 and reproduced, not always exactly, in LDOH (1947) at pp. 83, 22, 44, 69 [twice], 60, 101, 64, 85, 86 & 44. Trevor-Roper altered some of these quotations. For example, the original of the Speer comment on Bormann was: 'A few critical words from Hitler about Bormann, and all his enemies would have jumped at his throat.'

112. H.R. Trevor-Roper, *The Last Days of Hitler* (2nd edition, London, 1950), pp. lvii–viii.

113. SOC.Dacre 9/13, THE GERMAN INTELLIGENCE SERVICE AND THE WAR, p. 2.

114. Neitzel, *Abgehoert*, p. 12.

115. SOC.Dacre 10/2, C.S.D.I.C. (U.K.) G.G. [German Generals] Report S.R.G.G. [Special Reports German Generals]1288 © The following conversation took place between CS/2235 – General Berger (Chef des SS Hauptamtes & Chef des Gefangenenwesens) Captured BERCHTESGADEN 8 May1945 and a British Army officer Information received: 5 Jun 45.

116. SOC.Dacre 10/2, Narrative of GOTTLOEB BERGER, taken at Nurnberg [sic], Germany, 26 March 1946, 1400 to 1530, by Major H.R. Trevor-Roper. Also present: Mr. Charles J. Gallagher, Court Reporter. An interrogation to establish correct relations between

certain events to which Berger already referred in previous interrogations while in custody of the CSDIC (UK).

117. SOC.Dacre 10/2, C.S.D.I.C. (U.K.) G.G. Report S.R.G.G. 1288©; LDOH (1947), pp. 134–9.

118. Michael Wildt, *Generation des Unbedingten. Das Fuehrungskorps des Reichssicherheitshauptamtes* (Hamburger Edition, 2003), p. 11.

119. SOC.Dacre 10/2, C.S.D.I.C. (U.K.) G.G. Report S.R.G.G.1322 © The following conversation took place between CS/2262 – SS Gruppenfuehrer Ohlendorf (Ministerial Direktor im Reichswirtschaftsministerium) Captured FLENSBURG 21 May 1945 and a BAO [British Army Officer] Information received 7 Jul 45.

120. SOC.Dacre 10/2, Trevor-Roper to Professor S. Zuckerman, 8 April 1946. Solly Zuckerman (1904–93) was a scientist from Christ Church Oxford serving in the RAF. He was an influential figure who had helped shape Allied bombing strategy.

121. SOC.Dacre 10/31, untitled manuscript of *The Last Days of Hitler.*

122. LDOH (1947), p. 57.

123. SOC.Dacre 10/2, BRIGADEFUEHRER SCHELLENBERG Amtschef VI, Autobiography, compiled during his stay in Stockholm, June 1945, p. 8; LDOH (1947), pp. 94–5. Schellenberg later drew on this autobiography in preparing his memoirs: Walter Schellenberg, *The Schellenberg Memoirs* (London, 1956).

124. LDOH (1947), p. 105. Speer thought highly of Schwerin von Krosigk: 'he was one of the cleanest people we had, and he always took a firm and decent line as Minister of Finance': SOC.Dacre 10/4, U.S Group Control Council (Germany), Office of the Director of Intelligence, Field Information Agency, Technical, Intelligence Report nos. EF/Min/1, p. 29. Trevor-Roper did not follow Speer's lead concerning Krosigk.

125. LDOH (1947) NOTE ON SOURCES, p. 267.

126. Karl Koller, *Der letzte Monat. Die Tagebuchaufzeichnungen des ehemaligen Chefs des Generalstabes der deutschen Luftwaffe vom 14. April bis zum 27. Mai 1945* (Mannheim, 1949), p. 7. Koller's publication was the same in essentials as the 1945 version, although during the intervening years he had recalled or devised additional telling ripostes to Hitler's complaints about the Luftwaffe.

127. SOC.Dacre 10/16, A.D.I. (K) Report No. 348/1945 [THE COLLAPSE VIEWED FROM WITHIN] THE MEMOIRS OF GENERAL KOLLER, [THE GERMAN CHIEF OF AIR STAFF]

128. SOC.Dacre 10/16, A.D.I. (K) Report No. 348/1945 THE MEMOIRS OF GENERAL KOLLER p. 38; LDOH (1947), p. 189.

129. LDOH (1947), pp. 89–91 & 110.

130. LDOH (1947), pp. 193–203.

131. For an appraisal of Trevor-Roper's use of *Hitler Speaks* see Chapter 5.

132. Count Folke Bernadotte, *The Fall of the Curtain. Last Days of the Third Reich* (London: Cassell, 1945). In LDOH (1947) this book is cited as *The Curtain Rises*, an error corrected in the second edition. By 1953 Trevor-Roper thought that Bernadotte had greatly inflated his own role in saving prisoners, arguing he had only been a transport officer. Himmler's Finnish masseur, Felix Kersten, not Bernadotte, was 'the real centre of the system' to rescue Scandinavians and others from concentration camps late in the war: H.R. Trevor-Roper, 'Kersten, Himmler and Count Bernadotte', *The Atlantic Monthly* vol. 151 No. 2 (February 1953), p. 45. See also Gina Thomas, 'Himmler's Masseur' in Blair Worden (ed), *Hugh Trevor-Roper*, pp. 207–17.

133. LDOH (1947), pp. 162–3 & 162 note 1.

134. LDOH (1947), p. 183.

135. Parker and Douglas, 'The Search for Hitler', S. 165 note 2.

136. H.R. Trevor-Roper, *The Last Days of Hitler* (New York, 1947). Trevor-Roper had made hundreds of changes to the content, wording and phrasing of his book between the first draft and eventual publication. A thoughtful paragraph comparing Hitler with Stalin was overlooked during the typing of the manuscript.

137. LDOH (1947) p. 27, LDOH (American 1st edition, 1947), p. 24.

138. LDOH (1947) p. 37 & note 2, LDOH (American 1st edition, 1947), p. 34 & note 37. For American readers Trevor-Roper also amended a footnote about Himmler and the July Plot: p. 35 note 39. Subsequent British editions retained the original version of the reference.

139. LDOH (1950) Introduction to the second edition, p. lx. For the second British edition Trevor-Roper also amended a footnote on Himmler's indifference to the deaths of Russian women by adding

detail from Felix Kersten on the SS Leader's opposition to blood sports: LDOH (1950), p. 22.

140. SOC.Dacre 10/12, The Last Days of Hitler: textual changes relevant to Hanna Reitsch. In addition to substituting one for four paragraphs about Reitsch Trevor-Roper made eleven further changes elsewhere in the text concerning her role. Reitsch's account of her visit was published in various German, American and British papers and in William L. Shirer, *End of a Berlin Diary,* (London, 1947), pp. 156–73.

141. LDOH (1947) p. 18 & LDOH (1950) pp. lvi & 18–19; SOC.Dacre 10/29, Bernard Bassett SJ to Trevor-Roper, 30 May 1947; F.W. Pick to H.R. Trevor-Roper, 26 May 1948; Trevor-Roper, *Hitlers letzte Tage* (Frankfurt am Main, 1965), pp. 52–3.

142. SOC.Dacre 10/30, White to Trevor-Roper, 18 March and 17 May 1946.

143. 'Sir Peter Ramsbotham', obituaries in *The Daily Telegraph* and *The Independent*; *The Foreign Office List and Diplomatic and Consular Year Book 1951* (London), p. 416; *Who's Who* 1973 and 2009.

144. Parker and Douglas, 'The Search for Hitler', p. 163.

145. Hugh Trevor-Roper, *The Last Days of Hitler* (3rd edition, London, 1956), p. lxii.

146. *The Last Days of Hitler*, Preface to the Seventh Edition (London, 1995).

Index